*Routledge Revivals*

# Planning and Urban Growth in Southern Europe

First published in 1984, this book addresses key questions about the pattern of urban development in Southern Europe and the mechanisms employed to control and regulate this development in individual countries.

The book examines five countries – Greece, Italy, Portugal, Spain and Turkey – that have experienced different scales and rates of urbanization and industrialization. It identifies common problems arising from these processes, as well as the successes and failures of the planning policies employed to regulate development.

This book will be of great value to geographers interested in Southern Europe and urban and regional planners interested in comparative patterns of development.

# Planning and Urban Growth in Southern Europe

Edited by
Martin Wynn

First published in 1984
by Mansell Publishing Limited

This edition first published in 2017 by Routledge
2 Park Square, Milton Park, Abingdon, Oxon, OX14 4RN
and by Routledge
711 Third Avenue, New York, NY 10017

*Routledge is an imprint of the Taylor & Francis Group, an informa business*

© 1984, Mansell Publishing Limited and the Contributors

All rights reserved. No part of this book may be reprinted or reproduced or utilised in any form or by any electronic, mechanical, or other means, now known or hereafter invented, including photocopying and recording, or in any information storage or retrieval system, without permission in writing from the publishers.

**Publisher's Note**
The publisher has gone to great lengths to ensure the quality of this reprint but points out that some imperfections in the original copies may be apparent.

**Disclaimer**
The publisher has made every effort to trace copyright holders and welcomes correspondence from those they have been unable to contact.

A Library of Congress record exists under LC control number: 84007859

ISBN 13: 978-1-138-08297-7 (hbk)
ISBN 13: 978-1-315-11231-2 (ebk)
ISBN 13: 978-1-138-08300-4 (pbk)

# Planning and Urban Growth in Southern Europe

edited by

MARTIN WYNN

An Alexandrine Press book

MANSELL, London and New York

This book is part of the series
*Studies in History, Planning and the Environment*
edited by Professor Gordon E. Cherry and Professor Anthony Sutcliffe

First published 1984 by Mansell Publishing Limited
(a subsidiary of The H. W. Wilson Company)
6 All Saints Street, London N1 9RL
950 University Avenue, Bronx, New York 10452

© Mansell Publishing Limited and the Contributors, 1984

This book was commissioned, edited and designed by
Alexandrine Press, Oxford

All rights reserved. No part of this publication may be reproduced or transmitted in any form or by any means, electronic, or mechanical, including photocopy, recording, or any information storage and retrieval system, without permission in writing from the Publisher.

British Library Cataloguing in Publication Data

Planning and urban growth in Southern
Europe.——(Studies in history, planning
and the environment; 5).——(An Alexandrine
Press book)
1. City planning——Europe, Southern——
History
I. Wynn, Martin  II. Series
711'.4'094    HT169.E8/

ISBN 0-7201-1608-2

Library of Congress Cataloging in Publication Data
Main entry under title:

Planning and urban growth in Southern Europe.
(Studies in history, planning, and the environment)
"An Alexandrine Press book"
includes bibliographical references and index.
1. City planning——Europe, Southern——History.
2. Cities and towns——Europe, Southern——Growth——History.
I. Wynn, Martin.  II.Series.
HT169.E84P53 1984    307'.12'094    84-7859
ISBN 0-7201-1608-2

Text set in 11/12pt Ehrhardt and printed in Great Britain by Henry Ling Limited, Dorchester, bound by Green Street Bindery, Oxford

# Contents

1. Introduction
   MARTIN WYNN   1

2. Greece
   LOUIS WASSENHOVEN   5

3. Italy
   DONATELLA CALABI   37

4. Portugal
   ALLAN M. WILLIAMS   71

5. Spain
   MARTIN WYNN   111

6. Turkey
   GEOFFREY K. PAYNE and RUŞEN KELEŞ   165

7. Concluding Remarks
   MARTIN WYNN   199

Index   209

# 1
# Introduction

## MARTIN WYNN

THE PURPOSE OF THE BOOK

This book traces the history of urban planning and city growth over the past 150–200 years in five Southern European countries – Greece, Italy, Portugal, Spain and Turkey. It is a part of Europe scarcely covered in existing texts on European planning[1], and poorly researched by urban historians[2].

This dearth of information has contributed to the varying and sometimes contradictory images with which Southern Europe is associated. Geographically, proximity to Africa and the Middle East gives the countries, and particularly their southern extremities, a physical link with the developing world, with all but Portugal (unless one includes Madeira) having territory lying south of Tunis and El Diezair (formerly Algiers).

The association of Southern Europe with the developing world has also, perhaps, been encouraged by the dictatorships and military governments which have ruled for considerable periods in Spain, Portugal, Greece and Turkey in the post war era, and by the colonial and cultural associations between Spain and Morocco, Italy and Libya, and Greece and Egypt. Yet with Greece, Spain and Portugal joining Italy in the EEC in the 1980s, and with the longer term possibility of Turkey's entry, these nations are likely to become more closely aligned with the Western European democracies, following major political change in Portugal, Spain and Greece in the 1970s. Indeed, with an EEC context in mind, an understanding of the functioning of planning in these countries, and the urban growth processes they attempt to regulate, becomes all the more necessary and appropriate.

All five countries have well developed legal and institutional traditions, yet a superficial impression of development in many parts of Southern Europe suggests that planning systems have failed to control effectively the urban growth process. The well-known regional imbalances and the existence of shanty towns in many of the major cities give credence to the 'developing world' image alluded to above. This book, then, sets out to examine the evolution of urban planning in modern times in these countries, and to determine what impact planning machineries and authorities have had on the urban growth process in Southern Europe.

THE HISTORICAL SETTING

The political map of Southern Europe in the early nineteenth century was considerably different from that of today. In 1810, for example, at the height of Napoleon's power in Europe, all of Spain and mainland Italy were under French control, whilst the Ottoman Empire stretched from Asia Minor across the Dardanelles, to occupy all of what is today Greece, and most of the area to the north, up towards the Italian border and the Austrian Empire. Even by mid-century, Italy remained divided into its nation-states, and Greece, founded in the late 1820s, remained centred on the Peloponnese, with much of the northern provinces still lying in Ottoman hands. Indeed not until the late 1920s did Greece's boundaries come to coincide recognizably with those of today.

Industrialization came somewhat later to most of Southern Europe than to the major European powers to the north. In 1836, the iron and coal production figures of all five Southern European countries put together totalled less than half a million hundredweight each, compared with figures of 13 and 200 million hundredweight for Britain alone (table 1.1). Levels of urbanization varied somewhat, however. The Italian region-states had a long established network of urban centres, and in 1800 there were five Italian cities (Genoa, Milan, Rome, Naples and Palermo) with populations of 100,000 or more, with Turin and Venice passing this mark by 1850 (figure 1.1). In all Europe, only Istanbul, Paris and London had populations of over half a million in 1800, whilst Madrid, Barcelona and Lisbon were above the 100,000 mark at this date. Athens, which did not become the capital of the Greek State until the 1830s, had a population of less than 50,000 in 1850 which was still more than twice the size of Patras, the next largest Greek settlement. This compares with figures of one million for London in 1801, two million in 1851 and four million in 1881.

These figures, then, give some impression of the historical setting for this book. When the countries of Southern Europe emerged from the period of war and revolution in the first half of the nineteenth century, they were yet to experience the full impact of industrialization that was then being felt in Britain and, a little later, in other parts of north-west Europe. The levels of urbanization were also relatively low, with only Italy of the Southern European nations having more than 5 per cent of its population living in cities of 100,000 or more in 1850, compared with over 20 per cent in Britain. And the railways, which by 1850 linked most of the major cities of Britain and north central

TABLE 1.1. Population and iron and coal production in Southern Europe in 1836.

| State | Total Population (millions) | No. of Cities (over 50,000 population) | Iron (million cwt) | Coal (million cwt) |
|---|---|---|---|---|
| Spain | 14.03 | 8 | 0.2 | 0 |
| Portugal | 3.53 | 1 | 0.2 | 0 |
| Turkey (including Rumania) | 8.60 | 5 | 0 | 0 |
| Kingdom of Naples | 7.62 ⎫ | 2 ⎫ | 0 ⎫ | 0.1 ⎫ |
| Piedmont-Sardinia | 4.45 ⎬ 17.07 | 2 ⎬ 8 | 0 ⎬ 0 | 0.1 ⎬ 0.3 |
| Rest of Italy (excluding Lombardy) | 5.00 ⎭ | 4 ⎭ | 0 ⎭ | 0.1 ⎭ |
| Greece | 1.00 | 0 | 0 | 0 |
| Total | 44.23 | 22 | 0.4 | 0.3 |
| Great Britain (including Ireland) | 24.27 | 17 | 13 | 200 |

Source: Hobsbawm, E. J. (1962) *The Age of Revolution*. London: Mentor.

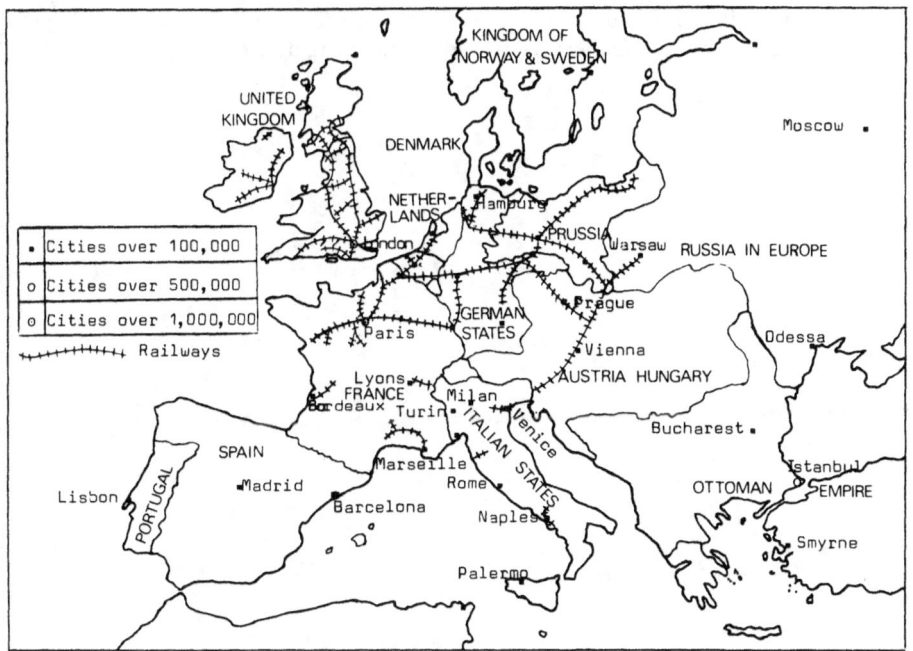

FIGURE 1.1. Europe in 1850.

Europe, were almost non-existent in the Mediterranean countries, save only for short stretches around Marseilles, Naples, Venice and Florence (figure 1.1).

Thus whilst the new industrial towns of Britain were suffering burgeoning population explosions[3], and the early public health legislation was being drafted, the major cities of Southern Europe were experiencing somewhat different growth processes, different both from Britain's and from each other's, which in turn elicited their own planning responses. It is here, then, that our story begins. . . .

NOTES

1. Of these, Clout, H. (ed.) (1975) *Regional Planning in Western Europe.* New York: Wiley, includes chapters on Italy and Iberia but, as the title suggests, the focus is *regional* planning and development; Garner, J. F. (ed.) (1975) *Planning Law in Western Europe.* Amsterdam: North Holland, has useful chapters on Italy and Spain but these are now rather out of date; and Haywood, J. and Narkiewicz, O. (1978) *Planning in Europe.* London: Croom Helm, completely omits Southern Europe.
2. Choay, F. (1969) *The Modern City: Planning in the 19th Century.* London: Studio Vista, briefly outlines the works of Cerda and Soria in Spain, and mentions early plans in Milan and Rome. See also: Gutkind, E. A. (1967) *Urban Development in Southern Europe.* New York: The Free Press.
3. Peter Hall, for example, cites the example of Rochdale in Lancashire, which grew from 15,000 in 1801 to 44,000 in 1851 and 83,000 in 1901. See Hall, P. (1975) *Urban and Regional Planning.* Harmondsworth: Penguin Books.

# 2

# Greece

## LOUIS WASSENHOVEN

THE SOCIO-POLITICAL BACKGROUND

The modern Greek State was founded in 1829 and recognized by Europe's major powers as an independent, autonomous kingdom three years later. The new state, however, encompassed but a small fraction of the Greek-speaking regions of the Ottoman Empire, i.e. only 36 per cent of what is today the Republic of Greece. Indeed, until the Balkan Wars of 1912–13, more than half of present-day Greece remained under Turkish rule[1], including nine of the country's twenty largest urban centres today. In 1860, only six towns had a population of 10,000 or more, and of these only three exceeded 11,000 – Athens (53,000), Patras (23,000), and Ermoupolis, on the island of Syros (18,500). By the turn of the century, Athens had a population of 200,000 and had reached the quarter of a million mark by the time of the 1907 census.

The sluggish expansion of Greece's major urban areas in the nineteenth century reflected the slow pace of economic and social change in the country. For the best part of the century, the national economy was generally stagnant, and following the War of Independence with the Turks in the 1820s, the emerging urban bourgeoisie and a nascent industrial sector suffered severe setbacks. Rather, it was the rural landed classes who tended to prosper, and their grip on local politics hampered the rise of the entrepreneurial urban classes and the growth of industry and manufacturing[2].

Upon emergence as an independent nation-state in the 1820s, Greece's urban history was only beginning. Although the city-states of antiquity achieved unprecedented levels of excellence in art, literature and political organization, urban development and an urban culture had for many centuries been either absent or insignificant in the lands which make up modern Greece. In the north, there were some long-established centres, such as Salonica

(Thessaloniki) and Jannina (Ioannina), of considerable importance. In contrast, Athens in the south was a mere village until, in 1833, the combination of historical attraction and pressure from local landowners persuaded King Otto to move the capital of the new state to the city of Pericles.

This low level of urbanization clearly did not favour the development of planning as a profession, and the absence of a genuine urban bourgeoisie within the frontiers of the kingdom also inhibited the development of an urban culture. At the same time, the influential and prosperous class of Greek merchants and businessmen based in Asia Minor, North Africa, around the Black Sea and Western Europe had little interest in the urban development of poverty-stricken Greece, although they did make handsome profits from real estate investments, particularly in Athens. In the capital, land speculation was rife even before the royal household moved its permanent residence there, under the shadow of the Acropolis, in the 1830s. In general, however, from the 1820s until World War I, the real economic capital of the country was not Athens, but rather Istanbul or even Alexandria, where the wealthy ex-patriate Greeks lived. The existence in foreign territories of a Greek bourgeoisie with wealth, modern ideas and political influence contrasted sharply with the situation within the Greek State. Nevertheless, as the power of the landed gentry began to decline towards the end of the nineteenth century, so the influence of this ex-patriate merchant class began, increasingly, to determine the course of political events within Greece. Until then, the dominant social classes within the country had regarded the State of Greece as if it were an alien presence (very much as in the period prior to Independence) with which some accommodation had to be found. On the other hand, the ex-patriate Greeks had until then been prepared to leave the government of the country to those at home – the landowning classes in the rural areas and to the impoverished petty-bourgeoisie of the towns.

Under these social-political conditions, it was unlikely, if not impossible, for town planning to emerge with the same reformist aspirations and welfare objectives as in many parts of north-west Europe. Town planning in these countries (Britain, France and Germany) grew out of the traditions, concerns and practices of institutions and social groups which were plainly absent in Greece (and this is as true of the twentieth century as it is of the nineteenth). The harmonious, controlled and efficient co-existence of industrial and residential activities, which was uppermost in the minds of urban reformers in the West, was not a major concern in the Greek State. What town planning ideology there was sprang from the need to manage the competing investment and land acquisition objectives of property speculators and the multitude of small urban landholders, and this concern has been at the centre of official Greek town planning activities ever since.

The ideological gap between the modern state and traditional Greek society was not the only reason why town planning did not evolve as it did in the West. There were other factors, although they were arguably all facets of the same contradictions. While local landed oligarchies managed to suppress the social unrest which was a contributory cause in the War of Independence, and have retained their local power until today, *formal* local government remained weak. Centralization of government power has been a key feature of the administrative system since the early days of Independence, and the French prefectoral system – introduced in the 1830s – has ensured that municipal authorities have lacked (and still lack) the powers that are taken for granted in many Western European countries. Town planning is one of these powers, and the central government is only now beginning to relax its absolute control over the spatial organization of towns and cities – a control which it has exerted since the first regulations were issued in the 1830s.

The social and political conditions which formed the backdrop to the emergence of the Greek State go some way towards explaining its ineffective governmental structures. The government of the country throughout the nineteenth century and during the first two decades of the present century was weak and inefficient, and generally lacking in any sustained policy concerning spatial or social change. The brave efforts of the Tricoupis administrations, towards the end of the nineteenth century, to create a more efficient and less corrupt public sector were thwarted by financial bankruptcy, the practice of political patronage, and Greece's troubled international relations. The ascent of the Liberals in the second and third decades of this century undoubtedly changed the picture, as is evidenced by their legislative work in the field of town planning, but the government's capacity to plan and then implement change has remained in doubt, even in recent years, in spite of the ever-growing arsenal of statutory and institutional instruments that the state machinery now has at its disposal. The disregard for governmental institutions within Greek society at large is the key to understanding this weakness, and the continued operation of the patronage system, even though less overt than in the previous century, in many ways characterizes the state-citizen relationship in Greece. The absence of a 'civic spirit' and of any readiness to face issues collectively, and the preference for personal, linear relations with friends and protectors near the centres of power, deprives the community of the moral and social prerequisites for collective action towards social and economic change. Under such circumstances town planning is but one more governmental function which is undermined through the network of family, extended kinship and political ties, and generally exploited for personal and political gains.

## THE FIRST TOWN PLANS
### AND THE NINETEENTH-CENTURY GROWTH OF ATHENS

The War of Independence ended in late 1827 and Governor Capodistria's administration took over control of the country in early 1828. Its capital was the township of Aegina, on the island of the same name in Saronicos Bay, now a favourite weekend retreat for many Athenians. Capodistria later moved his seat of power to Nafplion in the Peloponnese where he was assassinated in 1831 by members of the local ruling class (*kodjabashis*), who disliked his efforts to build a centralized, modern state. One of the actions of Capodistria's government had been to prepare simple town plans[3], essentially concerning street layout, for the expansion of the more important towns in the Peloponnese – Patras (the country's third city, today), Argos, Methoni, and Pylos (Navarino), in the bay of which the fleets of the allied powers had destroyed the Ottoman fleet in 1827 and sealed the fate of the war. The last two are now insignificant townships of archaeological interest only, but were then important ports. The authors of these early plans were Greek engineers, generally without any formal training, or foreign engineers attached to volunteer army units, which had assisted the Greeks in their revolt. A notable exception was the German-trained Greek architect, Kleanthis, who, in co-operation with the German architect Schaubert, was responsible for preparing the first plan for Athens in 1833 (figure 2.1). In 1834 he produced a plan for the expansion of Eretria, an ancient settlement on the island of Euboea. In both these plans, the design was in the neo-classical style of the Munich school, with gridiron street patterns, monumental squares, and radiating streets.

Capodistria was already dead when Greece was confirmed as an independent kingdom by the 1832 London Protocol signed by the Allied Powers (Britain, France and Russia), whose chosen King Otto arrived in Nafplion in 1833. The following year, the seat of the government was transferred, by royal decree, to Athens[4]. Corinth, Argos, Nafplion, Tripolis (all in the Peloponnese), Ermoupolis (the most important Greek port), and Megara (near Athens) had all competed for the privilege of accommodating the nation's capital. The ancient glory of Athens, however, had a powerful attraction, shrewdly perceived by the ex-patriate merchant class and foreign entrepreneurs, who had acquired large tracts of land there from the fleeing Turks and who then started pressing the government to move the capital to the cradle of ancient Greek civilization. Kleanthis proposed that the government should give him a commission, along with his partner Schaubert, to prepare a plan for the new capital. This was accepted in the summer of 1833. These events were an added incentive to yet more Greeks, both from abroad and from the provinces, to acquire land in Athens while prices were still relatively low.

The Kleanthis-Schaubert plan (figure 2.1) had the majestic quality that the capital of a kingdom deserved, in keeping with the ideology of the period and the authors' Germanic background. A monumental north-south central axis ('N' on figure 2.1), adorned with squares and gardens, linked the proposed site of the royal palace ('A') with the Acropolis (at the bottom of the plan). Two major avenues, converging on the palace at 45 degrees with the main axis, led to grandiose plazas on the outskirts of the plan area, thus forming a triangle with the palace at its apex. The palace precinct was enclosed by four major malls which denoted the official seat of government within the city.

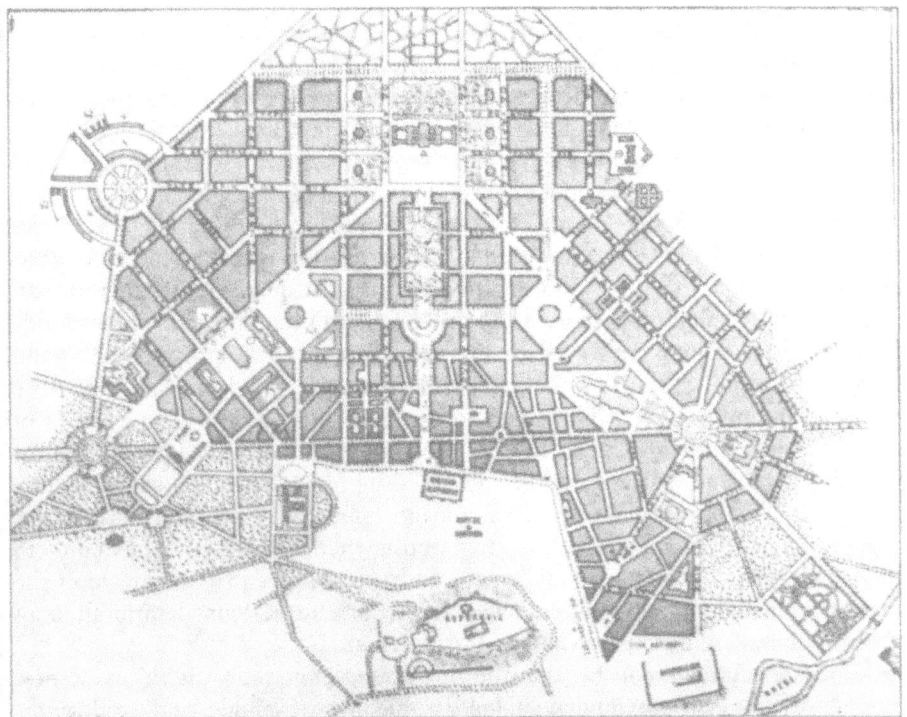

FIGURE 2.1. The 1833 Plan for Athens by Kleanthis and Schaubert.
The palace ('A') at the apex of the plan's monumental triangle (today Omonoia Square) was in fact ultimately built at the triangle's right hand corner (today Syntagma Square), and later became the seat of the country's parliament. The roads forming the sides of the triangle are still important and busy arteries of central Athens (Piraeus, Stadium and Hermes Streets). The main north-south axis, appropriately named after goddess Athena, patron of ancient Athens, is also a congested commercial street, where the town hall of the capital's central municipality is located.

The planners preserved a number of the existing narrow lanes of old Athens, around the Acropolis, and they respected the known ancient monuments, including the distinguished Byzantine churches of the capital. But beyond the vicinity of the Acropolis they created a new street pattern, the main streets of which were subsequently opened to form the road pattern which is recognizable today in central Athens. Sadly, overall implementation of the plan was thwarted by the power of local property owners who would have been adversely affected by the proposed development of the city. These interest groups managed to exert sufficient political pressure to get the Kleanthis-Schaubert plan suspended in 1834 in favour of a modification to be drawn-up by Leo von Klentze, a Bavarian architect. According to Costas Biris[5], this plan lacked the breadth of conception of the Kleanthis-Schaubert plan. Certainly, it covered a much smaller area, and no effort was made to safeguard the peripheral agricultural land from speculative development. The reduction in the planned area greatly benefited those who had recently acquired large tracts of land around Athens, but proved catastrophic for the city's expansion in later years. Von Klentze's plan did, however, retain proposals for the opening of a few new streets in the old city, which were subsequently opened, often only after forceful eviction of residents of houses earmarked for demolition.

Even as von Klentze's plan was being prepared, legislation was being approved which was to have a profound effect on the future pattern of urban growth in the capital. In 1834 the government sanctioned the division of land into extremely small plots in both the old town and the undeveloped surrounding terrain. Development decisions in the capital were taken by the King and his government, while the municipality of Athens, created in 1835, had little say in planning matters. The von Klentze plan was subjected to a series of modifications, most of which reflected lobbying by private landowners to turn public squares and gardens into private building plots. Although some of these attempts failed, several were successful and collectively resulted in a serious loss of valuable open space. It is worth noting that Athens today has no more than 2.0 m² of green space per person, and the absence of open space in the urban conurbation has been a major factor in the serious deterioration of environmental conditions in the last thirty years.

Land speculation soon became the dominant economic activity in the new capital. Fortunes were quickly made as the city expanded and landowners erected flimsy properties to rent out and the first illegal shanty settlement, aptly called Neapolis (New Town), sprang up in what is today a central area of the Athens agglomeration. In the 1870s, a new generation of speculators, former farmers from Attica, made their appearance on the periphery of the city, and this, combined with the inflow of ex-patriate Greeks from Egypt, created a pressing need for new housing which gave rise to a new boom in the commercial building sector.

While the business of building houses for sale was flourishing in central areas, land speculators were busily subdividing agricultural land on the fringes of the capital. *Some* of the resultant sub-plots would then be sold off for house construction, and corresponding plans for the development of *all* the original owner's land would be submitted to the authorities with a request that they be incorporated into the official town plan. By then, with development well underway, political pressure exerted by these technically-illegal builders was normally enough to get the plans approved, thus providing the original owner with the profits of speculation from the remainder of his property, which greatly increased in value as a result of planning approval. Between 1878 and 1907, according to Biris's figures[6], the official town plan area of Athens, originally based on the Kleanthis-Schaubert plan, grew by 500 per cent as a result of sixty separate extensions, randomly grafted onto each other, without any overall planning or co-ordination, and without any provision for service infrastructure or communal facilities.

TABLE 2.1 The population of Greater Athens and Greece 1907–81.

| | Greater Athens | | Greece | |
|---|---|---|---|---|
| Census year | Population | Percentage of Total Population of Greece | Area (1000 km$^2$) | Population (millions) |
| 1907 | 250,010 | 9.50 | 63.2 | 2.6 |
| 1920 | 453,042 | 8.19 | 150.2 | 5.5 |
| 1928 | 802,000 | 12.92 | 129.3 | 6.2 |
| 1940 | 1,124,109 | 15.30 | 129.3 | 7.3 |
| 1951 | 1,378,586 | 18.06 | 131.9 | 7.6 |
| 1961 | 1,852,709 | 22.09 | 131.9 | 8.4 |
| 1971 | 2,540,241 | 28.97 | 131.9 | 8.8 |
| 1981 | 3,016,457 | 31.08 | 131.9 | 9.7 |

*Source:* Census statistics. The 1981 figures are preliminary census results which appeared in the Greek daily press on 22 April 1981.

N.B. The country made considerable territorial gains between 1907 and 1920, attaining its present size at the international conferences of the 1920s, with the exception of the Dodecanese Islands which were acquired in 1947.

By the turn of the century, Athens was entering a period of rapid and sustained growth, in terms of both population and area, since when its primacy in the hierarchy of Greek settlements has become increasingly marked (see table 2.1).

Fluctuations in the city's growth in the early years of this century were by and large caused by external factors, notably Greek territorial expansion in the Balkan Wars of 1912–13 and the sudden arrival of Greek refugees in the aftermath of the Asia Minor military disaster of 1922. These events, however, were preceded by the mass exodus of migrants to America around the turn of the century[7]. Four hundred thousand Greeks, 90 per cent of them male, (i.e. 16 per cent of the population in 1896) migrated to the United States in the first two decades of this century. This was a terrible drain for the country, although the Greek Americans were later to become an important source of foreign currency and a politically powerful lobby both in Greece and in the United States.

## RESETTLEMENT AND THE URBAN GROWTH PROCESS IN THE INTER-WAR PERIOD

War and internal strife were almost constant features during the years 1912–22. Large Greek-populated territories were liberated in the Balkan Wars of 1912–13 and during the closing stages of World War I. For Greece, the war continued after 1918, in Asia Minor, where her military fortunes steadily declined until final defeat in 1922. A steady stream of refugees poured into Greece, probably as many as 1.5 million[8]. The 1928 census shows that 1.2 million refugees (i.e. almost 20 per cent of the total population) were then living in Greece, but many had died of hardship or had already migrated to America, Western Europe or Egypt. An international agreement, signed in 1923, ratified a large-scale exchange of minorities, which meant that substantial numbers of Greek refugees could settle in rural areas in the north of the country, vacated by Muslims returning to Turkey. Nevertheless, about half the total number of refugees settled in the country's cities, including about 0.25 m who chose to live in what is today Greater Athens. Between 1920 and 1930 the population of the capital doubled.

An international commission sponsored by the League of Nations was appointed to supervise the resettlement task in rural areas and the servicing of loans to the Greek government. The commission, in conjunction with government ministries, designed and built over 2000 rural settlement areas. Many of these were in fact merely extensions of existing villages, often catering for less than a hundred people each. But about 500 settlements constituted totally new villages, mostly designed by foreign architects (see, for example, figure 2.2), located in the rural regions of Macedonia and Thrace, which received 80 per cent of the rural settlers. In all, these new settlements provided accommodation for over 150,000 refugee families.

The resettlement in urban areas was less systematic; many of the self-built

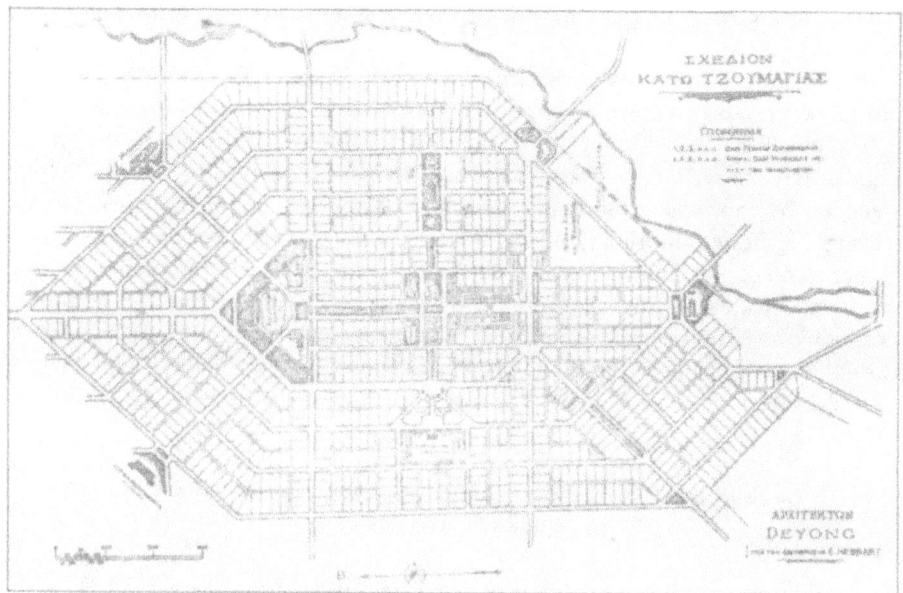

FIGURE 2.2. Kato Tzoumagia, Eastern Macedonia.
This rural settlement was designed for refugees by a foreign architect in the 1920s working under the supervision of French architect Ernest Hebrard.

refugee shanties were not cleared until long after World War II, and some of the 'temporary' hutments built by the authorities survive to this day (for example in the Kaisariani district of Athens). A large number of housing estates were built by the government, usually well outside the city limits, which increased the refugees' problems of integration and contributed to the general failure of these schemes[9]. In Athens, twelve substantial new settlements and thirty-four small estates were built one to four kilometres beyond the existing built-up area. One hundred and twenty-five of these urban refugee overspill estates, including the larger settlements around Athens, were built in Greece as a whole in the 1930s, comprising 27,400 dwellings in all. From 1930 onwards, responsibility for resettlement passed to the Greek Welfare Ministry, which proceeded with the direct building of apartment blocks for rent or long-term sale, and with the provision of land and credit to eligible families. An additional 127 government-sponsored estates were thus built in the 1930s in urban areas, to accommodate 36,500 families. It was an important building programme but was undertaken without co-ordination between the International Refugee Settlement Commission, the Ministry of Welfare and the town planning authorities of the day (i.e. the Ministry of Transport and the municipalities). Speculative private development in the city peripheries continued apace, often in the guise of 'housing co-operatives' for refugees, legalized after their construction without reference to any city-wide comprehensive planning.

Several of the refugee developments, both private and public, constitute serious social and planning problems today. Not only have they remained socially segregated areas, but they have deteriorated, structurally and environmentally, to the point where intervention of some kind is urgently required. The rehabilitation of Kaisariani, with an area of 86 hectares and a population approaching 30,000, located near the expensive neighbourhood of the Athens Hilton, is now one of the main projects on the agenda of the Public Corporation for Housing and Urban Planning (DEPOS), a central government agency created in 1976. So also is treatment of the Alexandras Avenue settlement, located just a few minutes' walk from the new Palace of Justice.

There were few attempts to produce new town plans for existing cities in this era, and most of these were made necessary by the destruction of large areas through fire or natural disaster. One such plan was that drawn up for Salonica, today Greece's second city, which was ravaged by fire in 1917. Ernest Hebrard, French architect and town planner, and professor in the newly formed School of Architecture at Athens Technical University, was commissioned by the central government to prepare a reconstruction plan for the city. His 1921 plan (figure 2.3) focused on the city centre, which had been completely destroyed by fire. A new monumental main street was designed to act as a central axis to link the old city with the port area, with a series of broad avenues crossing it at right angles and running parallel to the coast. Under the supervision of the central government, the street pattern of Hebrard's plan was adhered to in the reconstruction of the city centre in the early 1920s (figure 2.4).

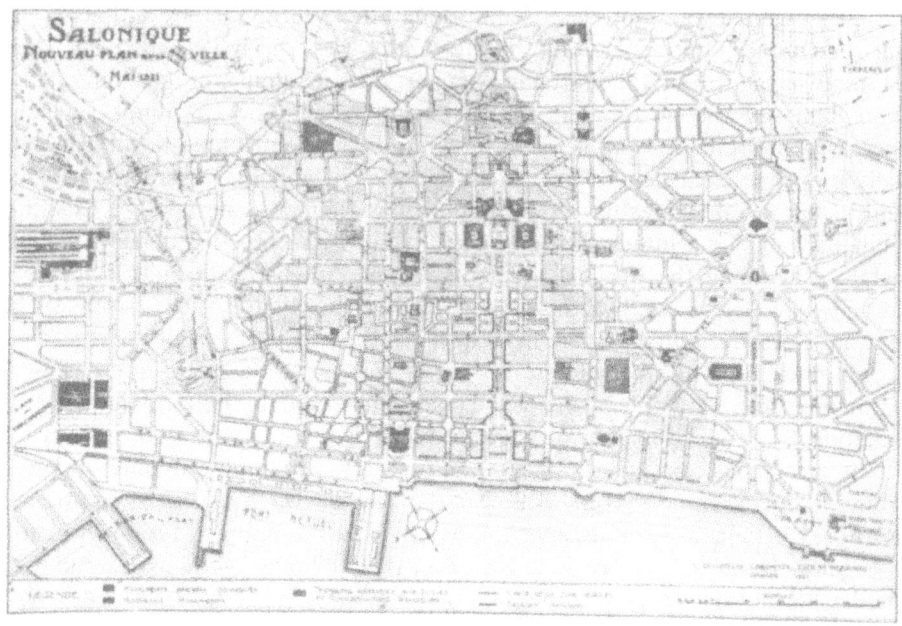

FIGURE 2.3. The 1921 Plan for Salonica, by Ernest Hebrard.

FIGURE 2.4. Aristotelous Street, Salonika's monumental mall, designed by Hebrard in the 1920s.

Leaving aside the replanning of the Salonica city centre and the new resettlement estates built on the outskirts of the nation's cities, planning and development in the inter-war period was characterized by piecemeal additions to existing town plans (normally after construction had taken place), the spread of 'illegal' developments which were never officially recorded, and the general lack of comprehensive city planning. When the government finally commissioned the drawing up of urban plans in the 1960s, most cities still had obsolete plans dating back to the beginning of the century or before. For example, in Kalamata, the second most important centre in the Peloponnese, the town plan of 1905, which was officially in force until 1968, encompassed only 57 per cent of the existing built-up area. As a result, about 36 per cent of the city's population were living outside the city's official limits, as defined in the 1905 plan, in illegally erected, typically three-storey, buildings. Similarly in Patras, the first city in the Peloponnese and the third in the country as a whole, it was found that 40 per cent of the population was illegally housed when the master plan for the city was being drawn up in the mid-1960s. Further, the old plans often contained many ambiguities and contradictions. In the Kalamata case, for example, subsequent *ad hoc* additions to the 1905 plan had designated valuable orange groves for residential development, whilst the densely built-up areas on either side of the main access road into the city were not shown on the plan at all, and thus remained illegal[10].

Planning practice, such as it was, was very much a concern of architects in this period. The School of Architecture of Athens Technical University produced a generation of graduates deeply influenced by the ideas of the modern architectural movement, as expressed in the series of congresses held in the 1920s and 1930s by the Congrès International d'Architecture Moderne (CIAM). Indeed, one of these congresses was held in Athens in 1933, and produced what became known as the Athens Charter[11]. The charter reflected many of Le Corbusier's ideas and the growing awareness among architects of the ills of anarchical growth and inner-city decay, a message carried into university teaching in the postwar era by many of the young architects of this period. Despite this growing awareness amongst the architects of the time, little was done in practice to ameliorate the deficiencies of the urban growth process.

During the inter-war period, many of the old city centres were already showing signs of serious decay and suffering from the congestion brought by the narrow village-like streets dating from Ottoman times. In other cities and towns, like Chania, in Crete, old centres had been built around Venetian fortifications, Jewish or Turkish quarters, reflecting the turbulent history of Greece's past. The prosperity brought by the export of tobacco and currants in the nineteenth century had seen the growth of elegant bourgeois neighbourhoods, often comprising two-storey neo-classical residences, in towns such as Kavala and Kalamata (figure 2.5) (in the Peloponnese), Chania (in Crete) and Volos (in Thessaly). These residential zones, generally located just outside the old city centres, were engulfed by the *ad hoc* expansion of the inter-war years,

16  PLANNING AND URBAN GROWTH IN SOUTHERN EUROPE

FIGURE 2.5. Kalamata, in the Peloponnese.
The railway station and the old Great Britain Hotel provide examples of a fast disappearing provincial townscape, dating from the prosperous years of the last century. The railway station has now been declared a listed building.

bequeathing a legacy of congestion and piecemeal development to the postwar planners and administrators.

### THE 1923 TOWN PLANNING ACT: THE PREPARATION, APPROVAL AND IMPLEMENTATION OF URBAN PLANS

In 1914, overall responsibility for town planning matters was taken from the Ministry of the Interior and given to the Ministry of Transport, although the former remained in charge of local government in general. This administrative schism tended to weaken the representation of municipal authorities in upper-tier planning decisions, but the Transport Ministry, under the dynamic leadership of the leading Liberal, Alexander Papanastasiou, was nevertheless responsible for the preparation and introduction of important new planning legislation. Indeed, the bases of statutory planning in Greece, for at least up until 1978, were the product of the 1920s[12]. Of greatest significance was the 1923 Town Planning Act, which laid down regulations for the preparation of town plans and their subsequent modification, and remains the most important piece of planning legislation on the Statute Book today. This not only reflects the comprehensiveness of the Act, but also indicates the extent to which it has provided the legal framework for the bulk of government action in the urban planning field ever since.

The 1923 Act established that municipal authorities, government ministries, national agencies, housing co-operatives or private developers could draw up urban plans, be they plans for entire cities or merely for isolated blocks. Plans drawn up by municipal authorities or the private sector have first to be approved by the municipal council which must give notice of its intention to approve any plan through the press, the town hall noticeboard and by letter to those directly affected by planning proposals. Members of the public can present objections which must be considered by the council before its approval is given. Plans have then to be submitted, via the Provincial office to the central ministry of the day responsible for town planning matters, for approval, modification or rejection[13]. The Minister, with the consent of his advisory committee, can reject a municipal or private sector plan and substitute one prepared by the ministry itself.

If the plan originates in the ministry, the plan approval process is more direct. The affected municipality(ies) have to be consulted, but their role is purely advisory; and no notice has to be given to affected individuals. The autonomous nature of ministerial plan-making is even more marked in the case of municipal building regulations which can be issued by central government without even consulting municipal authorities. In practice, municipal authorities have generally been precluded from drawing up plans themselves by their lack of technical and human resources; rather they have tended to commission private consultants – more often surveyors than qualified planners – or requested the central government to carry out the task.

The burden of implementation of public service infrastructure (roads, schools, green areas etc.), included in approved plans, rests mainly with the municipality, which poses enormous problems given the inadequacy of municipal financial resources[14]. Municipal councils, for example, are responsible for land acquisition for such infrastructure and the payment of compensation to affected landowners. Yet if there is no construction within six months of plan approval, landowners are entitled to apply for permission to build on such land – i.e. that zoned for roads, green spaces, schools etc. in the approved plan. The perennial financial crises of all municipalities, most of which are usually on the verge of bankruptcy, means that plan implementation proceeds without the provision of much of the service infrastructure contained in the plan, above all the public open spaces. This critical and well-known obstacle to the effective provision of service infrastructure has often been disregarded by central government ministries during the past twenty years, when the bulk of the country's urban plans have been approved. In practice, ministerial approval has often served only to increase private land and property values because of the added kudos of development with 'town plan' status; and the public interest, rather than benefiting from urban planning as the 1923 Planning Act suggested it should, has only suffered, again and again.

In some of the smaller towns, where the shortage of qualified staff is most acute, approved urban plans sometimes fail to specify land uses, merely distinguishing between public domain and private property, often superimposed on an inaccurate base-map. Accidental or deliberate 'errors' result in 'unexpected' advantages for some property-owners; or in the destruction of buildings of great architectural value. The functioning of the planning machinery established by the 1923 Act must, then, be viewed against a background of corruption, personal patronage and inefficiency of the state bureaucracy. There are countless ways in which planning laws and regulations can be contravened or by-passed, usually through the network of family ties and political patronage. The expropriation process is notoriously slow and ineffectual, with cases of landowners waiting for twenty-three years for a state valuation of the land in question[15]; and state authorities have repeatedly gone back on their pronouncements, damaging their credibility in the public eye[16], and shown inconsistency in their judgement on planning matters. This is particularly true of their ambiguous attitude to peripheral development and illegal housing, where making political capital has been the main criterion of successive governments. It is, of course, in these peripheral zones, beyond the city limits, that the major areas of unauthorized development have sprung up, built by urban migrants who left the Greek countryside in the postwar period.

### House Construction and Urban Migration in the Postwar Period

After the liberation of Greece from German occupation in 1945, responsibility for town planning was moved to the newly created Ministry of Reconstruction under the directorship of a thirty-five year old architect, Constantine Doxiadis[17]. Doxiadis had previously been appointed head of the Athens Planning Agency in 1937, within a special ministry created the same year by the dictatorship (that ruled the country from 1936 to 1941) to take responsibility for the government of the capital; he had also worked as head of a Town and Regional Planning Research Agency (within the Ministry of Public Works) during the German occupation. Twenty-five per cent of the nation's housing had been destroyed in the war against Italy and Germany[18] and more destruction was to follow in the civil war of 1946–49. Greece was faced with a massive reconstruction programme which relied mainly on private initiative with government support. But the 1940s was also a period of great opportunity for the planning of Greece's main cities and for building up land reserves for future use. This opportunity was sadly lost and the rapid urban growth of the following decade quickly wiped out the chances of securing the conditions for a satisfactory urban environment in the future. Doxiadis himself left the ministry in 1951 and town planning responsibilities were moved from one ministry to another until being relocated within the Ministry of Public Works, where they remained until the late 1970s.

Reconstruction in the immediate postwar period was dominated by the private sector, a tendency in the house construction industry in general which became increasingly evident in the 1950s and 1960s[19]. Since the war, investment in housing has accounted for 40 per cent of the gross total of private investment, whilst public investment in this sector has averaged only 2–3 per cent of the total expenditure budget per year. The construction industry has been dominated by the small-scale developers, who have been able to reduce the initial requirements for capital outlay by means of the so-called *antiparochi* (exchange in kind) method. Under this system, the developer makes a legal pact with the landowner, whereby the former can develop the land and pay off the landowner with a percentage of the newly-built floorspace. In this way, the landowner becomes a joint owner of this condominium property[20], along with subsequent purchasers of shops or apartments in the new building. Landowners have typically gained 40–50 per cent of floorspace in the new high-rise blocks through this method, with huge windfall profits accruing from subsequent rents.

The need for new housing after the war was not, of course, a result only of war damage, but was also brought about by the massive movements of population from the countryside to the major cities. Between 1951 and 1971 the number of Greeks living in settlements of 10,000 inhabitants or more rose from 37 per cent to 53 per cent of the country's population[21]. The vast majority of this shift in population to the urban areas went to the country's two major cities – Athens and Salonica – whose population totals in the 1950s and 1960s were growing at much faster annual rates than the country as a whole; and so marked has been the dominance and attraction of Athens and Salonica within the urban hierarchy, that between 1961 and 1971, the tenth and eleventh

TABLE 2.2 Population growth in Greece's major cities 1951–71.

| Urban Area | Annual % change in Population 1951–61 | 1961–71 | Total Population 1971 |
|---|---|---|---|
| Greater Athens | 3.00 | 3.21 | 2,540,241 |
| Greater Salonica | 2.32 | 3.88 | 553,655 |
| Greater Patras | 0.95 | 1.54 | 119,096 |
| Greater Irakleion | 1.85 | 1.93 | 84,710 |
| Larisa | 3.05 | 2,70 | 72,336 |
| Greater Volos | 0.35 | 0.55 | 71,245 |
| Kavala | 0.56 | 0.38 | 46,234 |
| Greater Chania | 2.05 | 0.35 | 45,547 |
| Jannina | 0.80 | 1.38 | 40,130 |
| Serres | 0.86 | −0.04 | 39,897 |
| Greater Kalamata | 0.06 | −0.21 | 39,462 |
| Total Country | 0.95 | 0.44 | 8,768,640 |

largest urban areas in the country (Serres, north of Salonica, and Kalamata, in the Peloponnese) actually suffered a population loss (table 2.2). Indeed, on the basis of 1961 census data and migration patterns in the 1950s, Kayser[22] concluded that thirty-nine of Greece's fifty-five urban centres (those with populations of 10,000 or more) were either in decline or stagnating.

The weakness of urban centres in the country's periphery is evident not only in demographic indicators (low rates of growth, ageing population, literacy), but also in indicators of their industrial base. If we compare Greater Athens with the next seven most important industrial centres in the country, we find that between 1958 and 1973, these seven centres remained static in terms of their share of national industrial employment, at about 16 per cent, whilst Athens increased its share substantially from 41 per cent to 46 per cent. Out of the 266 industrial plants in the country as a whole, which in 1973 employed more than 200 workers, 147 were located in Greater Athens, with an additional twenty-two in its own prefecture (Attica) and a further twenty-four in its immediate sphere of influence, a total representing more than 72 per cent.

These facts and figures, then, give some idea of the way in which the attraction of Athens had drawn in the bulk of inter-regional (and intra-Attica) migrants in the postwar period. According to official statistics, about a quarter of a million migrants moved into Greater Athens during each of the five-year periods 1956–61 and 1966–71[23]. During the 1960s, however there was an equally significant international migration of Greeks, mainly to West Germany. Between 1959 and 1965, 537,000 people emigrated, with 117,000 (1.35 per cent of the national population) leaving the country in 1965 alone. Some regions, particularly in the north, became depopulated to the point where more people were forced to leave because not enough remained to sustain economic activity. The country's rural economy was severely weakened and the apparent 'attraction of the centre' enhanced; and this process has tended to be reinforced by the remittances of emigrants to their relatives remaining in Greece, as most of this money has found its way into investment in real estate in the capital. This 'migrant' foreign currency is thus indirectly supporting what is sometimes described as the hidden 'parallel' economy in Greece, along with the flow of undeclared and untaxed (or 'black') money from within the country itself. Apartment blocks, built in the cities through the *antiparochi* development system described above, and land ripe for development on urban peripheries or in tourist areas, have been used as an investment outlay for much of this money. This connection is so strong that every time governments tried to tax real property or to investigate whether it was acquired with untaxed money, they were forced to retreat, tacitly acknowledging that the hidden sector keeps the economy moving.

The steady flow of migrants towards the country's major urban centres demanded a consistent and comprehensive housing policy from the national government. Instead, however, government policy, mainly revolving around the availability of credit facilities for house constructors and buyers, has been

FIGURE 2.6. Kypseli, a neighbourhood of Athens.

inadequate and haphazard, and has generally discriminated against low-income groups. Rather, it has been left to unauthorized house construction to provide homes for the bulk of in-migrants in the urban areas. In the period 1945–66, 45 per cent of the net population increase of Greater Athens (almost half a million people) were housed in illegally constructed dwellings; and in 1976, the Greek Centre for Planning and Economic Research estimated that 600,000 new dwellings would have to be built in the period 1976–81 to compensate for current and on-going housing deficits[24]. Legislation regarding shanty dwellings has been similarly inconsistent and politically-motivated. Just prior to the 1977 election, legislation was enacted to legalize illegal housing, only to be subsequently declared unconstitutional by the Council of State.

In summary, then, the housing needs of a rapidly growing urban population, encamped above all in the periphery of Greater Athens, have not been satisfactorily provided for. The miserable legacy of inter-war planning and development has been made worse still by the failure of government policy to deal adequately with the requirements of a massive migration into the major urban agglomerations. By the 1960s, the country's urban housing was characterized by a rapidly deteriorating physical environment, high-density living (up to 2000 people per hectare – see figure 2.6), high pollution levels, and poor service provision. Let us now turn to examine the evolution of town planning practice over the past twenty years, and the role this has played in the development process.

## NEW DEVELOPMENTS IN PLANNING IN THE 1960s AND 1970s

The 1960s in many ways marked a watershed in the evolution of planning

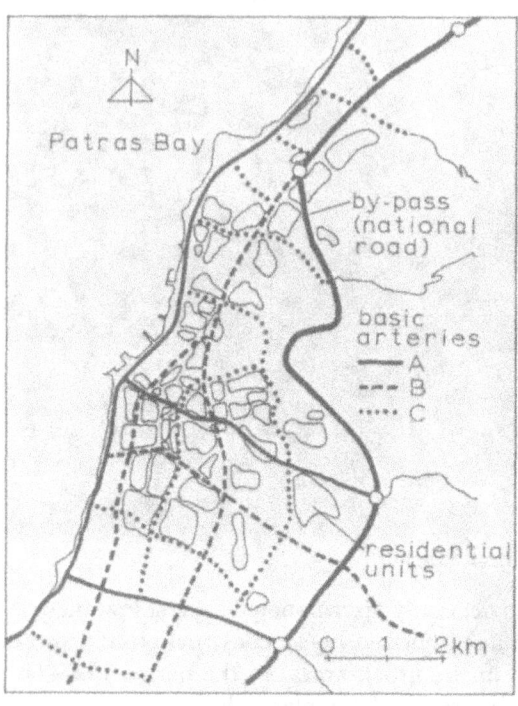

FIGURE 2.7. The 1967 Master Plan for Patras.
The plan was drawn up by G. A. Skiadaresis and Associates for the Ministry of Co-ordination and had a population target of 122,000 by 1986. Patras, third city of the country, was designated a 'twin pole of development' in 1979 along with the town of Aigion when a new comprehensive plan was commissioned for the two centres.

thought in Greece this century. A series of comprehensive urban plans were drawn up, and the first regional plans appeared; and a serious attempt at national regional-economic development planning was made[25]. The impetus for these developments in governmental planning undoubtedly came from the liberal government of 1964–65, although they can be traced back to studies on spatial planning undertaken in the School of Architecture and in the Centre for Town Planning Research at Athens Technical University[26] in the early 1960s, and most of these planning concepts have remained a feature of urban and regional planning in the country until the present day.

The mid-1960s, then, saw the appearance of a spate of urban plans, very much in the mould of the English master plans of the day. A Planning Directorate for the Athens area was established within the Ministry of Public Works in 1965, but the majority of city plans were drawn-up by consultants commissioned by the government. In this way new urban plans for Patras, Irakleion, Chania and Jannina were approved; and a series of tourist development plans were also contracted out to private consultants, most of them concerning the island of Crete[27].

In the 1967 Master Plan for Patras (figure 2.7), an attempt was made to counteract the haphazard residential development and absence of identity in urban neighbourhoods, which characterised the built-up area. Residential or 'ecological' units were identified within the existing urban structure and related to the proposed road network. The Master Plan for Chania (figure 2.8), the

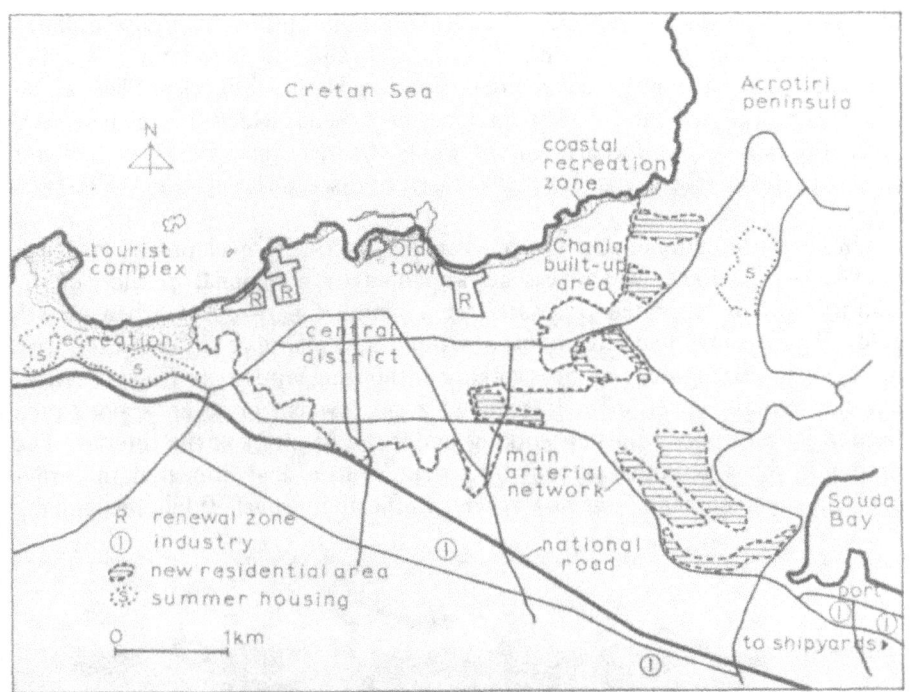

FIGURE 2.8. The 1967 Master Plan for Chania in Crete.
The plan, produced by Th. Argyropoulos and A. Tritsis for the Ministry of Co-ordination, had a population target for the Chania-Souda area of 68,000 by 1985. Regional policy in the 1960s and 1970s consistently designated Irakleion, the largest city in Crete, as one of the main regional development centres of the country. The two cities, which have often competed in the past for investment and government services, were each given a new university when it became impossible to settle the issue of where the University of Crete should be located.

main urban centre of western Crete, also encompassed the outlying port of Souda, with its naval base, shipyards and industry, treating both settlements as part of one future urban agglomeration. Three major zonal and functional growth areas were planned. A recreational and tourist zone was to stretch along the northern coast to the east and west of Chania old town, whilst a primarily residential zone was to link the existing Chania built-up area with that of Souda to the south. Finally an industrial zone was planned further inland along the national road.

In 1967, when these plans were being published, a military dictatorship took over the government of the country and remained in power for the next seven years. Under the military administration, there followed a period of hectic planning activity, accompanied by endless administrative reforms and the issue of planning documents, legal texts and decentralization decrees which were little more than illusory rhetoric in a period of tight and overcentralized dictatorial control. In 1972, Doxiadis Associates (under its founder Constantine Doxiadis), were commissioned to produce both a National Physical Plan, which was never approved, and a plan for Greater Athens, which in fact had been underway within the Department of Public Works since 1965 and did not appear until the late 1970s. We shall return to discuss the planning of Athens below.

Under the dictatorship, a fifteen-year 'perspective' Development Plan was worked out in 1972, which was accompanied by a regional division of the country and incorporated proposals for a national network of urban growth poles. The country had already been divided into planning regions, each with its regional development agency working within the Ministry of Co-ordination, but the military government introduced a new system of seven regions each headed by a Deputy Minister working under the Minister of the Interior. The proposals for a national network of urban centres had appeared in earlier government documents, but now received official approval. While recognizing

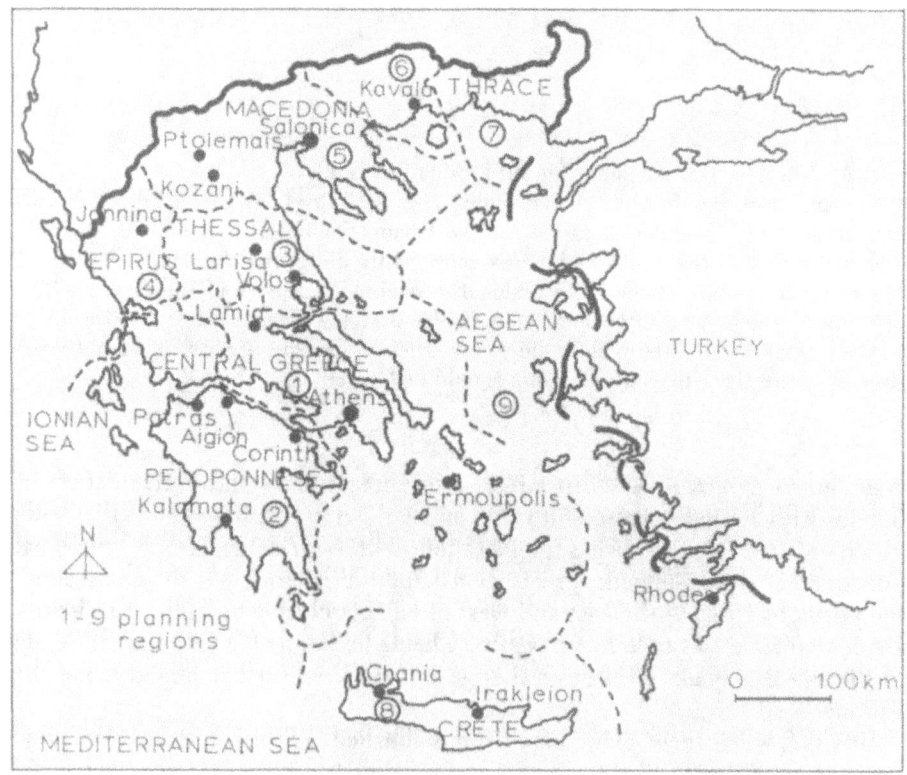

FIGURE 2.9. The Regional Division of Greece, established in 1977.
In 1977 the number of planning regions was raised from seven to nine, each with a Regional Development Service.

the dominance of Athens (the growth of which was to be checked) and Salonica (growth to be sustained), the plan advocated an eight-pole spatial model of development, and the concentration of investment in the six provincial growth centres, some of which were characterized as 'twin poles' (for example the cities of Volos and Larisa). The plan also insisted that there should be a network of second-tier zones and urban centres, but failed to specify them in any detail. Earlier planning documents issued by the Centre of Planning and Economic Research had designated fifty-six sub-regions, each based on an urban area with a population of 10,000 or more, which were to act as growth centres in the future development of each sub-region[28]; and the division of the country into planning regions changed again after the end of military rule. In 1977, the need to pay special attention to the undeveloped 'frontier zone' was the major reason for the creation of the separate regions of Thrace and Eastern Macedonia. The total number of regions thus rose to nine (see figure 2.9) and the Regional Development Services were reconstituted under the Ministry of Co-ordination, but without effective decision-making power[29].

Following the fall of the dictatorship in 1974, the 1975 Constitution[30] contained important new clauses on planning and development. The responsibility of the state for planning and development in the country's towns and cities was explicitly recognized, with the stated objectives of achieving a better functional organization of urban areas and improved living conditions. Then, for the first time, the principle of the obligation of landowners in urban areas to cede land to the authorities, without compensation, for public use was established; and, on the basis of approved plans, landowners could be required to place all their land at the disposal of the municipal authorities, and receive, in exchange, other land, of equal value, or part ownership of condominium properties (possibly erected on their former land).

These basic principles, contained in the 1975 Constitution, marked a significant psychological change in the state's attitude to planning, property and development. In 1976, the Public Corporation for Housing and Urban Planning (DEPOS) was created within the Ministry of Public Works to turn these principles into policies and plans, which might form the basis for subsequent intervention in the development process. In particular, this agency was charged with providing low- and middle-income housing in existing urban areas or new towns, and with studying the broader issues of urban development and housing policy. In practice, however, DEPOS initiatives were often thwarted by ministerial power struggles and the duplication of responsibilities. The Ministry of Co-ordination, which already had overall responsibility for economic planning and public investment programmes, was also given responsibility for 'regional planning and the environment' in 1976; and in the same year, a National Council for Physical Planning and the Environment (NCPPE) was set-up as a sub-committee of the Cabinet, with ultimate authority to approve all physical plans and related policy. DEPOS was also faced with the reluctance of the Treasury to provide the necessary finance to carry out its housing programmes, and, to date, it has not successfully asserted itself as either policy-making unit or housing and planning agency.

This overlap and confusion in agency roles and responsibilities was scarcely improved by the creation of the new Ministry of Physical Planning, Housing and the Environment (MPPHE) in 1979, and the setting-up of a Public Real Estate Company, within the Ministry of Finance, the same year. Nevertheless, 1979 did see the approval of the Urban Development Areas Act, which consolidated and extended the principles of planning and development embodied in the 1975 Constitution. The general failure of this legislation, however, highlights many of the problems currently facing planners and politicians in the urban management field, and we shall now turn to examine this in some detail.

### Politics and Planning in the late 1970s: The 1979 Urban Development Areas Act

The 1979 Urban Development Areas Act was inspired by the French *zone d'aménagement concerté* concept. The Act attempted to 'overcome' the lack of land and funds available for the provision of community facilities and service infrastructure by ensuring that all future urban development took place within designated 'urban development areas' (UDAs) or 'operational zones' as they have come to be known; most importantly, private landowners were required, collectively, to contribute up to 30 per cent of their land for public use, and additionally pay 10 per cent of their property value to cover the cost of public service infrastructure in any development project within a declared UDA.

Prior to UDA designation, the guidelines for future development have to be drawn up and approved. These could comprise detailed plans for development of a virgin site or complete renewal of an existing built-up area, boundary readjustment proposals, or simply land subdivision proposals accompanied by a set of building regulations and standards, to be adhered to in the future development of the area.

The 1979 Act, then, was the first major modification of the machinery established in the 1923 Town Planning Act for the planning and implementation of new development. The instruments and control mechanisms were made available to enable the public authorities to manage the planning and development processes, without the large demand on public finances which had previously precluded the provision of adequate public service infrastructure and facilities. In practice, however, the functioning of the UDA mechanism was violently opposed by the small landowners who for decades had viewed town planning as a means for speculative increase in real estate values, above all through the piecemeal extensions to the official town plan. At the same time, the authorities brought problems on themselves by failing to differentiate satisfactorily between the large- and small-scale landowner in the application of the Act, and in attempting too much, too soon. Hundreds of 'operational zones' were designated simultaneously, especially in coastal areas, without the necessary administrative machinery to handle the complexities of the operation; and with the 1981 election in sight, and objections to UDA designations flowing into the Ministry in their thousands, the government announced the abandonment of the 1979 Act, the suspension of legal actions against those who had proceeded with illegal construction in the periphery, and a return to the '1923 system', under which such developments could be legalized by *ad hoc* additions to town plans.

The failure of the 1979 Urban Development Areas Act highlights the contradictions and dilemmas facing the national and local governments in the field of planning and urban development. A government totally committed to the free market philosophy had been forced by the pressures of a rapidly deteriorating urban environment and the need to control the growth of speculative building and property development activities, to introduce measures that contradicted the principles of *laissez-faire* development. As a result, many of the government's supporters became disillusioned to the point of accusing ministers of undermining the foundations of bourgeois society, whilst opposition parties made political capital out of the suspension of the Act.

The failure of the Urban Development Areas experiment is likely to prove

FIGURE. 2.10. Chania, on Crete. The old harbour neighbourhood was one of the city's first nuclei of growth. Today, it forms a somewhat dilapidated, if picturesque, part of the city.

FIGURE. 2.11. Acadimias Street, Athens.
One of the few surviving interwar three-storey buildings is mirrored in the glass facade of a modern office block, in central Athens.

as serious for the future of area renewal and improvement as it is for the chances of curbing speculative peripheral growth. Some of the refugee settlements dating back to the inter-war years now form the nuclei of suburban neighbourhoods which are densely populated, rapidly deteriorating and in desperate need of community facilities such as schools, medical centres, and green spaces. At the same time, building densities in the city centres were allowed to rise under the dictatorship so that congestion and the deficiencies in green space and service infrastructure were made even more acute (figures 2.10 and 2.11). Since 1977, curbs on the density of city centre redevelopment have been introduced, and legislation was enacted in 1978 to facilitate the 'transfer of development rights' from plot to plot in an attempt to prevent the demolition of city centre properties of architectural or historic value. A developer wishing to demolish and redevelop on the site of an old building can be denied permission but given the opportunity to build a similar amount of floorspace in a less congested part of the city. Although this measure has been widely recommended and supported in subsequent planning documents, the problem of *area* renewal and rehabilitation in the city centre remains. The 'operational zone' of the 1979 Urban Development Areas Act constituted a planning and legal mechanism that could have proved invaluable in the re-equipping of both the city centre and the periphery. The socialist administration has now introduced a revised version of the Act, which shifts the burden of land contributions to large landowners and provides for financial assistance to local authorities in the implementation of plans. It must be hoped that the government will have the political will to carry this reform through to the implementation stage.

## The Plan-Making Process in Athens

During the postwar years the municipality of Athens, which houses only one-third of the population of Greater Athens[31], put forward a series of suggestions to the Ministry of Public Works for a new plan for the city. Only in 1965, however, did the Ministry start work on a new city plan; then, under the dictatorship, the Ministry of Co-ordination commissioned Doxiadis Associates to draw-up an alternative plan for the capital. So began the production of a series of paper plans and documents for the Athens metropolis which in fact have had almost no bearing at all on the development of the city.

The Doxiadis plan was presented in 1975, soon after the end of military rule. It was extremely ambitious in its provision of new public service centres and infrastructure throughout the city, and following a wave of adverse criticism, was quickly shelved. Work on the Ministry of Public Works plan for the city continued under the dictatorship and into the first years of democracy until in 1978, after thirteen years, the Ministry set a five-month deadline for the finalization of the plan. At the same time, however, five private consultants (including Doxiadis Associates) were also asked to submit plans for the future development of the capital, and a number of research and professional bodies were invited to submit their views. After a two-day conference in which the six proposals were discussed, Ministry staff were asked to produce a *pot-pourri* within thirty days, incorporating the best features of all six plans.

This extraordinary plan-making process produced, in January 1979, a short document entitled 'Capital 2000' for government discussion (see figure 2.12), and a more glossy version for public consumption a few months later. Following a further round of consultations with the Mayor of Athens (representing local government) and professional bodies (representing planning expertise), the Ministry of Public Works finally approved an eighteen-point programme consisting of generalities and hackneyed platitudes. The plan, which was to regulate the future growth of the city of Pericles, was thus reduced to a few boring and empty paragraphs to which everybody could afford to remain profoundly indifferent!

Despite the almost laughable inadequacies of this planning process, the government pressed ahead with its development of policy for the planning and growth of the capital. On the basis of population estimates that have subsequently been proved grossly inaccurate[32], the Ministry of Public Works announced an estimated population figure of 6.5 million for the capital in the year 2000 assuming the then current trends in growth continued. The NCPPE

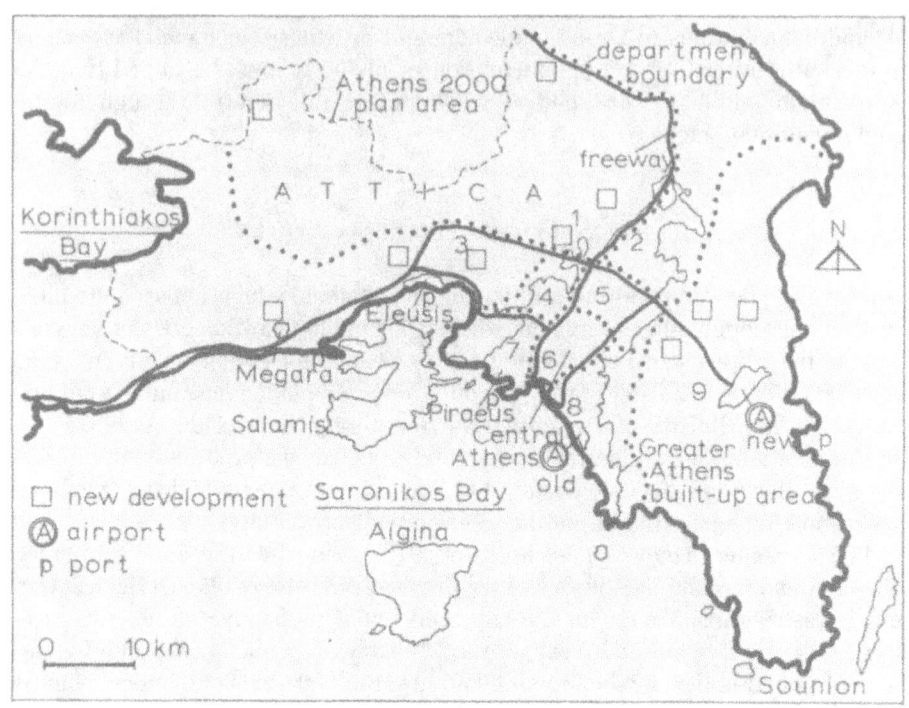

FIGURE 2.12. The 1979 'Athens 2000' Plan.
The plan put forward by the government for public discussion covered an area of 1500 km², much larger than the statistical unit of Greater Athens (210 km²). The target population for the year 2000 was 4.3 m, assuming a vigorous regional policy to check rural migration to the capital. The study area was divided into nine 'departments', each of which was to have its own centre for the decentralization of activities within the prefecture of Attica and away from central Athens.

set, instead, a target population of 4.3 million for the turn of the century, and argued that all Athens-bound migrants had to be diverted away from Athens towards nine selected growth poles or 'counter-magnets' around the country, which were given extremely ambitious population targets for the year 2000[33]. To date, however, little has been said about how this decanting of population from the Athens metropolis is to be achieved.

A more promising proposal to have come out of the 'Capital 2000' agreement is the suggestion that secondary service centres should be established within Greater Athens, above all in the western part of the city, which houses some of the lowest income groups, is ill-serviced and relatively inaccessible and neglected. Given the failure of the Urban Development Areas Act, however, it is again difficult to see how such a policy will be successfully carried through. Nevertheless, nine separate service plans, each one for a different 'department' of the capital, were drawn up under the guidance of the Ministry of Public

Works in 1980 and 1981, and it remains to be seen if these initiatives produce any actual results on the ground under the present socialist government. It must be said, however, that the record to date does not give rise to any great optimism, especially since the government has shelved both the 'Athens 2000' plan and the plans for the nine 'departments'[34].

It is worth adding also, in this context, that two decisions of critical importance for the future growth of the Athens Region – the location of its new airport and the proposed underground network lines – were taken by the Ministries of Co-ordination and Transport, respectively, without consultation and co-ordination with the planners in the Ministry of Public Works. Indeed, the lack of co-ordination and the political rivalries between ministries and individuals are well known, and experience has shown that a modest programme of pedestrianization in Athens has proved too much for effective inter-ministerial co-ordination, so fundamentally do ministries and their departments disagree on each other's powers and responsibilities.

### Concluding Remarks: Local Government, Planning and the Development Process

It is an attractive but optimistic thought to hope that urban plans might in the future effectively provide a framework for the control of urban growth by municipal authorities. In 1980–81 the central government started delegating development control powers to local authorities, but the majority of councils still remain woefully short of human, technical and financial resources, and inevitably rely upon upper-tier levels of government for all but the most undemanding of functions. In a country with a population of only 9.7 million, the large number of generally small municipalities (there are over 6000) impedes the effectiveness of local government in some areas, and the coalescing of some municipalities would seem a necessary prerequisite to any effective nationwide devolution of power and responsibilities to the local level. Until 1981 the Ministry of the Interior, which retains overall supervision of local government and the provincial governments, had shown itself opposed to giving mayors a free hand in staff selection, and this also hindered progress in some instances. The present government, however, is committed to freeing local authorities from this control.

The need to give local governments a greater degree of autonomy is becoming increasingly urgent, as the complexity of urban society heightens and the inability of the central authorities to come to terms with even the day-to-day problems of urban management becomes ever more apparent. Devolution of power is already proving to be a matter of practical expediency rather than ideology. Some of the larger urban municipalities are already developing initiatives that go beyond the scope of ministerial thinking; the Municipality of Volos, for example, is setting up an urban research, training and intelligence unit, the type of agency which is sadly lacking within ministerial departments.

For the past 100 years, then, the administration of the country has been over-centralized, and the urban growth process has been dominated by the Athens metropolis. Within the administrative machinery, urban planning has been undertaken in almost ritualistic fashion, and yet it has failed dismally to control or channel the urban growth process effectively. It is possible to explain this failure with an anti-planning bias: given the political-economic system in the country, planning has acted as something of an ideological smoke screen, but in reality it has only served the interests of the 'dominant classes' in society. This all too popular interpretation, however, ascribes to planning and planners a premeditated functional role, which unrealistically exaggerates the capacity of the government to govern, and of the ruling classes to plan. Rather, the failure of the planning system to get to grips with the problems of urban growth reflects the general inadequacy of the administrative and governmental machinery, and, indeed, the lack of adequately trained planners practicing in the country.

In connection with this latter point, it is perhaps worth briefly assessing the current state of planning education in Greece today. The teaching of planning at undergraduate level takes place within the Athens and Salonica Universities, but not as a main subject. Rather, it is taught as part of the architecture and, to a lesser extent, the civil engineering and general surveying degrees. In his Athens Centre for Ekistics, Doxiadis introduced post-graduate training courses, but these failed to attract Greek students in significant numbers, since the Centre's qualifications were not officially recognized. The Centre however has undoubtedly made a positive contribution towards the broadening of awareness within the Greek planning profession, but the aspiring planner still has to travel to France, Britain, the United States or Germany to acquire degrees and post-graduate qualifications. Greece desperately needs new educational and research centres to train its nationals, and to undertake (in conjunction with national and local governments) the planning and research projects which must inevitably play a part in the effective planning and management of the nation's urban areas. The reform of both local government and educational systems, then, may be highlighted as basic prerequisites if urban planning is in the future to become more than an ineffective bureaucratic procedure or mere ideological rhetoric. It is a hopeful sign that the present government is now legislating the introduction of post-graduate education in all universities, which have so far failed to offer such courses (and not only in planning). The National Technical University of Athens has prepared a course in Urban and Regional Planning; and the creation of an Association of Greek Urban and Regional Planners in 1982, with 200 members, is another factor which is accelerating the growth of the profession and will enhance its influence. It is hoped that these developments will make a positive contribution towards more effective planning and so help the improvement of the Greek city environment.

# GREECE

NOTES

This chapter centres on the developments in Greek urban and regional planning prior to the election the socialist administration in October 1981, although passing reference is made to the initiatives of the new administration.

1. For a concise history of Greece, see Clogg, R. (1979) *A Short History of Modern Greece*. Cambridge: Cambridge University Press; Woodhouse, C. M. (1968) *The Story of Modern Greece*. London: Faber and Faber; and Heurtley, W. A. *et al.* (1967) *A Short History of Greece from Early Times to 1964*. Cambridge: Cambridge University Press.
2. On the development of Greek society in the nineteenth and twentieth centuries, see Mouzelis, N. (1977) *Modern Greece: Facets of Underdevelopment*. London: Macmillan; Mouzelis, N. and Attalides, M. (1971) Greece, in Scotford Archer, M. and Giner, S. (eds.) *Contemporary Europe: Class, Status and Power*. London: Weidenfeld and Nicolson; Svoronos, N. (1972) *Histoire de la Grece moderne*. Paris: Presses Universitaires de France; Philias, V. (1974) *Society and Authority in Greece—Vol. I: The Spurious Urbanization 1800–1864*. Makryonitis (in Greek); Moskof, K. (1972) *National and Social Conscience in Greece 1830–1909: The ideology of compradorist space*. Salonica (in Greek); Moskof, K. (1979) The formation of modern Greek society. *Anti*, No. 127, 9 June (in Greek).
3. The basic sources on the history of town planning in Greece (all in Greek), consulted in the preparation of this chapter are: Biris, Costas (1966) *Athens, from 19th to 20th century*, 2 volumes, Athens: Foundation for the Planning and History of Athens; Voivonda, A. *et al.* (1977) The regulation of space in Greece. *Architectonica Themata (Architecture in Greece)*, 11, pp. 127–54 (with English text); Sarigiannis, G. (1979) *The Concept of Town Plans* and *The Production of Town Plans*, Athens National Technical University of Athens. Information on Greek town planning can be found in several issues of the annual publication *Architecture in Greece*, which provides extensive summaries in English.
4. On the history of Athens in modern Greece, the standard text is Biris (1966) *op. cit.* (see note 3). Diverse though rather anecdotal information can be found in Markezinis, S. B. (1966–68) *Political History of Modern Greece, 1828–1964*, 4 volumes. Papyros (in Greek). See also Leontidou-Emmanuel, L. (1981) Working Class and Land Allocation: The urban history of Athens 1880–1980. Unpublished PhD thesis, University of London; Karydis, D. N. (1980) Urban Development in Athens under Ottoman Rule. Unpublished doctoral thesis, National Technical University of Athens (in Greek); and Photopoulou-Lagopoulou, I. (1978) The Development of the Centre of Athens. Unpublished doctoral thesis, Univeristy of Salonica (in Greek).
5. Biris (1966) *op. cit.* (see note 3).
6. Biris (1966) *op. cit.* (see note 3).
7. See Polyzos, N. J. (1947) *Essai sur l'Emigration grecque: Etude demographique, economique et sociale*. Recueil Sirey; Philias, V. (1974) *Problems of Social Transformation: Studies*. Papazissis (in Greek); Valaoras, V. G. (1960) A reconstruction of the demographic history of modern Greece. *The Milbank Memorial Fund Quarterly*, 36, pp. 115–39. On emigration in the 1950s and 1960s, particularly to West Germany, see Nikolinakos, M. (1973) The contradictions of capitalist development in Greece: Labor shortages and emigration. *Studi Emigrazione*, 10, pp. 222–33; Nikolinakos, M. (1974) *Capitalism and Migration*. Papazissis, (in

Greek; first published in German); Nikolinakos, M. (ed.) (1974) *Economic Development and Migration in Greece.* Kalvos (in Greek); Bellini, F. (1966) L'emigration des traveilleurs Grecs. *Les Temps Modernes,* June; Botsas, E. N. (1969) Emigration and capital formation: The case of Greece. *Balkan Studies,* 10, pp. 127–34; Philias, (1974) *op. cit.* (see note 2); Kayser, B. (1971) *Manpower Movements and Labour Markets.* Paris: Organization for Economic Co-operation and Development.
8. The standard text on the refugee problem of the 1920s is Pentzopoulos, D. (1962) *The Balkan Exchange of Minorities and its Impact upon Greece.* Paris & Athens: Mouton and Athens Social Centre. See also Eddy, C. B. (1931) *Greece and the Greek Refugees.* London: Allen and Unwin. On the settlement of refugees see the article by Papaioannou, J. (1975) in *Housing in Greece: Government Activity.* Athens: Technical Chamber of Greece (in Greek, English, French and Russian). See also Vlachos, G. *et al.* (1978) Housing the Asia Minor refugees in Athens and Piraeus. *Architecture in Greece,* 12, pp. 117–24.
9. The social segregation encouraged by government housing schemes is bitterly criticized in two unpublished studies by the Greek National Centre of Social Research, *Housing in Greece* and *Sociological Study of Housing.*
10. Much of the material in this section is taken from the planning studies of Kalamata (1971), Chania (1967) and Volos (1980), undertaken by the Centre of Town Planning Research (National Technical University of Athens), by Th. Argyropoulos and A. Tritsis, and Th. Papayannis and Associates. Professor Argyropoulos provided additional information on Chania and Volos.
11. For the text of the Athens Charter see *La Charte d'Athenes.* Nendeln, Liechtenstein: Kraus Reprints, 1979.
12. The most up to date and by far the most comprehensive text on Greek planning law is Christophilopoulos, D. G. (1980) *Town Planning Legislation.* Athens: P. Saccoulas (in Greek), but new legislation was enacted in 1983.
13. Overall responsibility for town planning matters was transferred from the Ministry of Transport to the Ministry of Public Works during the war; to the Ministry of Reconstruction in 1945; to the Ministry of Welfare, briefly, in 1953; to the Ministry of Public Works the same year; and to the newly formed Ministry of Physical Planning, Housing and the Environment in 1979.
14. On the powers of local authorities and their problems, see *Local Self-Government in Greece.* Athens: Central Union of Municipalities and Communes of Greece, 1962; *The Present Role of Local Government.* Athens: Technical Chamber of Greece, 1978 (in Greek); *Local Government.* Athens: Centre of Planning and Economic Research, 1976 (in Greek). The municipal code was under revision in 1984 and the new socialist administration is pledged to give ample planning powers and resources to local authorities.
15. See Christophilopoulos (1980) *op. cit.*, pp. 154–5 (see note 12).
16. In 1978, for example, the Minister of Public Works announced that Alexandras Avenue in central Athens was to be extended to reach the capital's main railway station, necessitating the demolition of a number of apartment blocks. In many Western countries, this would have brought a wave of protest from affected property-owners; in Athens the proposal was met with calm indifference by affected individuals, who clearly failed to take the proposal seriously. To date, their indifference has been justified.

17. A special issue of *Ekistics* – No. 247, 1976 – was dedicated to the work of Constantine Doxiadis.
18. See Doxiadis, C. (1947) *Destructions of Towns and Villages in Greece*. Athens. See also Sweet-Escott, B. (1954) *Greece: A Political and Economic Survey, 1939–53*. Athens: Royal Institute of International Affairs, pp. 94–95.
19. On housing in Greece the interested and Greek-speaking reader should consult *Housing (Oikismos)* and *Housing (Katoikia)*, published by the Centre of Planning and Economic Research in 1967 and 1976 respectively; the papers of the conference on Construction in Greece, organized by the Technical Chamber of Greece in June 1979; the studies by Emmanouil, D. (1977) *Three Studies on Popular Housing*; and *Investigation of Categories of Tenants Uncovered by Existing Range of Housing Subsidies*. Athens: Public Corporation of Housing and Urban Planning (DEPOS), 1979; and Papaioannou (1975) *op. cit.* (with English text) (see note 8). There is of course, a very large number of articles and government reports on the subject. On the question of investment in housing see in addition Candilis, W. O. (1968) *The Economy of Greece, 1944–66*. New York: Praeger; Psilos, D. D. (1968) Postwar economic problems in Greece, in Committee for Economic Development (ed.) *Economic Development Issues: Greece, Israel, Taiwan, Thailand*. New York: Praeger pp. 1–77.
20. Condominium developments made their appearance in the 1920s, particularly after a 1929 Act permitted differentiated storey-ownership and made the apartment block with joint ownership of land a possibility.
21. On urbanization and urban growth in Greece, see Kayser, B. (1968) *Human Geography of Greece*. Athens: National Centre of Social Research (in Greek), also published in French as *Geographie Humaine de la Grece*. Paris: Presses Universitaires de France; Wassenhoven, L. (1980) The Settlement System and Socio-economic Formation: The Case of Greece: unpublished PhD thesis, University of London; Campbell, J. K. and Sherrard, P. (1968) *Modern Greece*. London: Ernest Benn; Beckinsale, M. anmd Beckinsale, R. (1975) *Southern Europe: The Mediterranean and Alpine Lands*. London: University of London Press.
22. Kayser (1968) *op. cit.* (see note 21); on internal migration in Greece, see Wassenhoven (1980) *op. cit.* (see note 21).
23. See Leontidou-Emmanuel (1981) *op. cit.*, Vol. II, p. 104 (see note 4). This information is provided in the 1961 and 1971 census returns and is based on responses to a questionnaire enquiring about the respondent's residence on the last day of 1955 and 1965 respectively. On internal migration in Greece see also: Moustaka, C. (1964) *The Internal Migrant*. Athens: Athens Social Science Centre; *Report on the Exploratory Survey into Motivations and Circumstances of Rural Migration* (1962), and *The Population Inflow into Greater Athens*. Athens: National Statistical Service of Greece, 1964; Baxevanis, J. J. (1972) *Economy and Population Movements in the Peloponnesos of Greece*. Athens: Greek National Centre of Social Research; Wagstaff, J. M. (1968) Rural migration in Greece. *Geography*, 53, pp. 175–9; Evelpidis, C. (1968) L'exode rural en Grece, in Peristiamy, J. G. (ed.) *Contributions to Mediterranean Sociology: Mediterranean Rural Communities and Social Change*. Paris & Athens: Mouton and Athens Social Science Centre, pp. 201–5; Sandis, E. E. (1973) *Refugees and Economic Migrants in Greater Athens*. Athens: Greek National Centre of Social Research.
24. For an analysis of the problem of unauthorized housing in Greece, see Romanos,

A. (1970) Squatter housing – Kipoupolis: The significance of unauthorised housing. *Architectural Association Quarterly*, No. 2, pp. 14–26. See also Emmanouil (1977) *op. cit.* (in Greek) (see note 19).
25. On the development of national planning in Greece, see Psilos (1968) *op. cit.* (see note 19).
26. The first such study appeared in 1961 as a diploma dissertation in the School of Architecture on the planning of the newly independent Republic of Cyprus. Several others followed, on various Greek regions (see, for example, Regional Planning scheme for the island of Crete, Diploma Dissertation, Technical University of Athens, 1965), usually stressing the need for the consolidation of rural settlements. Then, a number of regional and urban studies were produced by the Centre for Town Planning Research at Athens Technical University in the mid-1960s including a plan for the city of Kalamata.
27. These plans and studies are summarized in *Architecture in Greece*, 2, 1968, pp. 42–91.
28. Centre for Planning and Economic Research (1967) *Spatial Study of the National Network of Urban Centres*. Athens (in Greek). The concept of growth centres had been extensively used in plans drawn in the 1960s for the redevelopment of earthquake-stricken regions. See Aravantinos, A. (1970) Planning objectives in modern Greece. *Town Planning Review*, 41.
29. See Tsilenis, S. (1979) Regional division of Greece. *Synchrona Themata*, 6 (in Greek).
30. Sakoulas, A. N. (1975) *The Constitution of Greece* (1975). Athens (in Greek).
31. Greater Athens was defined at the time of the 1971 census as an agglomeration of fifty-eight municipalities, forming roughly a triangle with its base on the sea coast (see figure 2.12), and an area of approximately 210 km².
32. The population of Greater Athens was estimated at 3.68 million in 1978 by the Ministry of Public Works, based on a count of electricity metres undertaken by the Power Corporation. The 1981 census, however, gives a population figure of just over 3 million for Greater Athens, suggesting that the true 1978 figure was well short of the 3 million mark. The capital was not then, as government propaganda suggested, growing by 'one Patras' (100,000) a year through the 1970s. The true figure was, rather, less than 50,000 a year on average, and if current trends continue the population in the year 2000 will be 4.2 million, less than the government's target figure.
33. The nine 'counter-magnets' were Patras and Aigion in the Peloponnese, Volos and Larisa in Thessaly; Ptolemais and Kozani in Western Macedonia; Kavala in Eastern Macedonia, Jannina in Epirus and Irakleion in Crete (see figure 2.9). The population targets set for these towns were completely unrealistic, e.g. the combined population of Larisa and Volos were to grow from 200,000 in 1978 to 550,000 in the year 2000. This policy was abandoned by the government elected in October 1981.
34. A new plan for Greater Athens was produced in 1983 by the socialist administration.

# 3

# Italy

## DONATELLA CALABI

### INTRODUCTORY COMMENTS

The history of urban growth in Italy is characterized by a series of contrasts. Unlike many other European countries, the development of a hierarchy of urban centres preceded industrialization[1] and yet the expansion of Italy's cities this century has been somewhat sluggish (table 3.1), reflecting a slow economic growth in the country as a whole. In the historical evolution of urban systems, two distinct phases can be identified. The first, which began with the unification of Italy in 1861 and ended with the outbreak of World War II, was marked by a generally uniform growth in urban centres within the regional state system. Then, in the postwar era, a more rapid urban growth has seen the emergence of 'metropolitan' centres and the heightening of contrasts between the highly urbanized conurbations and the depopulated rural areas, and between the 'developed' and 'undeveloped' regions of the country.

Despite this rapid urban growth in the postwar years, however, Italian cities have tended to remain relatively small in comparison with their Northern European counterparts, partly because no *one* city has emerged as the country's dominant metropolis. In the north of the country, the long established settlements in the Po valley, Emilia, Veneto and lower Lombardy gave rise to a network of medium-sized (100–200,000) regional centres and the 'industrial triangle' of the north's three major metropolises – Milan, Turin and Genoa, with populations of 1.7 million, 1.2 million and 0.8 million, respectively, in 1980. Meanwhile in central Italy, Rome (2.9 million) has grown as the nation's administrative capital, whilst in Tuscany the expansion of industrial towns such as Prato and Pistoia this century has seen the decline in importance of the regional capital, Florence. In the south of the country, Naples (which in 1861 had a population of half a million and was the only city on a par with European

TABLE 3.1 Increase in Italy's urban population 1861–1961.

| Year | Total Population (millions) | Urban Population* (millions) | Urban Population as % of Total Population |
|---|---|---|---|
| 1861 | 25.02 | 4.89 | 19.6 |
| 1871 | 26.80 | 5.88 | 21.5 |
| 1881 | 28.46 | 6.72 | 23.7 |
| 1901 | 32.48 | 9.15 | 28.1 |
| 1911 | 34.67 | 10.82 | 31.3 |
| 1921 | 37.93 | 12.94 | 32.2 |
| 1931 | 41.18 | 14.41 | 35.1 |
| 1936 | 42.44 | 15.07 | 35.5 |
| 1951 | 47.16 | 19.39 | 41.1 |
| 1961 | 49.88 | 23.81 | 47.7 |

* 'Urban population' includes those permanently resident in settlements of 20,000 inhabitants or more.
*Source:* Carozzi, C. and Mioni, A. (1970) *L'Italia in formazione.* Bari: De Donato.

capitals) no longer dominates the south as before, as Bari, Catania and Salerno have grown as the centres of regions that have seen rapid industrialization in the postwar era.

Since unification in 1861, then, Italy has seen less obvious correlations between city growth and industrial development than in many Northern European countries, notably Great Britain and Germany. This chapter focuses on the urban growth process during this period and examines the role planning has played. The next four sections (pp 38–52) concern the period up to World War II, and the following three (pp 52–66) concentrate on the postwar period. Finally some concluding remarks are made in the last section.

## THE EARLY DEVELOPMENT OF PLANNING THOUGHT

The Napoleonic conquest of Italy in the early nineteenth century was followed by an influx of new cultural and scientific ideas and a reorganization of the country's administrative system. Under the guidance of the French, newly trained engineers drew up a classification of the national road system and opened new trans-alpine passes; the prefect system was introduced for the government of newly-defined 'departments' within the country[2]; and in Milan, the architect Giovanni Antolini was commissioned by Napoleon to design a new 'Bonaparte Forum' to be built around the castle area.

Antolini's 1801 plan (figures 3.1 and 3.2) in many ways characterized the new design concepts of the Napoleonic era[3]. The city extension comprised a series of civic buildings – museums, baths, stock exchange, customs hall,

FIGURE 3.1. Layout of the customs hall, part of Antolini's 1801 plan for the Bonaparte Forum in Milan. *Source:* Civica Raccolta delle stampe Bertarelli, Milan.

warehouses, theatre, assembly halls and schools – and in its grandeur and monumentalism sharply contrasted with the compact and minutely detailed morphology of the old medieval town. Much of the plan however, was never implemented; in 1807, when *Commissione d'Ornato* (planning commissions) were set-up within the country's major city councils, the Milan Council resolved to draw up a new plan, which focused on reform of the old city. Again, however, little of the plan was ever carried out – a few new town-gates and public buildings were erected – although other components do reappear in later plans for the city. Similar town expansion and old city reform plans were drawn up for other Italian cities in this era, and although only partly implemented, they nevertheless represented a new initiative by local authorities to intervene in the planning and growth of the country's major urban areas.

In 1815, following the fall of Napoleon, Italy was redivided into eight independent states, but aspirations towards achieving national unity remained

FIGURE 3.2. Facade of the museum and pantheon in Antolini's plan for the Bonaparte Forum in Milan.
*Source:* Civica Raccolta delle stampe Bertarelli, Milan.

strong amongst the intelligentsia and elements of the middle classes. As in Germany, the need for a customs union and national road and railway networks had become questions of national concern. In the town planning field, the most significant developments were connected with rebuilding and renewal in the various state capitals, above all to accommodate the coming of the railway. New building generally adhered to the neo-classical philosophy of 'order' and 'harmonious variety', and it was these concepts that tended to guide the leading architects and engineers (including Antolini) until the middle of the nineteenth century.

By the 1860s, the development of the railway network and the spread of new industries had been accompanied by a generally haphazard growth of many cities beyond their medieval walls and an increase in building densities in the old cities themselves. Factors relating to hygiene, building density and transport links became of the utmost importance in the functioning of the city, and yet many of the country's leading theorists continued to stress the importance of aesthetics in their designs and small-scale plans.

It was not until the early twentieth century that the development of planning theory and practice progressed from the *ad hoc* piecemeal treatment of urban growth that characterized the nineteenth century. The German concept of town building (*Städtebau*) came to dominate planning thought in Italy; town planning became an essentially technical activity, governed by regulations and laws relating to site dimensions, street patterns, traffic flows and building typology; the political, social and economic requirements and consequences of intervening in the urban growth process were afforded lesser attention[4]. Nevertheless, in the decade preceding the First World War, town planning emerged as a discipline distinct from those of architecture and engineering although the dichotomy between its aesthetic architectural origins and the more recent concern with the technical concepts related to civil engineering remained. In 1915, in a manual which is more or less a direct translation from Stübben's *Der Städtebau*, Caccia noted that 'in Italy, above all, is the confrontation between the two schools of thought particularly apparent. On the one hand, engineers see anything which is not closely related to construction as worthless; on the other hand, artists consider the subject of planning from an essentially aesthetic point of view'[5].

There were other outside influences and concepts which featured in the development of planning thought in this era. The Socialist Schiavi[6] founded a tenants' society (*Lega Inquilini*) which propagated the social implications of the British Garden City movement and the problems of city decentralization. Exploitation of the tenant by the small landowner was attacked and the benefits of co-operative housing schemes, such as the Società Umanitaria in Milan, were advocated. Others, such as Giovannoni, developed a school of thought that derived largely from the architectural tradition. Attention was focused on the 'variety of movements and contrasts' and on 'proportions'; and a regular and picturesque design and layout in town development and old city reform plans was favoured. The old cities were seen as historical centres where redevelopment should be limited; the suburbs, however, were the areas where new building techniques could be tried out, without any reference to the need to house the working classes, who by and large remained encamped in the old city centres[7].

It was this mix of ideas and concepts, then, in part from outside the country and in part stemming from Italy's own architectural and engineering traditions, that shaped the development of the planning profession in the early decades of this century. During the 1930s, the first undergraduate and post-graduate urban planning courses were set up at the University of Rome; and the Istituto Nazionale di Urbanistica (National Town Planning Institute) was established, which, amongst other things, published the journal *Urbanistica* and a book series on planning-related themes, both under the editorship of Giovannoni. Let us now turn to see how the evolution of planning thought was matched by developments in the planning machinery and legislative framework in the nineteenth century.

### PLANS AND PLANNING LEGISLATION IN THE NINETEENTH CENTURY

As already noted, *Commissione d'Ornato* were established to function within Italy's major town councils by Napoleonic decree in 1807[8]. Their major responsibility was to draw up a comprehensive set of bye-laws to regulate both the construction of roads and waterways (until then undertaken exclusively by civil engineers) and the design of public service infrastructure such as hospitals, theatres, cemeteries, slaughter houses (traditionally the work of architects). The work of the *Commissione* in the early nineteenth century helped bridge the gap between the two professions, although after 1815 the Austrian Administration reintroduced a system of provincial building offices (largely comprising architects) and municipal public works departments (mainly consisting of engineers) to co-exist alongside the *Commissione*[9], which thus tended to play a more limited role than in the Napoleonic era. They became concerned with the restoration of ancient buildings and with artistic and architectural control, as the numerous *Uffici* (offices) of the Austrian Administration precluded any more wide-ranging role.

It was also in the post-Napoleonic period that the practice of contracting out municipal works to private companies started. This arrangement for the building and management of public works such as slaughter houses, roads, railways and bridges came to be increasingly employed by municipal authorities in subsequent decades.

Following the unification of Italy in 1861 two significant pieces of legislation in the planning field were introduced by the new national government. The National Administration Act of 1865 attempted to standardize the disparate local authority building regulations, and introduced regulations aimed at curbing overcrowding and high building densities in cities with populations of 10,000 or more. More importantly, the Expropriation Act passed the same year reflected the government's desire to initiate public authorities and redevelopment schemes in the country's major cities. Public authorities were empowered to expropriate the necessary terrain for such projects, with minimal compensation paid to landowners. At the same time, two main types of plan were introduced: *Piani Regolatori edilizi* (redevelopment plans sometimes called 'alignment' or 'slum clearance' plans) could be drawn up to plan the clearance and redevelopment of the shabbier parts of town; whilst *Piani di ampliamento Urbano* (expansion plans) were intended to be used for the planning of piecemeal new development around the city periphery. Nowhere, however, was reference made to any concept of comprehensive city planning, nor was land-use zoning introduced.

The 1870s witnessed a concerted effort by many city councils to use the regulations introduced in the 1865 National Administration Act to improve standards of public hygiene and control new development. At the same time redevelopment plans, as introduced in the 1865 Expropriation Act, were used in many cities for the *ad hoc* opening and straightening of roads, the provision of water and sewerage systems, and the clearance and redevelopment of parts of the old city. In Florence (national capital 1864–71), the city council implemented a series of small-scale expansion and renewal schemes, framed within two distinct plans – an 1865 expansion plan and an 1885 redevelopment plan – both drawn up by the architect Guiseppe Poggi. Similarly, following the conferring of capital status on Rome (at the expense of Florence) in 1871, a redevelopment plan was approved in 1873 for the clearance and redevelopment of Rome's central areas.

Meanwhile, in Naples, the cholera epidemics of the early 1880s led the national government to pass the 1885 Naples Act, which speeded up expropriation procedure in the city (on the 'declaration of public utility'), and made special government funds available for the clearing and reconstruction of large areas of the old city. At the same time, redevelopment and expansion plans were drawn up and approved in 1888 to act as a framework within which redevelopment and new building could take place. These plans made provision for a new sewerage system and the realignment and raising of major streets, and earmarked areas for both industrial development (around the park) and the construction of new housing estates (mainly to the east). The plan area was divided into a series of 'concessionary zones', which were let out to private developers who had to follow the guidelines laid down in the plan[10].

Following the Neapolitan example, other towns – Turin, Bologna and Venice amongst them – drew up similar plans to clear inner-city slums and develop new areas on the city periphery. None of these plans, however, were comprehensive in their treatment of the city; rather they made provision for piecemeal and generally unco-ordinated intervention in the centre and outskirts of the city. In the 1891 Plan for Venice for example, it was noted that the plan comprised 'a limited number of definite projects and a study of partial changes which comply with general concepts, but are not connected to, or dependent on, one another'[11].

In many of the smaller and medium sized Italian towns, a similar pattern emerged. City centre reform was limited to *ad hoc* localized renewal, which often saw the construction of public or private service buildings and transport networks. As regards city expansion, plans generally catered for piecemeal additions to the built-up area, which tended to reinforce the monocentric structure which characterized most cities[12]. Even in these plans, detailed functional land zoning is rarely evident until after 1900; until then, building regulations were used to regulate land use and implementation was often hampered by the lack of any agreement between the local council and the affected landowners on how development should proceed. Such agreements tended to be restricted to those towns with a strong entrepreneurial tradition, or where affected landowners had sufficient capital to act as developers themselves.

### City Growth 1850–1918: Some Examples

The regional differences in the historical evolution of Italian towns make it difficult to generalize about the urban growth process or to talk of 'typical' examples. Here, however, an attempt is made to give some insights into the dynamics and mechanics of city growth in the period up to World War I by

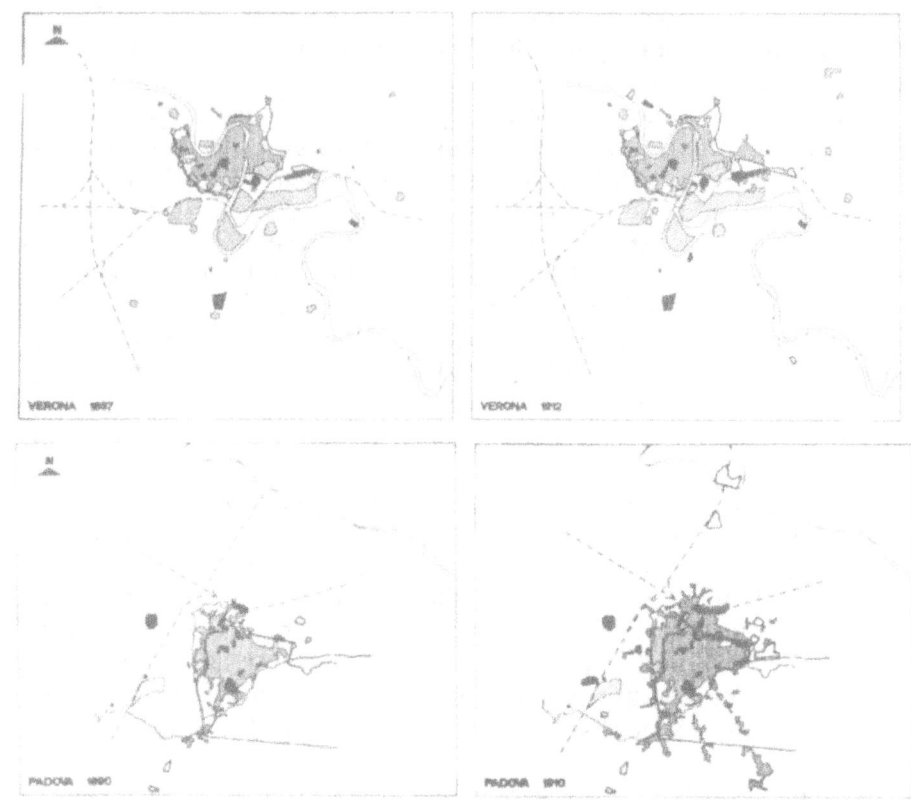

FIGURE 3.3. The growth of Verona (above) and Padova (or Padua) around the turn of the century.
Source: Carozzi, C. and Mioni, A. (1980) *Suolo Urbano e Popolazione*. Milan: Angeli.

examining carefully selected examples. First, four neighbouring towns in Central Veneto[13], which may be considered as fair examples of the 'medium-sized' towns referred to earlier, are examined together. Then, the urban growth process in Turin, today one of the country's leading industrial centres with a population of 1.2 million, is studied.

The towns of Central Veneto – Padua, Vicenza, Verona and Treviso – lie inland from Venice, in the northern half of the river Po floodplain. All four towns are within 80 km of each other, and at the end of the nineteenth century had populations ranging from 10,000 (Treviso) to 45,000 (Verona), and built-up areas of between 120 and 430 hectares. Growth until the late nineteenth century was minimal, but from then until the inter-war years, all four towns experienced a similar pattern of rapid change (see, for example, figure 3.3).

One of the major new developments in this period concerned the road network. The railway stations and goods warehouses had been built outside these towns in the 1850s, only later to be linked with the town centres by road, in

# ITALY

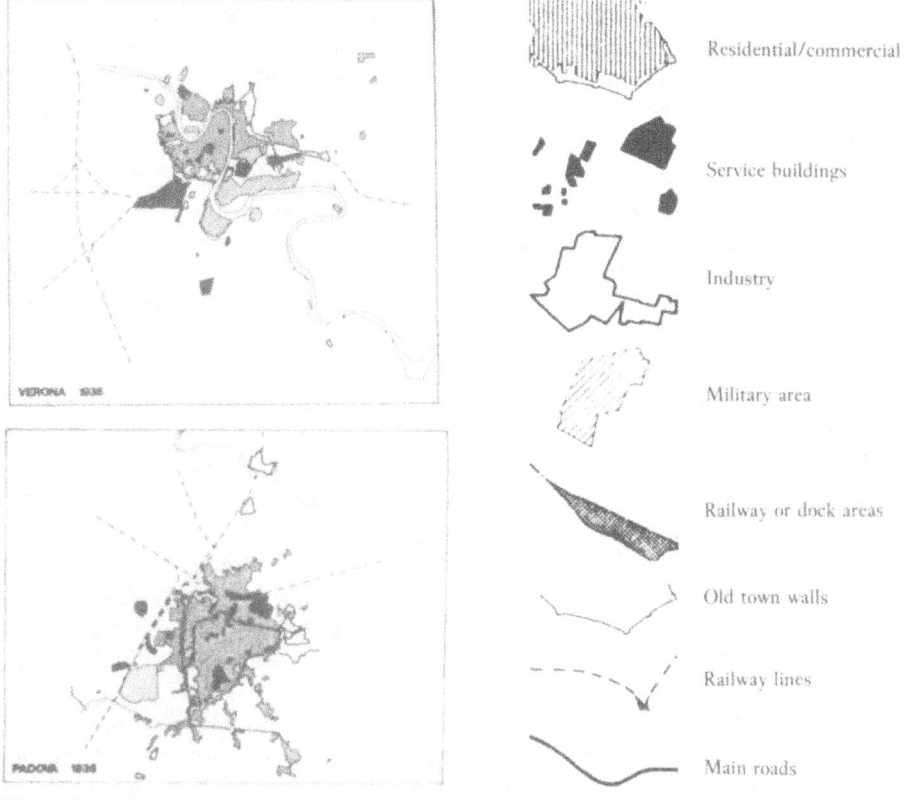

Note the location of the railway stations (shaded black) *outside* the old medieval walls (left) and their subsequent envelopment as the towns began to expand towards the end of the last century.

the 1880s and 1890s. These new roads were financed by the local councils and represented their major budgetary outlay; they involved breaking the town walls (as in Treviso), or demolition of town-gates (Padua), and in some cases the outer-wall roads ran alongside the walls themselves, to form a partial or full ring road. Again, however, these extensions of the road network were not part of overall town plans but were rather the result of a series of council resolutions to extend the road system in short stretches.

Rebuilding within the medieval walls was generally limited to modifications and extensions of public buildings or private premises. Some new roads were opened, canals were filled in and some limited demolition and clearance took place. Such building was governed in part by municipal building and public health regulations, drawn up by municipal councils in the latter half of the nineteenth century, and in part by the 1865 National Administration Act.

Outside the walls, new development consisted largely of new public service buildings (barracks, hospitals, cemeteries, asylums), whilst some new industrial premises were erected; again breaches in the walls were often made to facilitate new road links. New housing was limited to haphazard development along the outer-wall roads, particularly the ring roads. None of these developments, either within or without the old city walls, was undertaken within the framework of redevelopment plans, as established in the 1865 Expropriation Act. Indeed, the only such plan to be approved by any one of the four town councils in the nineteenth century was the 1865 Redevelopment Plan for Padua, which included proposals for the widening of the town's main streets. The plan was never implemented, however, largely because it made no provision for the financing of such intervention. These plans were the work of council planning departments rather than the *Commissione d'Ornato*, which remained largely concerned with the restoration of historic buildings and aesthetic control.

In all four towns, the second half of the nineteenth century also witnessed the installation of new public service infrastructure systems – gas-fed street lighting, electricity, and water supplies. These 'public works' were in fact undertaken by private companies, working in 'concessionary areas' under the direction of the municipal authorities. The gas pipelines, to feed the street lighting network, were installed by a Lyonese company in all four towns in 1845. Water and electricity networks followed in Padua, Vicenza and Verona after 1850, and cross town railway connections had been built in all four towns by 1900. Municipal sewerage systems, however, did not appear until some time later, the earliest designs coming in the 1930s.

In the first two decades of this century the urban population of Central Veneto towns experienced a sharp increase, and the resultant pressure on the nineteenth century urban fabric brought a number of new local level plans. These redevelopment plans were largely aimed at slum clearance and rebuilding in the old city centres, and were accompanied by legislation based on the 1885 Naples Act, making central government funds available for speedier redevelopment. In some areas, the results were quite dramatic; in Santa Maria in Vanzo (in Padua), for example, an old degraded part of the city was transformed into a middle-class residential zone, significantly different from the working-class housing provided in redevelopment schemes in other northern towns; but in the main, these plans were not carried out on the ground, being thwarted by the landowning interests that opposed them.

In the early nineteenth century, Turin experienced steady growth as it was first the capital of the State of Piedmont (up until 1861) and then, for three years, the capital of Italy, and by 1864 had a population of 218,000. After 1870, however, the expansion of the city slowed somewhat, exhibiting a growth model rather different from the Venetian towns discussed above.

Until the mid-nineteenth century, the development of Turin was characterized by the well-established eighteenth-century pattern of large compact blocks within a grid-patterned street layout, interspersed with grandiose squares and gardens. The compactness of the city also owed something to its siting on the north bank of the river Po; the eighteenth-century citadel, together with the

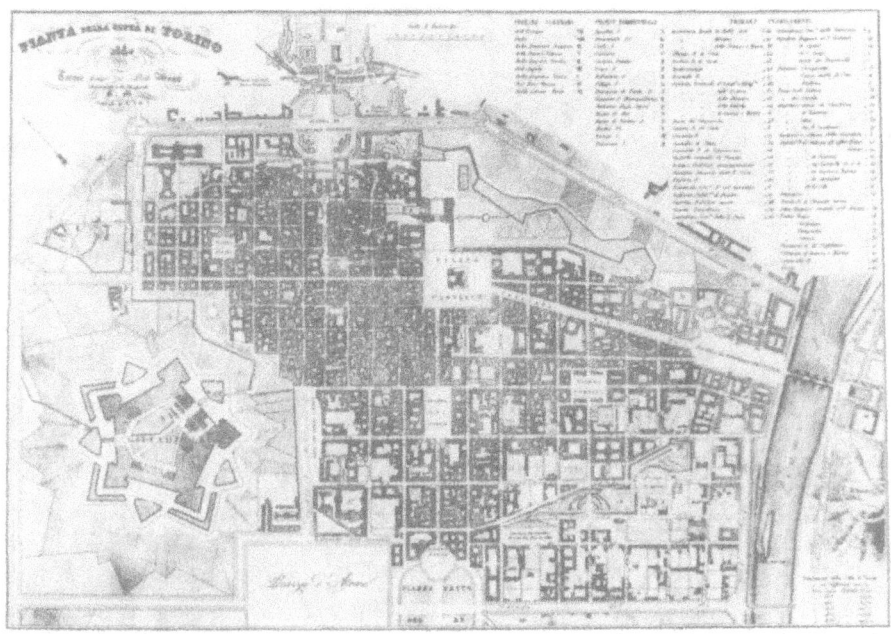

FIGURE 3.4. Biasioli's plan of Turin, 1840.
*Source:* Biblioteca Civica, Turin.

ring roads (running alongside what remained of the medieval walls), provided an urban space which had been largely occupied by 1840. Indeed, by this date, as Biasioli's plan of the city shows (figure 3.4), new areas of block development were beginning to appear to the south of the city, between the Piazza d'Armi and the river Po.

The need for a planned extension of the built-up area was recognized by the local council who in 1852 commissioned the architect A. Antonelli to draw up a plan for the expansion of the city. Antonelli's plan (figure 3.5) included proposals for the expansion of the city in the area of the citadel (which was to be destroyed) and along the banks of the river Po and a canalized and straightened river Dora. A railway network was also planned, with two alternative sitings for the railway station (on opposite banks of the river Dora) being provided.

Following the approval of Antonelli's plan, the urbanization of the citadel area went ahead, more or less as indicated in the plan. But the general absence of any functional specification for the planned blocks of development, and the lack of any firm control policy from the municipal council, meant that development on the city fringes reflected the existing landownership patterns rather than the grid pattern established in the plan. Only existing building and health regulations were used to control this new development. Nevertheless, the council did intervene to provide a number of public service buildings (the slaughter

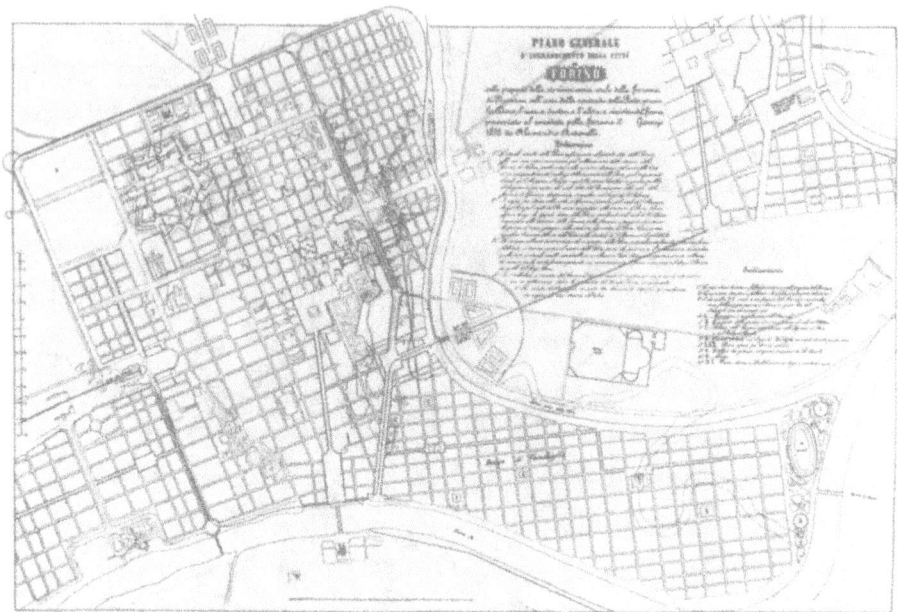

FIGURE 3.5. Antonelli's plan for the expansion of Turin, 1852. The plan contained proposals for the urbanization of the Citadel area, the canalization of the Dora river, and large tracts of new block development along the banks of the Po and Dora rivers. Alternative proposals for the siting of a railway station were also included.
*Source:* Collezione Lanzone, Turin.

house, cattle market, barracks, and prison) in the 1850s and 1860s, although not all these components had been included in Antonelli's plan. Taking all things into consideration, however, the efforts of the city council represented a concerted attempt to carry out a planned programme of new development, which contrasted markedly with the general *ad hoc*, piecemeal interventions of other big city councils in this period.

With the loss of capital status in 1864, Turin's civic pride was somewhat dented, and its administrative and economic activities were correspondingly reduced. The period after 1870 did, however, see certain innovations with regard to the problematical power supply situation in the city. A new network of canals was built to take water from the Dora and Po rivers to power the city's main industries (textile mills, food and wood processing, military workshops); and an elementary form of zoning was apparent in the council's attempt to keep the new industrial 'working areas' away from the residential, commercial and administrative functions of the 'town' area.

The last decades of the century also witnessed the approval of a series of small-scale redevelopment plans (within the legislative framework of the 1865 Expropriation Act) for the clearance of slum areas and opening and widening of new and existing streets. These developments reflected the town's civic will to re-establish the *imago urbis* (town image) in an era of rapid social and political change, and responded to the need for both new functional relationships in the old city centres and for new qualitative standards in new development.

It was also during this period that the industrial base which was to make Turin an internationally renowned car producing centre was established. At the Velentino National Exhibition, held in Turin in 1884, electricity was heralded as the solution to the city's power supply problems, and this seemed to be confirmed by the location of Fiat and Lancia factories there in 1889 and 1906 respectively. Industrial production in the city rapidly increased as new car-related industries (coach building, tyre manufacture, headlight manufacture) were attracted to Turin, all to be powered by the low-price municipal electricity network. By 1911, Turin's population had reached 415,000, and a new town plan (the Quaglia-Marescotti Plan) was drawn up to plan and control the rapidly expanding industrial city. Whilst new developments in and around the old city were officially recognized (very different in layout from those envisaged in Antonelli's 1852 plan), new sites in the city's surrounding hill area to the north were brought into the plan area for subsequent development, and the central government officially approved a slightly modified version of the plan in 1920. It was thus that the noble citizens of Turin, descendents from the House of Savoy, gradually turned from the Art Nouveau style of city planning of the mid-nineteenth century to the logic of a more functional zoning of the existing built-up area, which, since the early years of this century, has included large zones of industrial development and working-class housing.

### PLANNING UNDER FASCISM IN THE INTER-WAR YEARS

In 1922 the Fascist government of Mussolini came to power in Italy and remained there until after the outbreak of World War II. These two decades of Fascism stand out as a clearcut phase in the history of urban planning in Italy[14]. It was an era in which emphasis was placed on rural development, and 'peasant Italy' was idealized as the alternative to the ills of urban living. Land reclamation and redistribution, and irrigation schemes were undertaken by the central government, while wheat growing and child-birth programmes attempted to re-establish the prestige of rural areas in the country as a whole.

The evolution of planning thought and practice continued in the planning of new rural settlements. The most renowned and costly of these was the Pontine Marshes Redevelopment Programme, in which five new townships were constructed in a hitherto depopulated, marshy coastal area, 80 km south of Rome. The programme also included the reclamation of marsh areas, antipestilence measures, and large-scale state expropriation; their successful co-ordination and implementation transformed the area into a productive agricultural region in less than a decade.

All five new settlements in the Pontine Marshes scheme[15] – Littoria,

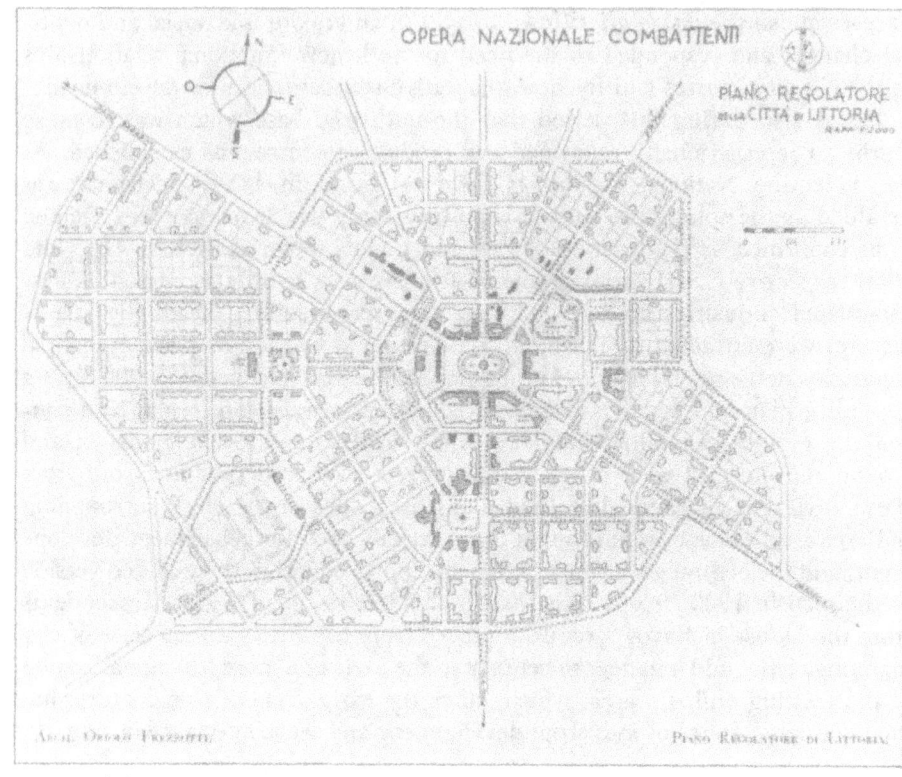

FIGURE 3.6. Development plan for Littoria, the capital of the Pontine Marshes.
The plan, drawn up in 1933 by Oriolo Frezzotti, included a wide variety of *plurifamiliar* dwelling types, but only one main centre in which the major services and commercial buildings were located.
*Source: Architettura,* September, 1933.

Sabaudia, Pontinia, Aprilia and Pomezia – exhibited common features as regards their planning and design (figures 3.6 and 3.7). They were based on a decentralized, yet essentially monocentric, concept of settlement development, with large residential areas surrounding one main centre which comprised the public buildings, market, hospital, main square, cinema, etc. In some of the plans (for example, figure 3.7) some of the more space-requiring public service facilities (sports areas, barracks) were located on the settlement outskirts. In general, these plans can be seen as early examples in Italy of comprehensive town plans that incorporate a form of land zoning to ensure the functional differentiation of space and residential decentralization.

The direct impact of the twenty years of Fascism on the development of the country's urban centres was limited to certain specific cases, such as in central Rome, where large areas of the old historic centre were demolished, and in Bologna, Brescia, Bergamo and Turin, where parts of the old town centres were destroyed to make way for new streets and office blocks, schools,

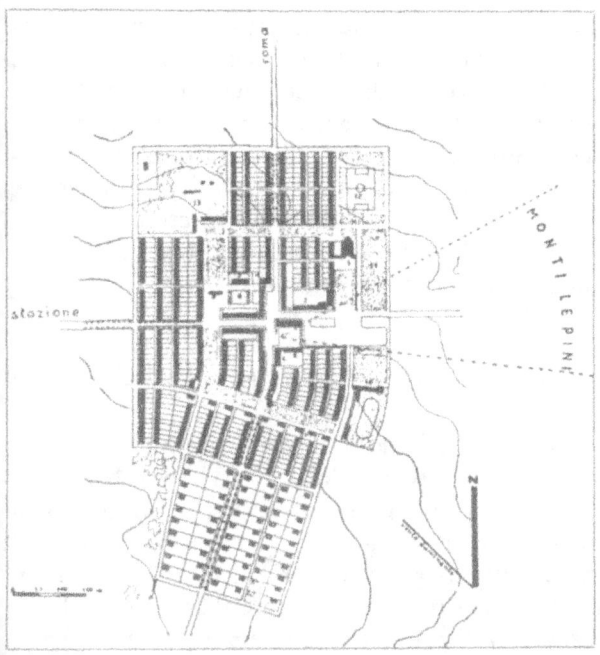

FIGURE 3.7. Development plan for Aprilia in the Pontine Marshes region.
The plan was drawn up in 1936 by the architects Piccinato and Montuori. Again dwellings are clustered around one main centre, although sports and recreational areas are included in the outer periphery.
*Source: Urbanistica,* November/December, 1936.

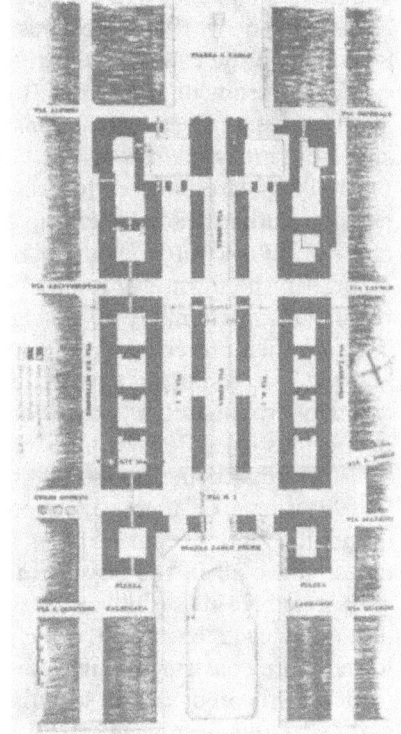

FIGURE 3.8. Plan for Via Roma, Turin.
An example of city centre demolition and renewal under Fascism: land bordering Via Roma was expropriated by the state and new buildings constructed, many of them destined for office and commercial use. It is worth noting, however, that the original plans pre-dated the First World War, although the complex was not built until the 1930s.
*Source: Architettura,* 1934.

banks and railway stations (figure 3.8). Despite the pro-agricultural bias of the government's official policy, the regime forged close links with the country's major financial and industrial groups – steel and power producers, car, chemical, and rubber manufacturers – and was instrumental in the creation of certain industry-related complexes, such as the industrial 'pole' in Venice-Marghera. This seeming contradiction in many ways epitomized the sterile years of the dictatorship, in which – notwithstanding the success of some of the larger-scale rural development schemes – little progress was made in the planning and management of the nation's urban centres.

### Planning and Reconstruction in the Postwar Era

The devastation caused by the Second World War left half a million houses in Italy in ruins, and a further 250,000 severely damaged. The war had paralyzed the construction industry and cohabiting and sub-letting became common features of postwar Italy. The 1951 census gives an average figure of 1.39 inhabitants per room for the country as a whole (1.21 in the north, 1.86 in the south), with 750,000 houses being occupied by more than one family. A total of 1.8 million dwellings were without an inside lavatory or water supply, and 220,000 families lived in dwellings defined as 'inappropriate' (huts, cellars, caves). Even by 1951, the housing deficit was still estimated at 2.5 million dwellings in the country as a whole.

The government's response[16] was to introduce a series of measures aimed at stimulating private sector construction, with minimal direct intervention by state authorities themselves. In a first building cycle, lasting from the late 1940s until 1964, state intervention consisted of the direct financing of quasi-public housing authorities such as the INA-CASA (National Institute of Housing) and the IACP (Autonomous Institute of Low Income Housing) and the subsidizing (in the form of loans and grants) of the private sector, whilst planning regulations, particularly in the big cities, were relaxed to allow a more intensive land use than prescribed in the approved town development plans (PRGs – see below). The result, in a period of rapid economic growth and unprecedented country-city migration, was a boom in the construction industry, unparalleled in previous eras. Between 1951 and 1955, an average 150,000 dwellings were built per year, rising to 380,000 in the period 1961–65 with a peak of 450,000 in 1964 alone. Of these, 5 per cent were planned and built by public housing authorities and the majority of housing estates built in the country's major cities, above all in the city periphery (figure 3.9), were privately built, many with state subsidies. Only after 1964, with the onset of an economic recession, did a new cycle begin[17], which saw a stricter adherence to approved plans, lower house construction figures and new attempts by the Socialist government to deal with problems of speculation and state acquisition of land (the 1967 and 1971 Acts, see below).

FIGURE 3.9. Residential district of Milan in the 1960s.
New high-rise residences in the background contrast with traditional working-class dwellings in the foreground.
*Source: Urbanistica*, Nos. 68–69.

Some of the housing projects after the war were framed within the 1942 Town Planning Act, which made provision for a hierarchy of plans at the extramunicipal, municipal and local (sub-municipal) levels, with both central government and municipal councils being actively involved in the plan-making and approval process. *Piani Regolatori Intercomunali* (PRI) could be drawn up by *ad hoc* groups of municipalities acting as one planning consortium, whilst *Piani Regolatori Generali* (PRG) were development plans at the municipal level. Finally *Piani Regolatori Particolareggiati* (PRP) were more detailed local-level plans to be drawn up within the framework of the approved PRG. It was made obligatory for the country's major city councils (named in the Act) to draw up their own plans, and procedural guidelines were set-out for the advertisement of plans and their final approval by the regional governments, who were empowered to modify plans as necessary. The 1942 Act was qualitatively on a par with most other planning Acts approved elsewhere in Europe in the postwar period but, as we shall see, it was largely ineffective in practice because of the economic and political forces which shaped the development process in Italy in the 1950s and 1960s.

The immediate postwar era, however, was an age of new hope and social commitment in the planning field[18]. 'Reconstruction' had political, social and cultural connotations beyond the mere building of new physical structures. The

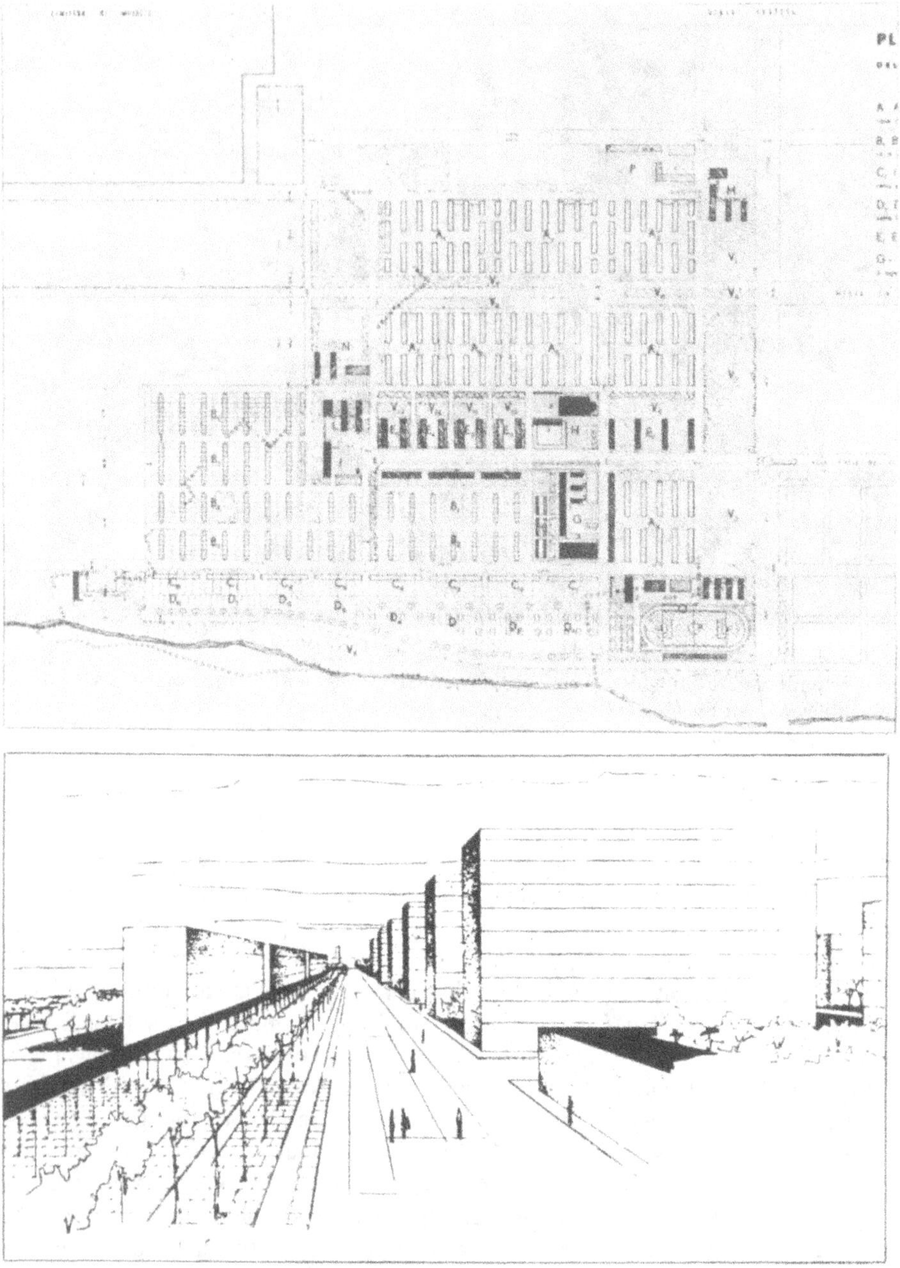

FIGURE 3.10. Layout and urban design in the Costanzo Ciano new town, 1942.
This was one of four new satellites planned for Milan in the early 1940s. It was the work of Albini, Camus, Cerutti, Fabbri, C. and M. Mazzocchi, Minoletti, Palanti, Pucci and Putelli, members of CIAM, some of whom worked on the plan 'AR' for Milan.
*Source: Controspazio,* October, 1973.

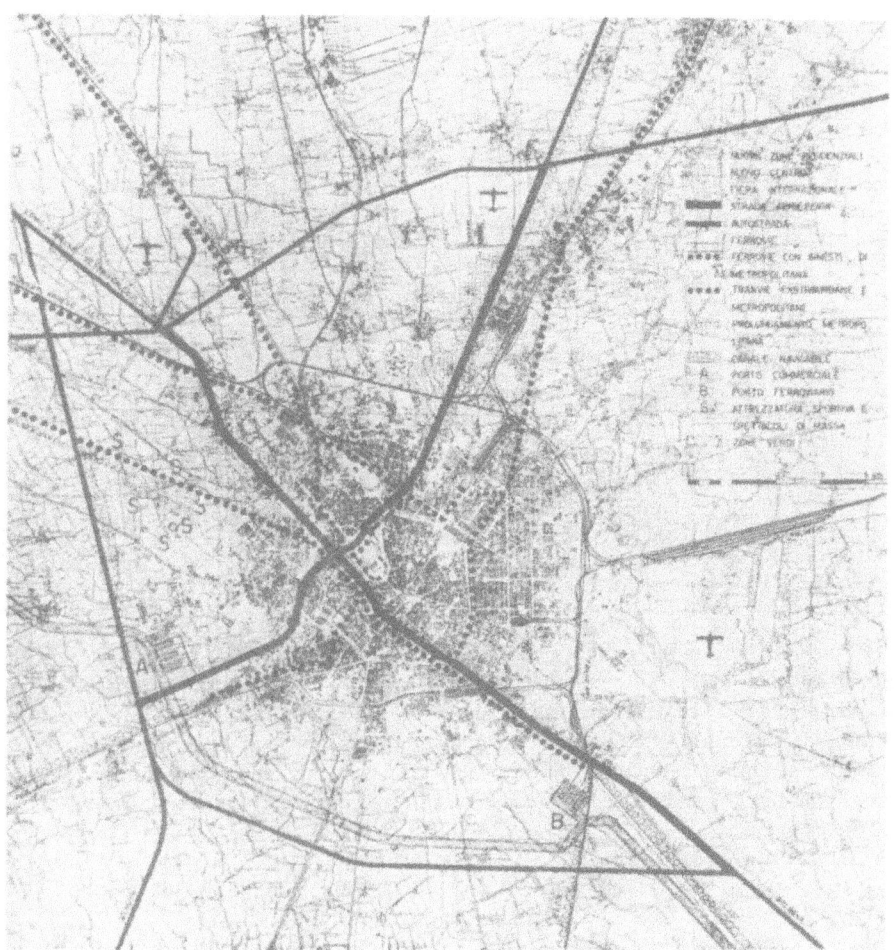

FIGURE 3.11. The development plan 'AR' for Milan, 1945.
The plan 'AR' drawn up in 1944 by a group of Italian architects belonging to CIAM and presented to the Milan Council in 1945 as a possible plan for the city. Its major objectives were the reconstruction and decentralization of the city and a restructuring of lines of communication. The key reads (from top to bottom): residential areas; new town centre; international exhibition area; metropolitan highways; national motorways; railways; railways linked to the underground; metropolitan tramways; underground; navigable canals; goods port (on canal); rail-canal port; sports areas; geen zones.
*Source: Costruzioni,* No. 194, 1946.

debate on the housing problem inevitably involved broader issues such as public intervention, devolution of power to the local level, development control and planning techniques and typology. In Milan[19], a project for the construction of four new satellite towns in 1942 (figure 3.10) was followed in 1945 by a

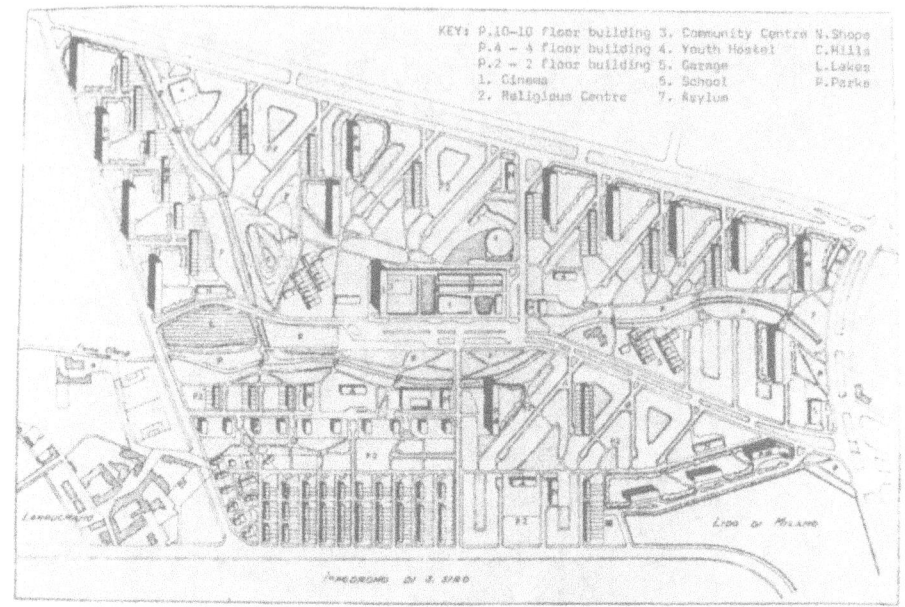

FIGURE 3.12. Plan for the 'QT8' housing estate outside Milan, 1948.
The plan was presented at the Triennale Art Exhibition in Milan in 1948 as a model neighbourhood for working people. It was designed by Piero Bottoni, who also worked on the plan 'AR' for Milan and, as a member of the Communist Party, unsuccessfully attempted to get a draft bill aimed at 'housing for all' through Parliament. There are various housing types included in the plan – semi-detached and multi-storey; and service buildings are intended for the use of surrounding communities as well as those of the estate.
*Source: Metron*, Nos. 21/22, 1948.

development plan (figure 3.11) drawn up in the political and cultural climate of the liberation from Fascism. The plan included proposals for a series of new housing estates on the periphery, redevelopment of large tracts of the city centre, and new cross-town road and rail systems. It was extra-municipal but the area covered by the plan ('Milan and its surrounds') did not correspond to any established administrative unit; the plan was never formally approved but the *Piano Regolatore* for the city, drawn up in 1948 by the Milan Councils, incorporated many of its features (for example, the metropolitan highways and the new town centre). And in the late 1940s the 'QT8' housing estate (figure 3.12) epitomized the new architectural and design concepts of the reconstruction era[20].

The postwar boom in the building industry and rapid recovery of the national economy brought sudden and sweeping changes in the urban morphology of the country's major cities, and exacerbated the regional imbalances between town and country and between north and south. Migrants from the south[21]

TABLE 3.2. Classification of population by settlement size and region 1951–71.

| Region | Settlement size | | | | | | | | | Total | |
|---|---|---|---|---|---|---|---|---|---|---|---|
| | up to 10,000 | | 10–100,000 | | 100–500,000 | | 500,000 or more | | | | |
| | 1951 | 1971 | 1951 | 1971 | 1951 | 1971 | 1951 | 1971 | | 1951 | 1971 |
| | | | | | (thousands of inhabitants) | | | | | | |
| North West | 6169 | 5747 | 2537 | 3500 | 357 | 779 | 2682 | 4892 | | 11715 | 14919 |
| North East | 4703 | 4187 | 3235 | 2783 | 1479 | 3029 | — | — | | 9417 | 9999 |
| Central Italy | 2992 | 2446 | 3866 | 3831 | 517 | 1228 | 1652 | 2800 | | 8668 | 10305 |
| South (Mezzogiorno) | 7306 | 6634 | 5991 | 7919 | 1727 | 2365 | 2662 | 1884 | | 17685 | 18802 |
| Total | 21171 | 19014 | 15629 | 18034 | 4080 | 7401 | 6996 | 9576 | | 47516 | 54025 |

*Source:* ISTAT, 1951 and 1971 censuses.

TABLE 3.3. Annual average percentage change in migratory population in Italy's major cities 1961–69.

| City | Rome | Turin | Bologna | Genoa | Milan | Florence | Palermo | Venice | Bari | Naples |
|---|---|---|---|---|---|---|---|---|---|---|
| Annual % change 1961–69 | +1.47 | +1.0 | +0.8 | +0.75 | +0.36 | +0.33 | −0.1 | −0.13 | −0.22 | −0.55 |

*Source:* Mainardi, R. (1971) *Le grandi città italiane*. Milan: Angeli.

flocked into the industrial triangle of Milan, Turin and Genoa (tables 3.2 and 3.3) as new high-rise housing estates sprang-up in the periphery, and commercial and managerial functions came to dominate the centre. In Turin, car production continued to be the major growth industry, with one-half of all inhabitants depending on Fiat for their livelihood, whilst in Genoa, coal, steel and port related industries provided the new jobs.

In the decade 1951–61, rural-urban migration assumed unprecedented importance in the urban growth process, with 78 per cent of total demographic increase in urban areas being due to in-migration. The nation's four largest cities – Rome, Milan, Turin and Naples – collectively experienced a population increase of 1.2 million during the decade, and the north's industrial triangle of Milan-Turin-Genoa absorbed an average 113,000 migrants a year in the period 1951–65. In an effort to stem the flow of migrants from country to city

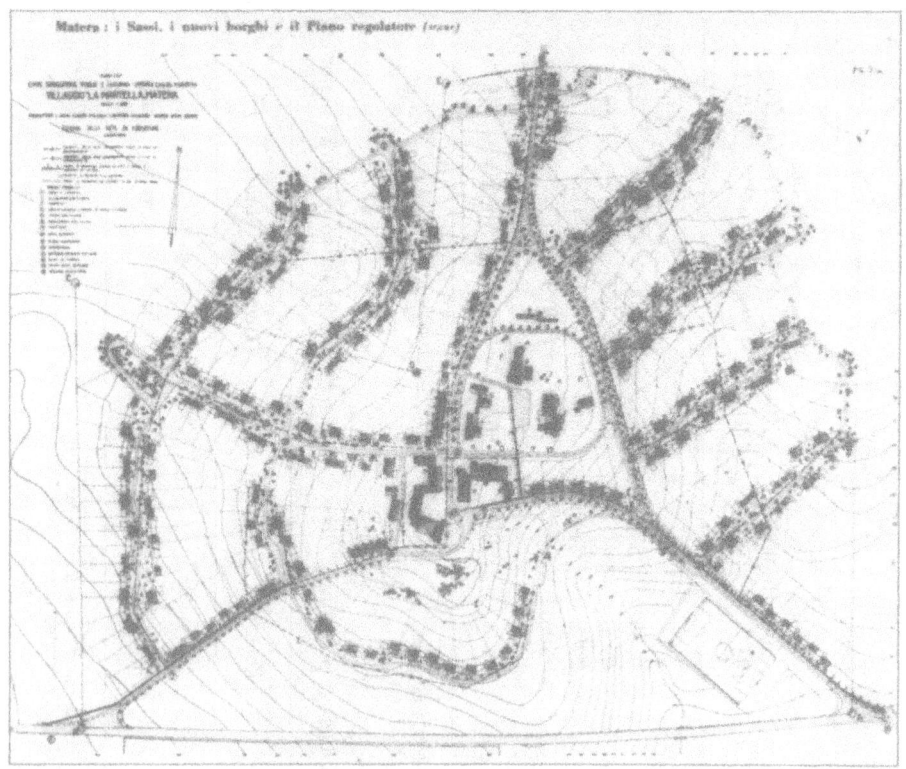

FIGURE 3.13. Plan for the development of La Martella, part of the general extension plan for the town of Matera (between Bari and Taranto).
The general extension plan for the Matera municipality included this plan for the development of La Martella, an outlying rural settlement. It was designed by Ludovico Quaroni, and is an example of the application of the neighbourhood concept of planning in the 1950s.
Source: Urbanistica, No. 15/16, 1955.

and, above all, from south to north, the government embarked upon a new era in national regional-economic policy in the 1950s through the Cassa per il Mezzogiorno, a special public body set-up to manage the economic development of the south. There is, of course, a great deal of literature[22] available on the history of the Cassa, and it is not within the scope of this book to examine in any great detail the functioning of the Cassa's development policies. In the 1950s, the major projects concerned public service infrastructure (roads, railways, aquaducts) and land reclamation and reform schemes, and only in the mid-1960s did the industrial policies, based on financial incentives to industry in selected 'areas' and 'poles', come to the fore.

The Cassa's policy also encompassed rural development programmes for 'special' areas, in which selected centres and smaller communities in their spheres of influence (for example Matera – figure 3.13) were singled out for sweeping new investments in infrastructure and new economic activities. Although these 'special' programmes were generally well managed, the urban development process in the south's established main centres (Naples[23], Bari and Palermo) continued apace, with Cassa policy doing little to control growth or co-ordinate investment. Rather, the 1950s and 1960s in these cities witnessed the speculative renewal of the old city centres and the anarchical sprawl of the suburbs, often in contradiction to approved urban plans. Ironically, some of the worst offenders in this context were public authorities, often financed by the Cassa, who built their housing estates on the periphery and paid scant regard to approved plans or planning legislation.

NEW DEVELOPMENTS IN PLANNING IN THE 1960s AND 1970s

Amongst the hopes and aspirations of the postwar era, the Italian planners of the day adopted and adapted certain new ideas and theories from overseas. Howard's Garden City concept was clearly evident in the 1942 'Four Satellites Project' for Milan; and the neighbourhood unit, with its provision of community service infrastructure, appeared in the plans for new housing estates and development projects in the 1940s and 1950s (for example, the QT8 estate – figure 3.12 and La Martella – figure 3.13), even if in practice much of the accompanying service infrastructure was belatedly or never built on the ground.

Towards the end of the 1950s, the need for a wider spatial and conceptual view of urban development, taking account of the complexity of political, territorial and social issues, brought the introduction of a number of new planning ideas and models. The 'city-territory', 'city-region'[24], and 'managerial centre' concepts were put forward in a range of planning literature and paper plans, which attempted to establish new roles for planning and the planner in an era of rapid transformation in Italian society in general. New supra-municipal plans for Milan, Bologna and Rome were drawn up and approved as were 'city-

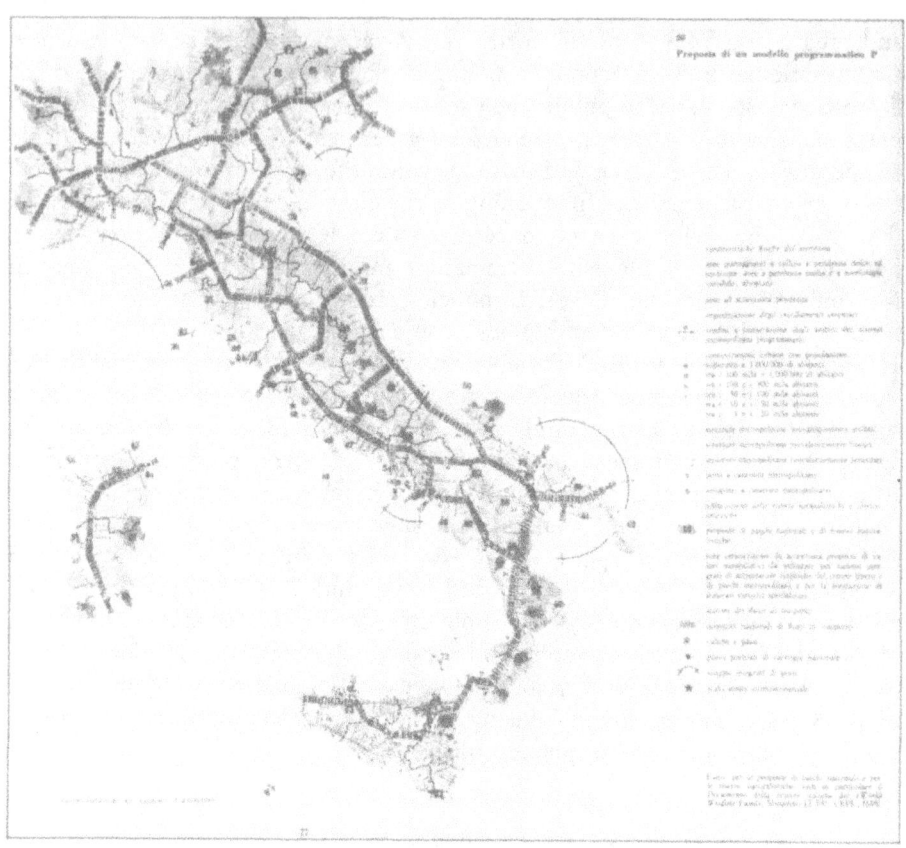

FIGURE 3.14. 'Progetto 80', the national territorial plan drawn up by the Treasury in 1971.
The plan specified major metropolitan areas, urban centres of different sizes, national parks, airports, major transport flows, etc.
Source: *Urbanistica,* No. 57, 1971.

region' plans for Rome-Latina and Messina-Reggio; and public competitions for new plans for *centri direzionali* (tertiary/quaternary service centres) in Turin, Padua and Milan were held[25]. The problems of the organization of space and the need for an 'urbanized continuum' were debated by planners and economists, as was the relationship between territorial planning and a national economic plan. *Progetto 80* (Project 1980 – figure 3.14) was drawn up by the Treasury in 1971, as a national strategic plan to guide and co-ordinate public and private sector investment. The plan borrowed from the French concept of *amenagement du territoire,* and although it was never given full Cabinet backing, it was indicative of how the spatial and conceptual development of upper-tier physical planning had progressed since the war, with its prescribed aim of bringing about a more balanced regional distribution of the country's 'urban systems' and 'metropolitan areas'.

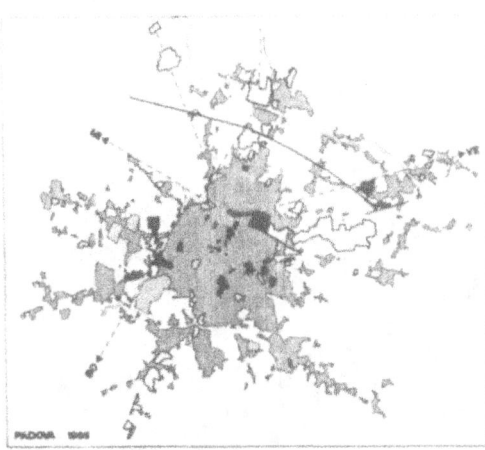
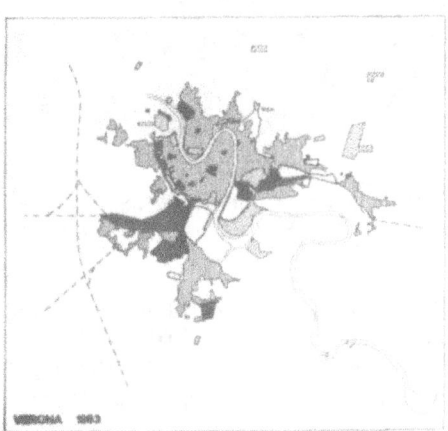

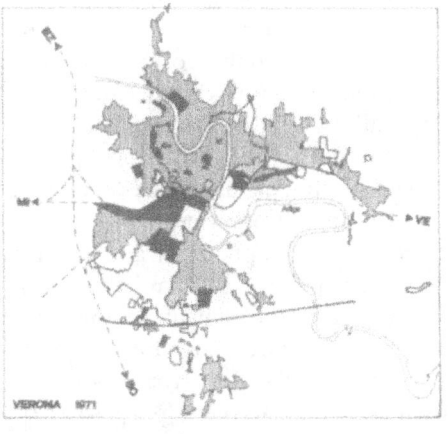

FIGURE 3.15. Patterns of growth in the postwar era in Padova and Verona. Note the general radiocentric pattern of growth along the road and rail lines of communication. (For key, see figure 3.3.)
*Source:* Carozzi, C. and Mioni, A. (1980) *Suolo Urbano e Popolazione.* Milan: Angeli.

FIGURE 3.16. Genoa in the 1970s.
A new urban motorway is constructed alongside the new *centro direzionale* (commercial, office and administrative centre).

The realities of the development process, however, followed a depressingly similar pattern, with the existing planning machinery doing little to control speculative development and the generally anarchical growth of the city periphery (figures 3.15 and 3.16). But in the 1960s the Coalition government announced its intention to draw up a complete revision of the country's planning legislation. In 1967, following a series of scandalous construction tragedies involving the collapse of illegally constructed and defective buildings, the so-called Legge Ponte (Bridging Act) was passed as a first step towards the proposed reform. Although this Act introduced a number of new control measures, and forbade all new construction in settlements without a development plan, it allowed for a one-year 'free for all' interim, before legally coming into force. During this interim, more building permits were granted in a period of a few months than in the previous ten years, and speculative development experienced a further surge in many of the country's urban centres.

The 1970s saw somewhat more successful attempts at framing new legislation to enable the public administration to plan and control the urban growth process more effectively. The 1971 Housing and Town Planning Act (Law No. 865) gave local authorities new powers to expropriate sites for state-subsidized housing projects, for public service infrastructure (roads, schools, parks etc.) and for inner-city conservation and improvement purposes[27].

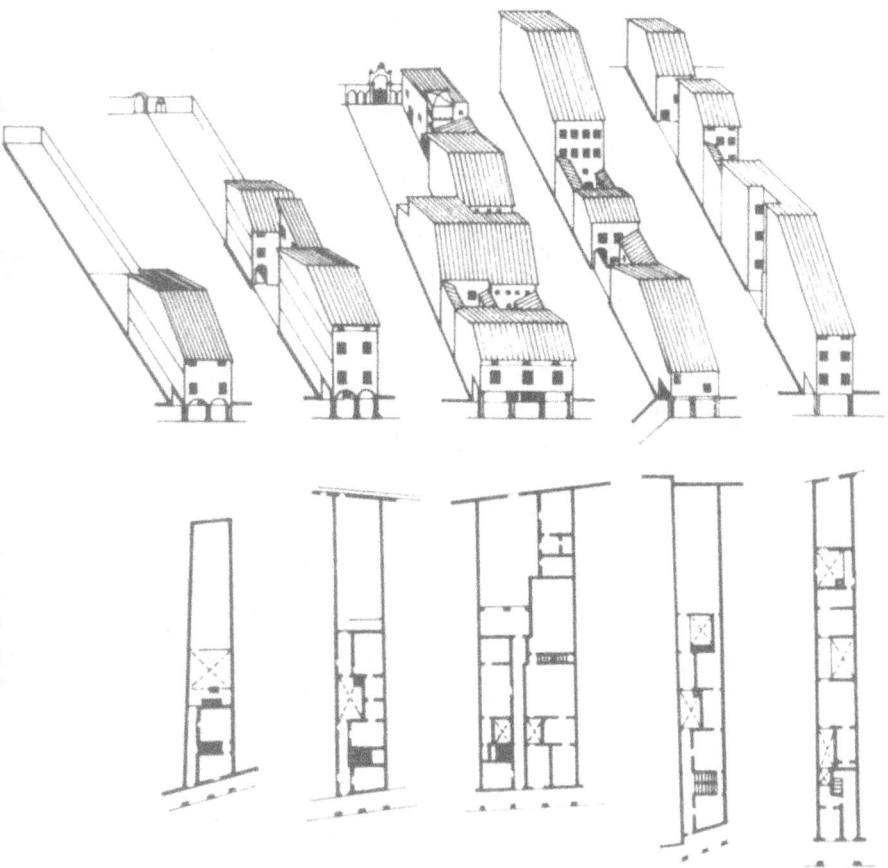

FIGURE 3.17. Housing types included in Bologna Council's 1973 historic housing centre plan ('Peep/Centro Storico').
*Source:* Bologna Council (1978) *Risanamento Conservativo del Centro Storico di Bologna.* Bologna: Bologna Council.

This last named aspect of local authority intervention came to the fore in the late 1960s following the initiative of Bologna Town Council, which financed a series of rehabilitation projects in the old city (see figure 3.17) and at the same time attempted to maintain the existing social and community structure. A number of 'special' Acts were subsequently approved for the financing and planning of inner-city rehabilitation and development for individual cities, sometimes based on the Bologna model, and sometimes following natural disasters (an earthquake in Ancona; floods in Venice).

The new powers given to local authorities in the 1971 Act were reinforced by the National Framework Act of 1972, which introduced a new regional authority structure to administer somewhat smaller regions (see figure 3.18), each with a proportionately greater degree of political and financial independence

FIGURE 3.18. The 1972 regional reorganization.
Each region comprises several provinces, and provincial capitals are shown on the map in smaller print. A series of regional planning Acts were approved in the late 1970s setting out the powers and responsibilities of regional authorities in different parts of the country.

than before[28]. This devolution to the regional level was subsequently extended by the 1977 Regional Government Act (Law No. 10), which empowered regional authorities to draw up their own regional planning acts to regulate planning, urban renewal and housing provision in the region. The late 1970s saw the approval of a spate of these regional planning acts although some regions still have no approved act.

The 1970s also witnessed a general mobilization of resident groups (particularly in the northern industrial cities and in Rome and Naples), stimulated by clashes with the police in 1972 (over illegal occupation of empty dwellings), and the increasingly efficient organization of political parties of the left. The urban conflict came to the fore in big cities and small towns alike, and democratization, participation and decentralization became central political issues in both local and national elections in which the Communist Party made significant gains in 1975 and 1976. Let us now turn to examine how the failure of urban planning and housing policies helped fuel this conflict in the national capital, Rome.

## Metropolitan Planning and Growth in the Postwar Era: The Case of Rome

Rome is neither a typical north Italian industrial city nor does it fit the model of a southern territorial centre, although it shares with the former the burgeoning development of the tertiary sector in recent years, and with the latter the preponderance of shanty and illegal housing in the outer areas. Between 1951 and 1971, its population grew by 68 per cent, from 1.66 to 2.78 million, a greater increase than in any other Italian city; it is today the bureaucratic centre of the country and the traditional capital of the Italian State.

In 1962, a new PRG for Rome was approved[29], based on a population projection of five million people and a new 10,000 hectare area of expansion to the south-east of the city. This new zone was to be built around the 'structural axis' of a motorway link with the Autostrada del Sole and include a series of *centri direzionali* housing a quarter of a million inhabitants and 300,000 office buildings. It was an attempt to break the monocentric growth of the capital, and to create a new centre, out to the south-east, towards the major industrial zone; and in 1966, the city council approved a low-income housing programme in which 700,000 new dwellings were to be built on over half the 10,000 hectares earmarked for new development in the 1962 PRG.

In reality, however, very little of the 1962 plan or the 1966 housing programme were implemented. Construction of the new motorway link, to be the structural axis of the new centre, was not embarked upon until the late 1970s and the existing city centre saw widespread renewal resulting in a dramatic increase in tertiary activities in the 1960s and 1970s. In the Rioni *centrali* (city centre districts), for example, the number of inhabitants dropped from 424,000 to 195,000 between 1951 and 1971 while the adjacent *quartieri* (inner suburbs) almost doubled their resident population, to a total of over two million in 1971.

This movement of population into the inner (and, to a lesser extent, the outer) suburbs was encouraged by the decision of the Rome Council in 1966 and 1969 to validate building densities included in the PRPs (district plans) approved in the 1950s, which contradicted standards specified in the 1962 PRG. These plans were drawn up whilst the old 1931 PRG for Rome was still in force, and generally included extremely high residential densities and poor provision of service infrastructure. The 1962 PRG recognized the land uses included in these plans, but set new standards and norms to regulate building density and service provision. In the 1960s, development in the new zones earmarked for city expansion in the 1962 plan was often blocked by PRPs that were always 'under study', thus preventing building permit cession; and so developers looked to the existing built-up areas where, with the resurrection of these old PRPs, intensive infilling could take place.

Meanwhile, in the areas earmarked for expansion, only 60,000 (of the programmed 700,000) low-income houses were constructed between 1966 and 1975, whilst over 5000 hectares were *illegally* developed largely as housing, hotels and industry, with scant service provision. The result, in housing terms, was that by the mid-1970s 650,000 people were living in the so-called *quartieri abusivi* – dwellings that were built illegally, without the necessary building permit, with a further 100,000 in the *borgate ufficiali* (state built low-income dwellings dating from the Fascist period) and a further 100,000 in the *borghetti*, the self-built shanty towns of the capital. In all, then, almost one-third of the capital's population was inadequately housed, and, although the Social-Communist governments of the late 1970s introduced new service provision programmes to provide roads, green areas, schools, etc. in these zones, the housing situation in the capital remains critical.

## Concluding Remarks

The history of urban planning and urban growth in Italy is not easy to summarize in a few sentences. It is a complex and contradictory story, in which certain cities have experienced growth patterns of their own, and in which the differences between north and south and between town and country have remained as great as ever.

In the historical evolution of planning legislation, the 1865 and 1942 Acts stand out as major landmarks. The 1865 Acts centred on the new expropriation powers made available to local authorities, and also established the two major types of plan (expansion and redevelopment) which were the forerunners of the PRG. Although conceptually fairly limited, this legislation enabled local authorities to make considerable progress in the opening up and expansion of old town centres, even if direct intervention by public authorities remained generally weak.

The early decades of this century did not see the new legislative and political initiatives in the planning field that were characteristic in several other European countries at the time, although the major public housing authorities – IACP, INA-CASA, GESCAL – were founded in this period, and the early estates were built. The 1942 Town Planning Act opened a new era in planning and provided the basis for subsequent legislation in the 1960s and 1970s although neither the 1942 Act nor its subsequent modifications provided any effective control of capitalist development, which has brought with it the dire consequences of over-congestion in the centre and ill-equipped anarchic sprawl in the suburbs.

A survey undertaken in the early 1970s[30] suggested that 62 per cent of the population lived in areas with approved urban plans, although the physical area covered may be as low as 25 per cent of the country. Only at the municipal level has planning taken place to any degree, although regional and sub-regional plans may now start to appear, following the approval of regional planning Acts for most regions. Only a very small number of municipalities have prepared PRPs (local-level plans) and this failure has clearly hampered the effective implementation of PRGs. In general, however, the history of planning and development in Italy can be characterized as two separate histories, sometimes but now always linked: one concerning the evolution of planning thought and practice, and the other charting the city growth process. It is a sad truth that the former has had relatively little impact on the latter, and the results of decades of speculative development and uncontrolled growth are evident enough in Italy's urban areas today.

### NOTES

1. See Gambi, L. (1975) Il reticolo urbano in Italia nei primi anni dopo l'unificazione, in Gambi L. et al. (eds.) *Dalla città pre-industriale alla città del capitalismo.* Bologna: Il Mulino.
2. Morachiello, P. (1980) Il prefetto Chabrol: Amministrazione Naopoleonica e scienza dell' ingegnere, in Morachiello P. et al. (eds.) *Le Macchine imperfette.* Rome: Officina.
3. Patetta, L. (1978) Architettura e spazio urbano in epoca napoleonica, in *L'idea della magnificenza civile. Architettura a Milano 1770–1848,* Catalogo dell' esposizione (Exhibition Catalogue), Milan, October/November, 1978. Milan: Electa.
4. See Ciucci, G. (1980) La città nella colonizzazione del territorio italiano, in *Architettura della casa in Europa. La svolta delle politiche sociali agli inizi degli anni '30*, Transactions of the International Conference, University Institute of Architecture, Venice, Dipartimento di Analisi Critica e Storica, April, 1980.
5. Caccia, A. (1915) *Costruzione, trasformazione e ampliamento della città* Milan: Hoepli. The subtitle is: *Compilato sulla traccia del 'Der Städtebau' di J. Stübben, ad uso degli ingegneri, architetti, uffici tecnici e amministrazioni municipali* (after *Der Städtebau* by J. Stübben, to be used by engineers, architects, technical offices and local authorities).

6. See Schiavi, A. (1911) *Le case a buon mercato e le città giardino.* Bologna: Zanichelli.
7. Giovannoni, G. (1931) Vecchie città ed edilizia nuova', in *Nuova Antogia.* Turin: UTET.
8. See Romanelli, G. (1980) La Commissione d'ornato: da Napoleone al Lombardo-Veneto, in Morachiello, P. *et al., op. cit.* (see note 2).
9. Castiglioni, P. (1861) *Sull' ordinamento del servizio sanitario comunale nel Regno d'Italia.* Turin.
10. Patamia, C. (1875) *Relazione al Consiglio Comunale sull 'ordinamento del servizio igienico-sanitario a Napoli.* Naples; Russo, G. (1959) *Il risanamento e l'ampliamento della città di Napoli.* Volume II. Naples: Società per il risanemento di Napoli nel settantesimo della sua fondazione; Alisio, G. (1978) Aspetti della cultura dell '800 a Napoli: II risanemento e l'ampliamento della città. *L'Architettura, Cronache e storia,* No. 255.
11. Quoted in Romanelli, G. (1978) *Venezia Ottocento.* Rome: Officina Press.
12. Exceptions to the monocentric pattern included towns where peculiar geographical features made more than one centre necessary (as in Cuneo and Cosenza), or where new development around the railway gave rise to a multi-nuclei structure (as in Bergamo and Terni).
13. A comprehensive study of the whole region can be found in: Mancuso, F. and Mioni, A. (1979) *Centri Storici: Veneto,* Milan: A. Pizzi.
14. In this context, see Ciucci, G. (1970) L'urbanista negli anni '30: un tecnico per l'organizzazione del consenso, in Danesi, S. and Patetta, L. (eds.) *Il razionalismo e l'architettura italiana durante il fascismo.* Venice: ed. La Biennale; Mioni, A. (1976) *Le trasformazioni territoriali in Italia.* Venice: Marsilio; Mioni, A. (1980) *L'urbanistica fascista,* Milan: Angeli.
15. For more detail on the five new towns see: Mariani, R.. (1976) *Fascismo e città nuove.* Milan: Feltrinelli; on Sabaudia, see Pensabene, G. (1933) Sabaudia. *Casabella,* October; Piccinato, L. (1934) Il significato urbanistico di Sabaudia. *Urbanistica,* January/February; Piacentini, M. (1934) Sabaudia. *Architettura,* June; Vago, P. (1934) Sabaudia. *L'architecture d'Aujourd' hui,* July; Dougill, W. (1936) Two new-towns in Italy, Littoria and Sabaudia. *Town Planning Review,* June. On Aprilia, see: Piacentini, M. (1936) Aprilia, *Architettura,* May; Aprilia realizzata. *Urbanistica,* May–June, 1938; Aprilia. *Architettura,* July, 1938.
16. For more detail on government policy in the postwar period, see: Graziani, A. (1972) *L'economia italiana 1945–1970.* Bologna: Il Mulino.
17. For more detail on the building cycles see Cacciari, P. and Potenza, S. (1972) *Il ciclo edilizio.* Rome: Officina; Indovina, F. (1974) *La spreco edilizio.* Venice: Marsilo.
18. Tafuri, M. (1964) *Ludovico Quaroni.* Milan: Comunità; Astengo, G. (1949) Attualità dell' urbanistica. *Urbanistica,* No. 1.
19. For more detail on planning in Milan in the immediate postwar era, see *Urbanistica,* no. 18–19, 1956, entirely dedicated to Milan.
20. Gazzola, P. (1946) La vicende urbanistiche di Milano e il piano A.R. *Construzioni,* No. 194; Bottoni, P. (1954) *Il quartiere sperimentale della Triennale di Milano.* Milan: Quaderno Triennale Domus; see also *Controspazio* No. 4, 1973, dedicated to the work of P. Bottoni.
21. Between 1950 and 1975, during which time the total population of Italy increased by 9 million, those in the agricultural sector decreased by 12 million and people

in the non-agricultural sectors increased by 21 million. During the same period those living in 'rural settlements' (less than 20,000 inhabitants) decreased by 3 million and those living in 'urban centres' increased by 12 million. By 1975 two out of every three Italians were urban dwellers. See: Carozzi, C. and Mioni, A. (1970) *L'Italia in formazione.* Bari: De Donato; and Mainardi, R. (1971) *Le Grandi Città Italiane.* Milan: Angeli.
22. Carabba, M. (1977) *Un Ventennio di Programmazione 1954–1974.* Bari: Laterza; Petriccione, S. (1976) *Politica Industriale e Mezzogiorno.* Bari: Laterza; Ferrari Bravo, L. and Serafini, A. (1972) *Stato e Sottosviluppo: il caso del Mezzogiorno Italiano.* Milan: Feltrinelli.
23. For more detail on the functioning of the development process in Naples, see *Urbanistica,* no. 26, 1959; and *Casabella,* no. 231, 1959, pp. 34–51.
24. See ILSES (1962) *Nuova dimensione della città. La città-regione.* Stresa; many articles in *Casabella,* in particular: no. 242, 1960; no. 264, 1962; no. 270, 1962 (Piccinato, Quilici, Tafuri, 'La Citta-territorio, verso una nuova dimensione'); also various authors (1967) *La citta-territorio,* Bari: Dedalo.
25. For more detail on planning in Turin in the postwar era, see *Urbanistica,* No. 1, 1949.
26. See Carabba, M. (1977) *Un ventennio di programmazione 1954–74.* Bari: Laterza; Ministero del Bilancio (1969) *Progetto '80.* Milan: Feltrinelli.
27. See Caccarelli, P. and Indovina, F. (eds.) (1974) *Risanamento e speculazione nei centri storici.* Milan: Angeli; in it, see particularly the rich bibliography on general terms, theoretical debates, and single case studies collected by Padovani, L., Documentazione bibliografica di alcuni aspetti del dibattito recente in Italia, pp. 210–220.
28. See De Lucia, V., Salzano, E. and Strobbe, F. (1973) *Riforma Urbanistica 1973.* Rome: Lega per le Autonomie e i poteri locali.
29. See Folin, H. (1979) Urban struggles: a critical commentary on the article by Della Seta. *International Journal of Urban and Regional Research,* 3, (1), March; Marcelloni, M. (1979) Urban movements and political struggles in Italy. *International Journal of Urban and Regional Research,* 3, (2), June.
30. Paris-Rome. Roma-Parigi. Paris Project. *Revue preparée par l'atelier parisien d'urbanisme (APUR),* No. 23–24, 1983 (number prepared by APUR with the Rome Municipality).

# 4

# Portugal

## ALLAN M. WILLIAMS

INTRODUCTION

Portugal, one of the smallest countries in Western Europe, is also one of the least urbanized societies. As late as 1864, the date of the first census, there were only two cities of any consequence. These were Lisbon, the capital, which had a population of 197,649 and Oporto, the regional capital of northern Portugal, which had a population of 86,761[1]. There was no other city of any real size or substance, and such places as Évora, Coimbra and Braga were little changed from medieval times. Even in 1940, only 33.2 per cent of the population lived in urban areas, and this was according to a very generous definition[2]. After the early 1950s there was more rapid urbanization, associated with the process of uneven regional development[3], but in 1970 the proportion of the population resident in urban areas was still only 38.3 per cent.

The country also possesses one of the most uneven distributions of urban areas, and the urban hierarchy is still dominated by the two major cities of Lisbon and Oporto. In 1970 the populations of the *cidades* (the administratively defined cities) of Lisbon and Oporto were 782,266 and 310,437 respectively, but the populations of the metropolitan areas were larger, being 1,596,406 and 837,610 respectively. As can be seen from figure 4.1, these two cities were of a completely different rank to the other urban areas. In 1970 no other city had a population which exceeded 70,000, and the next largest towns after the two metropolitan agglomerations were Coimbra (55,985), Braga (48,735) and Setúbal (46,670). The 1981 census indicated that the dominance of Lisbon and Oporto had been strengthened, for the proportion of the total population living in these two metropolitan areas had increased to almost a third by this date. The significance of these two cities in the urban development process means that they will inevitably figure prominently in the discussion which follows.

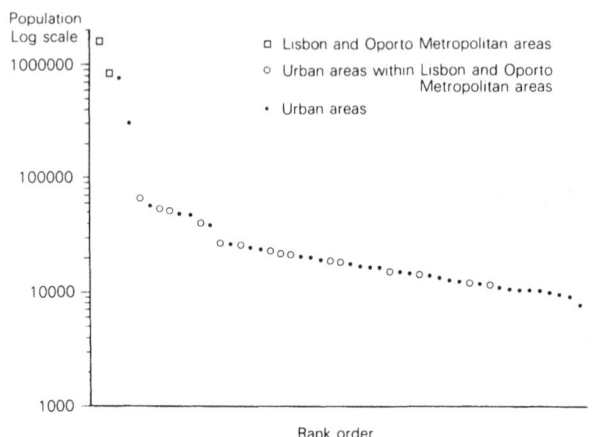

FIGURE 4.1. Rank order distribution of urban population in Portugal in 1970.

It is certainly true that most of the major examples of planned urban development since the late sixteenth century are to be found in Lisbon and, to a lesser extent, Oporto. Two such examples are the rebuilding of Lisbon after the earthquake of 1755 and the remodelling of the Praça da Ribeira in Oporto at the end of the eighteenth century. In general terms, however, urban planning has been fairly weak in Portugal, and this is true even of its two main cities, so that the country seems to have contributed little to the development of new ideas in planning thought and practice. Thus, although the Portuguese did play an important part in the transmission of urban planning ideas to cities such as Bahia (Brazil) and Luanda (Angola) in its overseas territories[4], the particular interest in studying urban built-form and planning in Portugal during the eighteenth, nineteenth and twentieth centuries is to appreciate how a variety of foreign influences were adopted and implemented in its towns and cities. French and Italian influences were probably the strongest, as can be seen in the work of such as Nasoni in the eighteenth century and Auzelle in the twentieth century, but at certain times both English (for example, Whitehead) and German (for example, Ludovice) architects have also been influential.

For the purposes of this chapter, urban development and planning in Portugal is subdivided into five periods. The first is the eighteenth and early nineteenth centuries which were akin to a 'golden age' in urban design and development in Portugal, when there were important attempts to remodel the urban fabrics of both Oporto and Lisbon. After this, and especially following the Napoleonic invasions, there were several decades of political, economic and military uncertainty in Portugal, and only at the end of the nineteenth century were there any real attempts to plan for the rapid expansion of the two main cities. The outstanding feature of this, the second period, was the Avenidas plans for Lisbon. The third period covers the early years of Salazarist rule from the mid-1920s. This was an era of low growth and moderate urban expansion when, under a highly centralized corporate state, the first tentative steps were taken to develop a legislative framework for urban planning. In the following period, which lasted until the Revolution of April 1974, this framework was tested and was found to be inadequate in view of the dramatic increase which occurred in economic growth and in rural-urban migration. New legislation was passed to attempt to remedy these deficiencies – evident most spectacularly in the uncontrolled development of *bairros clandestinos*[5] – but no satisfactory planning solutions emerged. Finally, after 1974, there have been a number of attempts to revise further and to democratize planning, the most important of which have been the measures to decentralize powers and finances to the local authorities. Each of these periods will be discussed in turn.

## The Eighteenth Century:
## The Renaissance and Urban Redesign

The late thirteenth century was one of the more fertile eras of town building in Portugal's history, when a number of frontier towns were established. These towns, such as Monsaraz and Vila Vicosa, were developed according to geometrical ground plans. They usually had a *rua direita* as a central axis between the main gate and a square or the castle, with other, lesser roads running parallel or at right angles to this[6]. Later, the period of the Discoveries in the fifteenth and sixteenth centuries brought considerable wealth to Portugal, but this resulted in architectural developments rather than any distinct phase in town planning. There were important changes in architectural form, culminating in the Manueline style (late gothic but influenced by the overseas discoveries), which is well illustrated, for example, by the Torre de Belém or the Christo Convento in Tomar, but urban expansion lacked a planned framework.

During the sixteenth and early seventeenth centuries both Lisbon and Oporto experienced infilling within their city walls and limited expansion beyond these. In Lisbon the early city had been sited on the easily defensible São Jorge hill, but as the wealth of the nation grew so the city expanded into the *baixa* (or lower areas). A number of important buildings such as the Casa do India and the Alfandega Real were constructed in the *baixa*, adjacent to the port and the commercial centre, the Terreiro do Paco. These developments resulted in a dense, irregular street pattern within the city walls while, later, growth spilled beyond the city walls forming early suburbs that had an irregular form, reflecting the landownership pattern and layout of existing estates. The one exception to this pattern of expansion was in the suburb of Bairro Alto, developed between 1520 and 1650 on the hill to the west of the *baixa*. This had a regular gridiron of streets which, at the time, were unusually spacious[7], but the Bairro Alto was an exception which had no direct parallels elsewhere in Lisbon or in Oporto. In the latter, growth was again dominated by the limits imposed by the city walls, especially the Fernandina Muralha (Ferdinand

Walls), built in the late fourteenth century. Within the walls, there was infilling of small, narrow and irregular streets, while beyond these walls expansion was based around the main roads from the city, and existing village nuclei such as Lordelo[8].

By the mid-eighteenth century, then, there was little tradition of planned urban development in Portugal in either the major cities or in the smaller towns. This was changed radically during the course of the century, especially by the earthquake of 1755. This massive earthquake, accompanied by a tidal wave and followed by uncontrollable fires, led to the destruction of about half the built-up area of Lisbon, including most of the *baixa* and its imposing public buildings. Thus was provided the opportunity for large-scale urban redevelopment at a time when Portugal was still fairly wealthy (mainly from the exploitation of Brazilian resources), and power was strongly centralized in a king who was dominated by a relatively progressive and efficient chief minister, the Marquess of Pombal. The king was faced with a number of alternative plans for the redevelopment of the city. These included a proposal to abandon the present site of the capital, various schemes to level and/or redesign the city, and one project to achieve an exact reconstruction of the old city. As a result of Pombal's influence, the king eventually chose a scheme to remodel the *baixa* in accordance with a geometrical pattern, in the spirit of renaissance ideals of town planning[9]. It has been suggested that Pombal's preference for this scheme was influenced by his own favourable impressions of Georgian town development in England[10], but there is no definite evidence to substantiate this.

The plan for the redevelopment of Lisbon had been prepared by Eugenio dos Santos and was based on a gridiron of seven north-south streets intersecting with seven east-west streets; these were located between two large squares, the Rossio at the north and the Praça do Comércio at the south (see figure 4.2). The whole scheme was meticulously planned and different widths were ordained for the streets, ranging from 40 to 60 feet. There were also detailed specifications for the houses, which were to have continuous frontages and uniform facades. The details of the facades varied from street to street but those in the main streets were to be three storeys and 80 feet in height. Such a radical scheme implied a massive redistribution of land, and although this aroused substantial opposition, the royal ruler was able to impose the plan on his citizens. Rebuilding started in the year following the earthquake but Santos's death in 1760 meant that overall supervision of the plan, as well as responsibility for the design of the Rossio, passed to Carlos Mardel[11]. Nevertheless, Mardel ensured that the dictates of Santos's plan were generally adhered to.

Although this was undoubtedly a radical scheme, with hindsight its gridiron pattern has been justifiably condemned as being 'rather unimaginative'[12]. In contrast, however, the Praça do Comércio has been judged to constitute a *place royale* of international standing[13]. It is an imposing *praça* which is

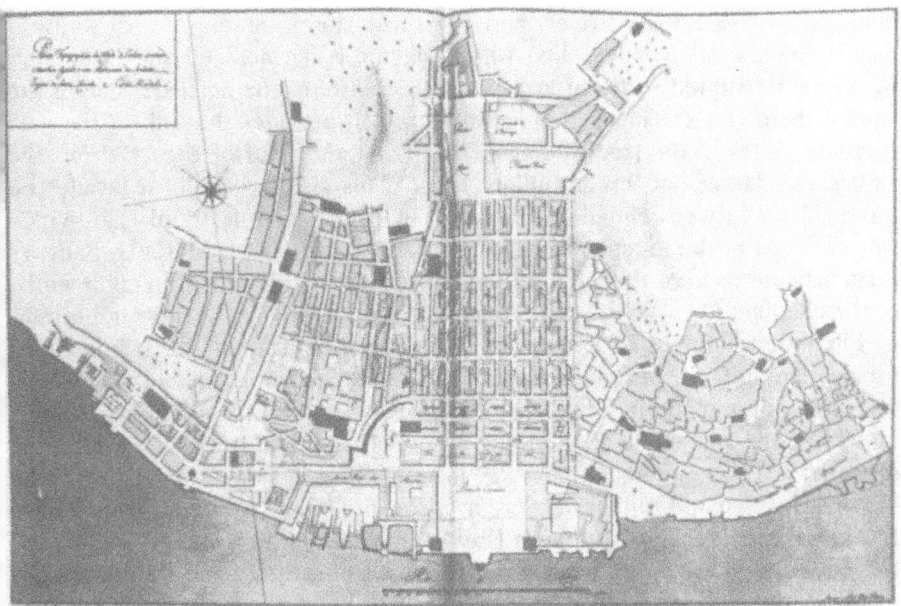

FIGURE 4.2. The plan for the redevelopment of Lisbon, by Eugenio dos Santos. The *baixa* is in the centre between the Alfama (right) and the Bairro Alto (left).

FIGURE 4.3. The Praça do Comércio on the edge of the river Tajo.

open on one side to the river, and has three-storey buildings with uniform facades on the other sides. The whole scheme is harmonized and integrated by an uninterrupted series of arches. In the centre of the northern side of the square there is a soaring triumphal arch, which provides the link to the Rua Augusta in the *baixa* (see figure 4.3). At the other end of the gridiron, the Rossio is a larger but less grandiose *praça*. This also has uniform facades on three sides and was defined on the north by the Palacio de Inquisição, which was replaced in the nineteenth century by the Teatro de D. Maria II. Santos's *baixa* scheme was not the only example of planned development in eighteenth-century Lisbon (c.f. the Praça da Algeria) but it was by far the most important.

The redevelopment of Lisbon also had wider implications for it influenced urban planning in a number of other cities. For example, in both Vila Real de Santo Antonio and in Olhão gridiron plans were used for urban expansions. However, the main influence of the *baixa* scheme was probably experienced in Oporto. The key person here was João do Almada (and later his son) who became the civil and military governor of the city in 1757. Under his influence the Junta dos Trabalhos Públicos (Public Works Board) was established, and made a start on the badly needed improvement of sanitary and water arrangements in the city. The Junta also undertook to improve circulation within the city by widening roads such as the Rua do Infante and the Rua das Flores, and providing for orderly expansion by laying out new roads such as in the Bairro da Rua de Almada[14]. A number of foreign architects, notably John Carr of York and John Whitehead, the British consul, were also important in designing palladian and neo-classical style public buildings in the city[15]. Whitehead was also instrumental in the enlargement and remodelling of the Praça da Ribeira, a small waterfront square which was at the commercial heart of the city. He seems to have been influenced by the designs for the Praça do Comércio in Lisbon, particularly in the use of a series of linked arches to harmonize the square.

Towards the end of the eighteenth century, therefore, as work progressed slowly on the various schemes mentioned, important steps were being taken in the development of orderly town planning. In combination with the late arrival of Renaissance concepts of architectural design, this led to some reshaping of urban structure. There was, however, a general failure to develop town planning more widely, and it was not until a century later that there were any further significant advances.

## The Nineteenth and Early Twentieth Centuries: Political Uncertainty, Industrialization and the Plans for the Avenidas

After the remarkable redevelopment of Lisbon in the late eighteenth century, the early years of the nineteenth century were an anticlimax in terms of growth and urban development. The independence of Brazil meant the loss to Portugal of a valuable source of raw materials and wealth, while at home the Napoleonic invasion, the Peninsular War, the political tensions of the 1820s, and the civil war of the 1830s all acted to inhibit economic development. The early nineteenth century, therefore, was a period of economic stagnation, and it has been estimated that by 1913 GNP per capita in Portugal had dropped to less than half the European average, having been above average in 1830[16]. A corollary of this was the high rate of emigration experienced throughout the period, rising from between 4000 and 11,000 per annum at mid-century to between 20,000 and 44,000 per annum in the 1890s[17].

This general pattern of stagnation was only partly broken by industrialization in the late nineteenth century. In common with other late-industrializing countries at this time, industrialization remained limited to a few sectors and to a few regions within the economy[18]. In the Portuguese case, this mainly involved the processing of raw materials which had been produced either internally (for example, cork) or in the African colonies (for example, cotton), and was limited to the littoral region, especially around Oporto in the north and, to a lesser extent, Setúbal in the south[19]. The concurrence of higher rates of industrialization and emigration in the later years of the century is probably a reflection of the crisis in Portuguese agriculture (which was itself linked to the crisis in world agriculture).

Portugal was not only a late-industrializing country, but was also late-urbanizing. Even in 1864, the year of the first official census, 71 per cent of the population lived in *frequesias rurais* (rural parishes), and the same proportion was recorded in the next census in 1878[20]. By the end of the century, however, there had been some increase in the level of urbanization. Although the census of 1900 revealed that the proportion of population living in *frequesias rurais* had fallen only slightly to 67 per cent, over the period 1864–1900 as a whole, there had nevertheless been a 77 per cent increase in the population of *cidades* (cities) and 30 per cent in the *vilas* (towns), compared with only 21 per cent in the *frequesias rurais*[21]. It was the industrial cities which experienced the largest rates of increase; the population of Setúbal doubled between 1878 and 1911, that of Aveiro doubled between 1864 and 1911, and that of Covilha increased by almost 70 per cent between only 1878 and 1890[22]. But the most substantial increases, albeit with lower rates of growth, were in the two major cities where populations increased between 1864 and 1900 from 197,649 to 356,311 (Lisbon) and from 86,761 to 167,955 (Oporto). The rate of increase was slightly greater in Oporto, reflecting its role in industrialization during this period.

These changes in the organization of the economy led to a profound transformation of the industrial cities. On the one hand, the sheer growth in absolute numbers created a demand for new housing which required substantial expansion of the built-up area. At the same time, there were changes in the social structures of these cities, and the growth of both the industrial working class and of the bourgeoisie led to the need for new types of housing. These changes can be illustrated in both Oporto and Lisbon, where urban expansion in the early nineteenth century was at a generally low level, reflecting the limited economic growth in these cities and in the nation as a whole. In Lisbon, for example, work was still proceeding very slowly on the Santos/Mardel plan for the *baixa* and the Rossio square was only completed in 1845[23]. However, from the middle of the century onwards, there was more rapid urban development.

In both Lisbon and Oporto, the influx of large numbers of rural migrants in the second half of the nineteenth century created an enormous need for low-cost dwellings. Although some employers provided tied accommodation in their own housing colonies[24], the greater part of the new housing was provided by the lesser bourgeoisie who invested in and rented out property. This resulted in distinctive housing areas being created in both cities. In Lisbon there were three main types of working-class housing in this period[25]. First, there were the *patios*, which were very high-density infill in the gardens of existing large houses; these areas were located around the edges of the *baixa* in such zones as Rato and Gracia. In 1903–5, an official enquiry into this type of housing in Lisbon showed that 161 of the 221 *patios* could be classified as being in 'very poor condition'. Secondly, terraces of single-storey dwellings were built facing each other across a narrow alleyway, which was at right angles to the main roads. Thirdly, there were the *vilas*, being large-scale suburban residential developments of working-class housing, as in Vila Sousa or Candida, which sometimes incorporated some elements of social and physical infrastructure. Such areas were usually found in close conjunction with the existing places of employment, especially along the river margins.

In Oporto, the provision of working-class housing was dominated by the *ilhas*, or slums, which were literally islands of infill development in the interior of long garden plots of the houses located on the main roads radiating out from the city centre. Entrance to the *ilhas* was restricted, being through narrow arches, and the houses – usually about twenty in number – were closely packed on one or both sides of a narrow alley. These terraces could be of either one or two storeys and frequently were of a back-to-back type. As a result, they were poorly-lit and badly ventilated and also lacked the basic amenities, usually being reliant on communal water supplies and toilets. An example of the layout of an area of *ilhas* is shown in figure 4.4, this being located in São Victor on the riverside to the east of the town centre. This illustrates both the typical *ilha* of back-to-back dwellings along a narrow alley, and also some recently improved *ilhas*, where alternative dwellings have been demolished in order to improve lighting and ventilation for the remaining houses. São Victor is only one of several areas of *ilhas* in Oporto, which are located in a semi-circle around the predominantly medieval core of the city. Their growth was quite remarkable: in 1844 there were no *ilhas*, but by 1899 100,000 people (more than half the city's population) were estimated to be housed in these dwellings[26].

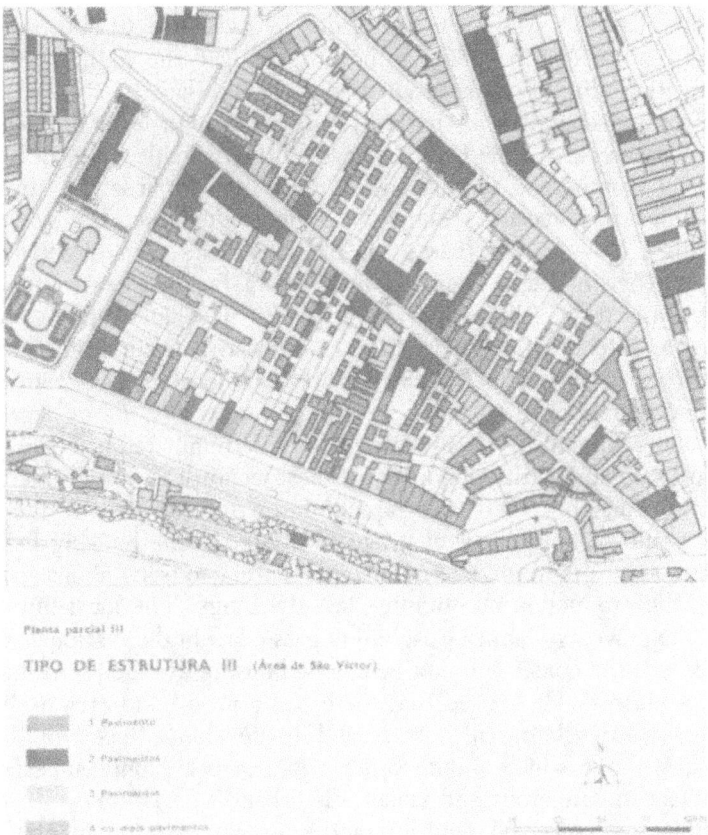

FIGURE 4.4. *Ilhas* in the São Victor area of Oporto.
The plan shows the number of storeys (*pavimentos*) in each building (after de Oliveira).

The *ilhas* and the *patios* were not the only forms of working-class housing in Lisbon and Oporto, but they are the best documented. Concurrent with the construction of these new dwellings was a process of invasion and subdivision of older houses in the higher-status areas of the cities. This occurred in Lisbon in the Bairro Alto, as new high-status housing was developed in the areas of the Avenidas (discussed below), enabling residents to vacate their properties in the former area. The process was even more accentuated in Porto, in the Ribeira-Barredo area; this had been the commercial heart of the city and it was also a nucleus of substantial houses for those controlling the city's commerce. Traditionally, the area had been very congested and inaccessible, especially because of its location on the very steep lower bank of the deep valley of the river Douro. As a result, there had been numerous attempts in earlier centuries to improve access to the port and the commercial area[27], although these only partly solved the difficulties. In the late nineteenth century, the construction of the D. Maria Pia rail bridge by Eiffel (1876) and the D. Luis I two-level road bridge in 1886 significantly changed the traffic flow through the Ribeira-Barredo. Previously, all road transport had to cross the Douro and pass through the Ribeira-Barredo, but these high-level bridges, which linked the plateaux above the Douro, bypassed the riverside zone. Accordingly, the centre of commercial activity shifted over time towards the upper level, and this move was accentuated by the redevelopment of the Avenida dos Aliados into a long square (based on Barry Parker's plan of 1915). Partly as a consequence of these changes, the Ribeira-Barredo ceased to act as a high-status area (especially as new suburbs were developed) and a process of subdivision and degradation occurred as recently-arrived rural migrants, many of whom were employed in the small workshops located in and around this zone, settled there[28].

Urban and economic development led to large numbers of people living in substandard and unhealthy conditions. These conditions were widely recognized at the time, but there was no significant intervention by the state in either the realm of housing or of urban planning. In the housing field, there were several attempts in the late nineteenth century to bring about state intervention in the production of working-class dwellings. The most important of these was the move by Deputy Fuschini to pass a law in the National Assembly in 1884 for '... the construction of economic housing destined for inhabitation by the poor classes'. He argued that there was a need '... to try to dilute the flagrant inequalities between classes, and to develop a just equilibrium of conditions, without which public order and peace are only superficial and always subject to dangerous and violent disturbances'[29]

This Bill never received approval and state intervention in housing was delayed for another thirty years. Instead, there were some voluntary associations which sought to provide public housing – as at Monte Pedral in Oporto during the first decade of the twentieth century – but these were insignificant in number.

State intervention in urban planning was equally ineffective. A decree of 1864 did provide the framework for urban planning: it became compulsory for municipal urbanization plans to be prepared for Lisbon and Oporto, and voluntary for other cities to do so. These were to be general urbanization plans and were to cover both the existing built-up area and extensions to the cities. Not surprisingly, no voluntary plans were prepared and that for Oporto was only started in the 1930s. Only in Lisbon was there any early progress in planning, and this was limited to plans for extending the built areas, the plans for the Avenidas.

In comparison with the uncontrolled development of urban working-class housing, there was a measure of planning in the development of the new residential areas for the bourgeoisie, especially in Lisbon. The plans for the Avenidas in Lisbon can, in fact, be divided into two separate but related phases, which together led to a distinctive extension in the built-up area away from

FIGURE 4.5. The Avenida Fontes P. de Melo, leading into the Praça Marques de Pombal. The Praça is the pivotal link between the Av. do Liberdade and the Avenidas.

the riverside to the north. The first phase was based around the development of the Avenida da Liberdade, which was the work of the Italian-born architect Pézerat, who had been impressed by Haussmann's work in Paris, and sought to create an elegant and imposing new boulevard in Lisbon. The plan meant the disappearance of the Passeio Público and its replacement by a massive avenue 1276 m long, which ran between the Rossio and the Rotunda da Pombal (see figure 4.5). The proposed loss of the Passeio gave rise to considerable opposition to the scheme and only when the powerful Rosa Araújo became President of the Câmara (city council) of Lisbon was it agreed to proceed with the plan. Work started on the Avenida in 1879 and even today it seems to dominate the city, linking the *baixa* with the areas of twentieth-century development. Although the plan is considered to show Haussmann's influence, a significant difference is that it was a scheme for expansion and not for redevelopment[30].

The plan for the Avenida da Liberdade is also important because it was a necessary precondition for the second phase of expansion of bourgeoisie housing, the scheme for the Avenidas Novas. This had been projected in general outline by Pézerat, but it was F. Ressano Garcia who prepared the detailed plan for the scheme in 1888. He proposed to develop an *avenida* to run north-east from the Rotunda da Pombal to the Praça de Saldanha, thence gaining access to the plateaux beyond the Avenida da Liberdade. From Saldanha he proposed that the Avenida da República be developed northwards to the Campo Grande (see figure 4.6). The *avenidas* were finally approved by

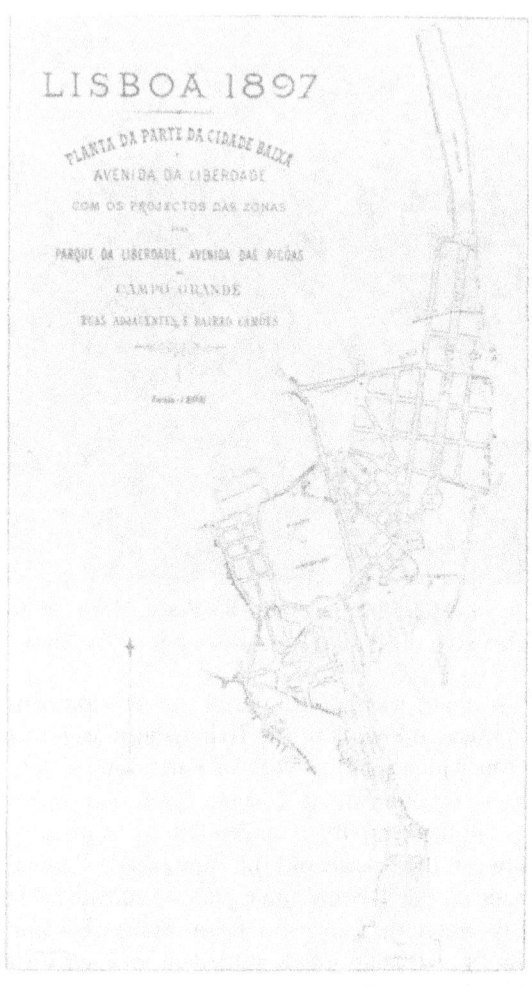

FIGURE 4.6. F. Ressano Garcia's plan for the *avenidas* of Lisbon.

the Câmara as part of a large package of urban improvement proposals in 1904.

The *avenidas* were of immense importance in the development of the city, for they provided the framework for the physical and social expansion of the city during the early twentieth century[31]. However, unlike Santos's earlier scheme for the *baixa*, they did not govern building design. Instead, only the layout of roads and of the building line was decreed, and the construction of individual buildings was left to private developers. The outcome was a socially homogeneous but architecturally heterogeneous residential area[32]. The main *avenidas* were lined by the more prestigious dwellings, and minor roads (built at right angles to the main axis) housed the lesser bourgeoisie. The *avenidas* also represented a decisive break with the fairly compact city which had existed prior to the nineteenth century and, partly because of this, a condition for their successful development was the availability of an efficient public transport sys-

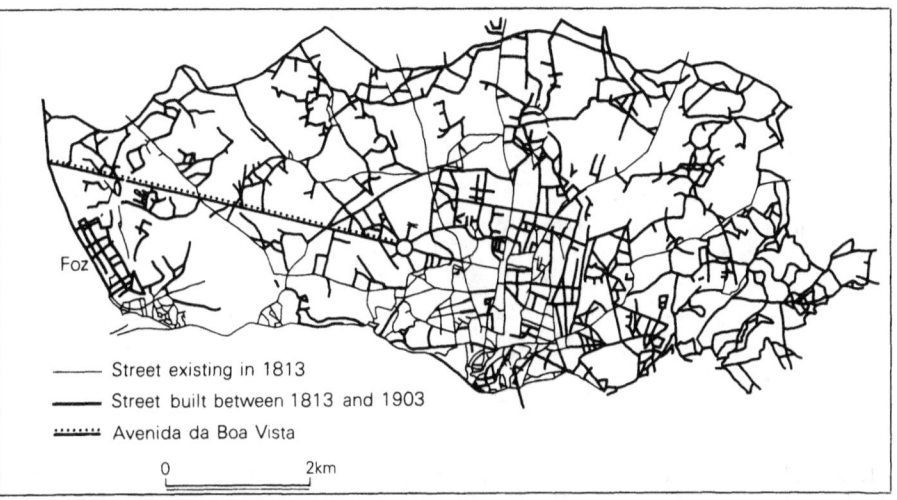

FIGURE 4.7. The growth of the road network in Oporto, 1813–1903 (after de Oliveira).

tem. Public transport had been introduced in 1873, but it was the development of the electric car system after 1901 which was decisive[33].

The difference between the expansion of Lisbon and Oporto is immediately evident if the plan for the *avenidas* (figure 4.6) is compared with the plan of actual road developments in Oporto (figure 4.7). There was no overall urban plan for Oporto or even a plan for the expansion of particular zones of the city. Instead, growth was piecemeal and orientated around long-established roads, creating an irregular pattern of development. Many suburbs, in fact, retained the characteristics of villages[34] and, as there were no controls on building design, architectural form tended to be fairly varied. There were, however, some exceptions to this irregular pattern, the most important of which was the construction of the Avenida da Boa Vista from the Praça Albuquerque to the west coast. This was on a lesser scale than the *avenidas* of Lisbon and it was also planned without consideration of adjoining roads, but it did provide a major axis for expansion. The other important examples of planned expansion were the high-status suburb of Foz, based on a set of streets running parallel to the coastal route, the Avenida do Brasil, and the area around the Rua da Constituição to the north of the city centre. In general, though, urban development in Oporto was very different to that in Lisbon, and it was the former which was typical of the remainder of the country. Thus at the end of the first phase of intense modern industrialization and urban growth, Portugal still lacked a coherent urban planning framework.

1926–1950: THE CORPORATE STATE IN ASCENDANCY

The early years of the twentieth century was a period of intense political instability in Portugal, and during the short-lived Republic of 1910–26 there

% Change 1920-1950

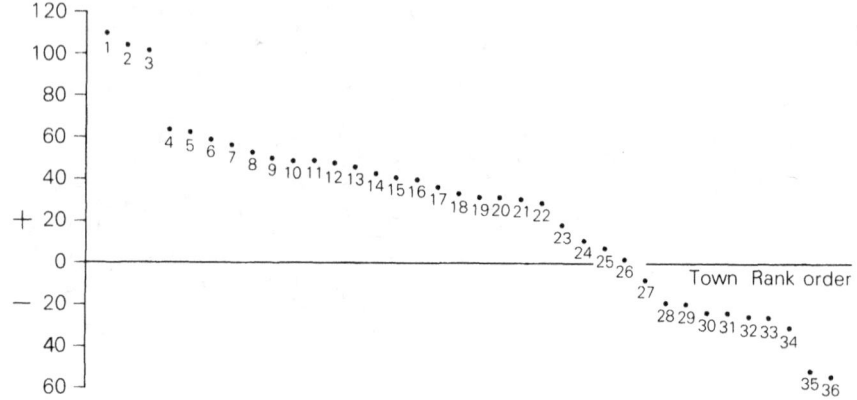

FIGURE 4.8. Rank order of urban population changes 1920–1950. 1. Barcelos; 2. Coimbra; 3. Guimarães; 4. Chaves; 5. Lisboa; 6. Viseu; 7. Evora; 8. Figueira da Foz; 9. Bragança; 10. Caldas da Rainha; 11. Vila Real; 12. Braga; 13. Covilhã; 14. Leiria; 15. Castelo Branco; 16. Porto; 19. Santarém; 20. Viana do Castelo; 21. Portimão; 22. Aveiro; 23. Setúbal; 24. Guarda; 25. Portalegre; 26. Tomar; 27. Elvas; 28. Lamego; 29. Miranda do D.; 30. Penafiel; 31. Lagos; 33. Pinhel; 34. Tavira; 35. Abrantes; 36. Silves.

were no less than forty-five administrations, many of which were brought to a close by political violence[35]. This was also a period of economic instability and high inflation, which was ended by the military coup of 1926. The military leaders appointed Salazar to be Finance Minister, and later to be Prime Minister. Slowly, Portugal moved towards becoming a corporate state and this was formalized by the drafting of a new constitution in 1932, which was based on the contemporary Italian model[36]. Salazar proved to be a very conservative Minister of Finance and he rigorously pursued anti-inflationary policies with balanced state budgets; these measures achieved economic stability but they also resulted in low rates of economic growth, made worse by the depressed state of international markets[37].

Although overall economic growth rates were generally low in this period, the process of uneven regional development continued, and there were still substantial population shifts from the interior to the littoral region, a trend which was reinforced by emigration. The regional redistribution of population was linked with migration flows from rural to urban areas, and the level of urbanization increased slowly during this period[38]. The pattern of urbanization is illustrated by figure 4.8 which shows the population changes in individual cities between 1920 and 1950. One of the largest increases was in Coimbra, which more than doubled in population (from 20,841 to 42,640) during this period, whilst other industrial towns located in the littoral, such as Aveiro, Braga and Guimarães, had growth rates of 30–100 per cent. Some towns in the interior also had relatively high growth rates, reflecting their roles as either industrial centres (for example Covilhã), or capitals of *distritos* (for example, Vila Real and Viseu). However, many of the towns of the interior, such as Lamego Élvas and Abrantes, experienced substantial losses of population, indicative of a strong tendency for a regional polarization of urban growth to occur. As ever, Lisbon and Oporto continued to dominate the picture of urbanization. There were strong but hardly spectacular growth rates in both cities between 1920 and 1950. The absolute increase, however, is more impressive; the population of Lisbon grew from 486,372 to 790,434, while that of Oporto grew from 203,091 to 281,406. The population changes in the metropolitan agglomerations are even more spectacular, with the Lisbon metropolis expanding from 619,831 to 1,092,453 and that of Oporto from 409,851 to 652,032. By 1950, the two cities accounted for 22 per cent of the country's total population.

The period 1926–1950 marks the beginning of formal urban planning in Portugal. Although there were earlier attempts at urban planning as in the *avenidas* projects, it was only under the corporate state that a framework for compulsory urban planning was developed. This was also a period when important steps were taken to consolidate state intervention in housing so that, in theory at least, the state assumed considerable powers to shape future urban development. In practice, these planning and housing controls did not always produce the anticipated results, but they were important landmarks in the evolution of urban planning. The advances in urban planning during this period can probably be accounted for by three factors: first, continuing urbanization was exacerbating the contradictions of unplanned development, especially in terms of land use; secondly, both housing and planning policies were ultimately used to centralize power within the state, and this was consistent with Salazar's strategic aims; and, thirdly, there was the profound influence of Duarte Pacheco, Minister of Public Works between 1932 and 1936 and again between 1938 and 1943, when he was also the President of the Municipality of Lisbon. Pacheco was an unusually dynamic and effective Minister who seems to have enjoyed the confidence of his Prime Minister. He was, therefore, in a strong position to pursue his twin aims of achieving industrial expansion and the orderly, planned development of the city; and housing and urban planning policies were inevitably important instruments in his attempt to achieve these objectives.

The state was already committed to a policy of providing public sector housing through a Decree Law (No. 4137) approved in 1918 allowing for the construction of *Bairros Sociais* (Social Housing). However, this was a very limited programme, and of greater importance was the 1933 sequel (Decree Law 23052), which empowered the state to construct *Casas Economicas* (Low-Income Housing). Under this provision, which was passed while Pacheco was Minister of Public Works, more than 8000 single-family dwellings were

FIGURE 4.9. Public housing in Alvalade, Lisbon.

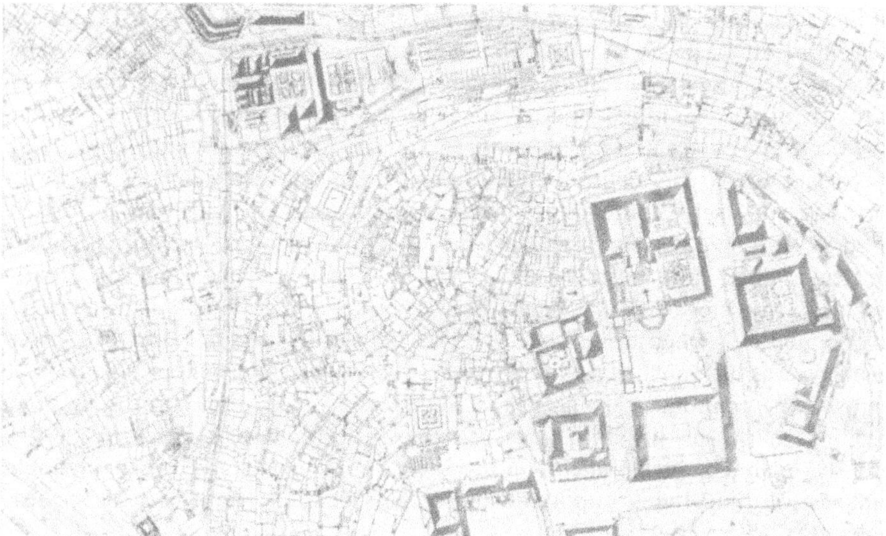

FIGURE 4.10. Town plan for Coimbra, drawn up in the early 1940s.
This section of the plan shows the proposed redevelopment of the Alto (old, upper part of the city) to accommodate new buildings for the University.

constructed for rent by the early 1950s[39]. The 1933 Act was later followed by a number of additional Acts in the period 1945–47 which provided for the construction of other types of state housing, such as the *Casas das Fámilias Pobres* (Poor Families' Houses) and the *Casas dos Pescadores* (Fishermen's Houses)[40]. Access to this housing was restricted both socially (to certain groups such as civil servants, fishermen or the inhabitants of shanty towns) and spatially (most of the houses were in Lisbon or Oporto), and only about 20,000 houses were built, in total, before 1950. However, a commitment had been made to state housing which was to become increasingly important after the Second World War.

The changes which occurred in architectural style in this period are also worth commenting on. In the years 1925–27 a group of young architects started to campaign for Modernist architecture[41]. For a while, Pacheco seemed to encourage this, with the group competing for design contracts (for example, for new secondary schools). However, in the late 1930s the award of the design for the Areeiro-Alvalade area of expansion in Lisbon to a traditional design (figure 4.9) signified the defeat, at least temporarily, of the Modernist movement[42]. Thereafter, the emphasis in housing design was placed on the *casa portuguesa*, the illusory myth of a typical, traditional Portuguese dwelling which dovetailed closely with Salazar's anti-urban ideology[42]. Nevertheless, while housing architecture remained 'traditional', there was a move towards a monumental style in the architecture of public buildings, inspired by the visit to Lisbon in 1941 of Spier with an exhibition of modern German architecture[43]. The result was the construction of massive public buildings in a classical style, including the new faculty buildings for Coimbra University on the ancient site of the Alto (the upper walled city). A large area of older housing, including many of the student 'Republics' (residences which were known as centres of political dissent) had to be demolished to make way for this scheme, drastically changing the urban morphology of the old city (see figure 4.10).

In addition to housing there were also important developments in urban planning. The major achievement was the introduction of the obligation of the country's major local authorities to prepare urban plans. The legislative framework for this was provided by the 1934 and 1944 Planning Acts (Decree Laws 24802 and 33921)[44]. The 1934 Act made it compulsory for all municipalities to prepare general urbanization plans for their areas, and municipalities were subsequently made responsible for the preparation and the approval of these plans. Municipalities with populations larger than 2500, the administrative centres for *concelhos* (districts), and those which were of interest for their touristic, recreational, spiritual or artistic value, had to prepare these plans.

The aims of the 1934 Act were unrealistic, both because of the large number of plans to be prepared and also because the local authorities lacked the technical and financial means to prepare urban plans. Salazar, as Minister of Finance, had already destroyed local financial autonomy in 1928–29 by removing the rights of local authorities to raise certain local taxes so that they lacked the resources to finance more than a rudimentary local administration. Beyond this, they were dependent on subventions from the state and, as these were limited, the municipalities generally lacked the means to develop the necessary technical resources for planning. This reliance on the central state was reinforced by the Administrative Code of 1936–40, which made most of the activities of the municipalities dependent on ministerial approval[45]. In effect, then, the 1934 Act made the central state responsible for urban planning, as only a very few of the larger authorities had the technical resources to prepare plans. Yet because of the large number of plans to be prepared and the lack of qualified planners in Portugal[46], the central state was able to produce only a handful of plans; it has been estimated that by 1945 work had commenced on only fifteen out of a total of approximately 500 plans which should have been drawn up[47].

In 1944, a new urban planning Act was passed; this repeated – in places, literally so – substantial parts of the earlier Act, and the obligations on producing urban plans remained unchanged. Approval of the plans, however, was transferred to the Ministry, hence reinforcing the already high level of centralized decision-making in planning[48]. The urbanization plans were to encompass four main items of physical planning. Existing built-up zones, the zones to be urbanized on the periphery of the town, and protected rural zones were to be identified, and transport links to adjacent centres were to be mapped out. The passing of the new Act did little to rectify the problems of its forerunner, and only ten more plans were approved in the next three years. Two other problems also remained unresolved; first, these were general urbanization plans and there was a need for complementary detailed land-use plans; and, secondly, only the areas of the urban municipalities were covered by the plans, whereas the most intense urbanization pressures were usually occurring in the urban-rural fringe beyond the administrative boundaries. In view of the special problems which existed in the areas adjacent to Oporto and Lisbon, the Administrative Code of 1936 had decreed that agglomerations of municipalities should be formed in these urban regions to prepare general urbanization plans; however, these plans were not produced during this period[50]. As yet, therefore, only a rudimentary framework for urban planning had been provided, although some progress had been made, especially with respect to land policies. The 1933 Expropriation Act (Decree Law 28797) gave the state compulsory purchase powers over land, and this was to be particularly important in shaping the development of Lisbon.

During the period 1926–50, Lisbon continued to grow rapidly, guided by the framework of the Avenidas plan. Large new *bairros* were developed by both the public (for example, Arco de Cego) and private sectors (for example, Benfica) but these were in the form of infill in the interfluves between the main radial roads. Probably the most significant event during these years was the acquisition by the Municipality of 2800 ha of land, under the provision of the

1933 Expropriation Act. This action, which was very much due to Pacheco's influence, meant that a third of the land surface of the city had been brought into public ownership[51]. The municipality then adopted a policy of gradual resale of plots of land at relatively low prices and under strict controls with respect to the type of building allowed. The result was that urban development within the city boundaries was more strongly controlled during this period than in any other since the late eighteenth century. Another end product was the creation of the Monsanto Forest Park which provides an enormous public park very near the centre of the city. However, despite the control exercised over development, Lisbon still lacked a coherent general urbanization plan for the entire city. Plans had been produced by Forrestier in 1928, by Agache in 1933, and by de Groer in 1938, but none was formally approved and implemented. The most influential was that by de Groer who proposed that development should be based on a series of radials from the centre linked by circular ring roads. He also proposed that the 'inner' circular route should be extended across the Tejo by a new bridge at Beato-Montijo, to the east of the centre. The plan included proposals for new industrial zones and for extending housing along existing lines of development. However, it was never approved and its main value was in stimulating discussion about the city's future form.

Urban development in Oporto was equally undramatic during this period. Growth was mainly limited to piecemeal and irregular extensions of the built-up area, within the framework provided by the few major planned roads such as Boa Vista[52].

Many of these suburban additions were still based on existing rural settlements, routes and landownership patterns, so that the emerging network of roads tended to be badly connected; this contributed eventually to the acute traffic problems which are evident in the city today. There were a few exceptions to this general pattern: for example, the Avenida do Marechal Gomes da Costa was developed to link Foz with the Avenida da Boa Vista (the previous lack of a link is evident in figure 4.7). In addition the development of a number of large, low-rise public housing estates, such as those at Condominhas and Carrical, was started during this period. As in Lisbon, however, there was no overall urban plan for these developments. Two plans for the city were prepared during this period by Antão de Almeida Garrett, of the Faculty of Engineering at Lisbon University (the Anteplano de Urbanizacão of 1947 and the Plano Regulador de Cidade of 1952), but neither was officially adopted.

In summary, this was a period characterized by three main elements. These were continuity, innovation and centralization: the continuity was evident in the regional pattern of urbanization and in the form of urban expansion in particular cities; the innovation occurred in the establishment of a legal framework for urban planning and the expansion of public housing; and the centralization was the almost insidious way in which decision-making was concentrated in the Praça do Comércio, headquarters of the Ministério das Obras Públicas (the Ministry of Public Works).

1950–1974: Growth and Urban Change

During the early years of the corporate state, Salazar had been committed to a policy of economic stabilization and limited growth, but after the Second World War the government pursued a policy of industrialization. At first this was based on encouraging indigenous industries, whether these were in new sectors, such as the development of the oil refinery at Cabo Riuvo, or were traditional sectors of established strength, such as the processing of raw materials like cotton, cork and timber[53]. However, in the 1960s, the onset of the colonial wars, which absorbed an increasing share of Portugal's resources, meant that the state itself no longer provided the main stimulus to growth, and the traditional policies of economic nationalism were relaxed and foreign investment was welcome[54]. At the same time, there was a considerable expansion of the tourist industry, especially in the Algarve and around Lisbon. The results were twofold – first, high growth rates in Gross Domestic Product (GDP) were sustained (annual average of 6.2 per cent in the mid-1960s); and, secondly, the proportion of employment in the primary sector fell from 50 per cent to 30 per cent between 1950 and 1970, while the proportions in the secondary sector and tertiary sectors both increased[55].

Economic development was accompanied by a process of uneven regional development, for the growth of new and traditional manufacturing industries and of service employment was concentrated in the littoral. Within this broad region, two sub-regions dominated economic growth, that in the north-west (the *distritos* of Aveiro, Braga and Oporto) and that in the south-west (the *distritos* of Lisbon and Setúbal). The south-west region alone accounted for 40 per cent of GDP in 1970, based on heavy industry around the Tejo estuary and the dominance of Lisbon in the tertiary sector (with 38 per cent of all employment in this sector). In addition, the north-west accounted for a further 28 per cent of GDP, based on highly land-intensive agricultural production, labour-intensive industrialization, and more limited service functions, especially in Oporto. The dominance of these regions was such that, in the period 1960–75, only these five *distritos* experienced population gains. All the other *distritos* lost population, and in the interior these losses amounted to more than 1 per cent per annum; the direct cause of these population shifts was rural-urban migration and emigration (an estimated 12 per cent of the population left the country in the 1960s). It may be concluded, therefore, that the commitment of Portugal to a more overtly capitalist path of development after 1950 led to an accentuation of trends which had existed in the spatial organization of the economy prior to this date[56].

There was also an acceleration of existing trends in urbanization: in 1950, it has been estimated, 19.7 per cent of the population lived in centres which had more than 10,000 inhabitants, but by 1970 this had increased to 27.1 per cent[57]. This was, of course, still a low level of overall urbanization, but the process had a distinctive regional pattern, with the towns of the littoral region

TABLE 4.1. The growth of population in Lisbon and Oporto.

| Year | Lisbon City | Lisbon Metropolitan Area | Oporto City | Oporto Metropolitan Area |
|---|---|---|---|---|
| 1864 | 197,649 | 260,677 | 86,761 | |
| 1878 | 227,674 | 297,084 | 105,838 | |
| 1890 | 300,421 | 380,876 | 146,739 | |
| 1900 | 356,311 | 452,094 | 167,955 | |
| 1911 | 436,326 | 557,341 | 194,009 | 393,865 |
| 1920 | 486,372 | 619,831 | 203,091 | 409,851 |
| 1930 | 594,390 | 768,136 | 232,280 | 407,962 |
| 1940 | 709,179 | 929,391 | 258,548 | 473,002 |
| 1950 | 790,434 | 1,092,453 | 281,406 | 652,032 |
| 1960 | 802,230 | 1,288,386 | 303,424 | 746,424 |
| 1970 | 782,266 | 1,596,406 | 310,437 | 837,610 |

*Source:* Instituto Nacional de Estatística, General Population Censuses 1864–1970.

experiencing the largest increases. Between 1960 and 1970 the population of Coimbra grew from 46,313 to 55,985, that of Setúbal from 44,435 to 49,670, and that of Braga from 40,977 to 48,795. In contrast, there was a fall in the number of settlements with more than 2000 inhabitants from 314 in 1960 to 257 in 1970, and most of the losses occurred in the interior[58]. Even some of the larger towns of the interior, such as Vila Real, Portalegre, Élvas, Viseu and Évora lost population during this period, reflecting the enormous drain of people from the interior. Many of the towns of the littoral were expanding beyond their administrative boundaries, so that the official statistics underestimated their growth, making the real difference between the east and west even greater than the figures suggest.

This general pattern of urbanization was overlain by the recurrent expansion and domination of Lisbon and Oporto. The populations of the two cities, as defined administratively, were in fact stagnant during this period, but this only reflected the fact that growth was dispersed more widely throughout the metropolitan regions. Thus the population of the metropolitan area of Lisbon grew from 1,092,453 in 1950 to 1,596,406 in 1970, while that of Oporto increased from 652,032 to 837,610 during the same period (see table 4.1). The higher growth rate in Lisbon reflects the massive polarization of growth which occurred around the city on both banks of the Tejo. In contrast, growth in the north-west was more spatially diffuse and this is accounted for by the regional differences in the organization of production[59], industrial growth having been located within the existing settlement pattern.

The unprecedented scale of economic change brought about enormous pressures on housing, land use and transport in the more rapidly expanding cities. The response of the state to this was completely inadequate in both the housing and urban planning fields, so that the private sector, largely unfettered, gained the ascendancy during this period. This was partly due to the early death of Pacheco, who had been the driving force behind the establishment of state control. It was also due to the sheer scale of urban growth which created development problems to which the state was incapable of developing an effective response. Nevertheless, an impressive array of regulations was placed on the statute book. The first important legislation in this era was the General Regulation of Urban Buildings (Decree Law 33,382) of 1951, which made it obligatory for all new buildings to be licenced by the local authority. This was designed to tighten up the control over speculative and illegal building, but it was largely ineffective because it depended on the existence of approved general urbanization plans which most cities simply did not possess. The complexity of the legislation also tended to obfuscate further the lack of clarity in planning controls[60].

The activities of private developers were also the concern of the 1965 Housing Development Act (Decree Law 46,573) which was the first Act to legislate for large-scale private development schemes. It became obligatory for promoters to submit their plans for official consent; if a general urbanization plan existed, then the municipality was empowered to grant approval, but otherwise this was the responsibility of the Ministry of Public Works. It was hoped that this Act would reduce illegal building and allow the state to supervise the installation of suitable infrastructure in new developments. In effect, however, the private sector was being granted the initiative in development, which increasingly contributed to unordered urban expansion[61]. The local authorities lacked the technical resources to evaluate and process applications, while reliance on the General Directorate of Urban Planning (within the Ministry) was inevitably ponderous. As a result, by the 1960s, the balance of power could be said to have swung firmly from the public to the private sector. There was an attempt in 1973 to tighten up control over private development, but new regulations (introduced in Decree Law 289) were evaded by the use of new forms of contracts which confused ownership and land-use issues[62].

One of the underlying problems of urban planning was that many local authorities did not possess approved general urbanization plans, as was obligatory under the 1944 Act. Recent research has revealed that, even in 1980, only 100 out of 275 *concelhos* (municipalities) had approved plans, while a further forty either had conditionally approved plans or plans awaiting approval. In contrast, plans were still being prepared for eighty-five areas and no work had yet begun on the plans for the remaining fifty more than thirty-five years after the 1944 Act. This slow progress stems not only from the time taken to prepare the plans but also the delays in their approval (see figure 4.11). Some plans have taken up to twelve years to prepare and others have taken just as long to receive approval from the Ministry. The largest number of plan approvals occurred between 1945 and 1955, which was more than the total of approvals during the following twenty years of more intense urbanization[63].

The two most interesting examples of plans prepared under the 1944 Act

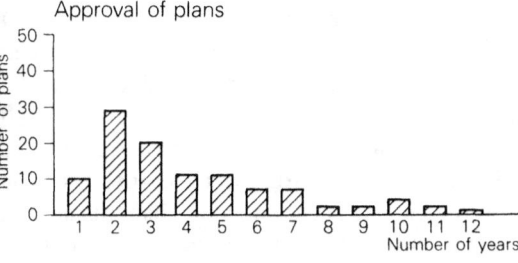

FIGURE 4.11. Time taken to prepare and approve general urbanization plans, under the 1944 Urban Planning Act.
*Source:* Gabinete de Planeamento e Estudos do Ministério da Habitacão e Obras, Públicas.

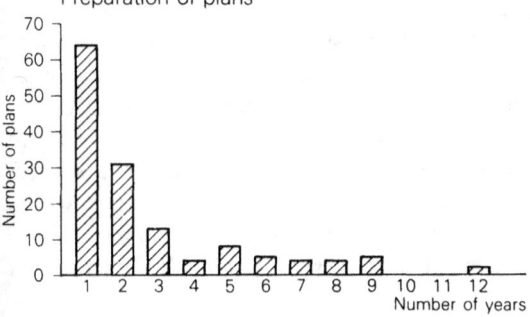

FIGURE 4.12. The *Plano Director* for Lisbon approved in 1976.

are those for Oporto and Lisbon. The *Plano Director* for Lisbon (figure 4.12) completed in 1967 but approved by the state only in 1976, focused on the need for the orderly expansion of the city and aimed at a comprehensive zoning of land and development of the transport system. Three themes were identified as being particularly important. First, tertiary employment was expected to grow by 55 per cent between 1960 and 1985 and room for expansion of the commercial areas was therefore required; it was recommended that this should include the relocation of public sector offices from the *baixa* to a new sub-centre. Secondly, the population of Grande Lisbon was expected to continue growing at around 12,000 per annum, and most of this expansion was to be channelled into two western zones, along the western river bank and the route to Sintra with the Monsanto Park acting as a buffer between these zones. Thirdly, a thorough redesign of the road system was considered to be necessary to manage the expected increase in road traffic and to relieve congestion in the centre. The basic proposal was to divert traffic away from the centre, channelling it on to peripheral routes or on to a new motorway spur which linked the Tejo bridge (completed in 1966) and the northern motorway. There were also to be seven radial roads from this motorway, linking it with the rest of the road network.

The *Plano Director* of 1964 for Oporto was basically quite similar to its Lisbon counterpart, reflecting their preparation under the overall supervision of Robert Auzelle from Paris (another example of French influence). The main aim of the plan was to provide for the orderly expansion of the city to accommodate its changing economic role, as its service functions increased. It was also recognized that existing population decentralization trends were likely to continue, especially as the housing policies of the *Plano do Melhoramento* (the housing improvement plan for the city) of 1956 would result in further reductions in density in the pre-twentieth century urban zones. The plan therefore identified suitable zones for expansion and made proposals for the provision of social infrastructure.

In economic terms, Oporto was expected to become increasingly important as a centre of tertiary activities; land would have to be obtained in the central areas to facilitate this, and it was recommended that some functions, such as warehousing, would therefore be decentralized. Finally, to facilitate the efficient functioning of the tertiary sector and to allow for the journeys-to-work of the dispersed population, plans for redesigning the road system were proposed. New east-west and north-south routes were to be completed, deflecting through-traffic away from the centre and the Dom Luis bridge and on to the newly opened Ponte da Arrabida. A new inner-ring road, the *via cintura*, was to deflect internal traffic from the commercial core to a ring of adjacent car parks. This plan was only conditionally approved so that the central government was able to retain control over all major decisions.

Both the Lisbon and Oporto plans were only partially successful in achieving their aims. The process of plan preparation and approval was very slow, so that policies tended to be overtaken by events. Furthermore, the plans also very much reflected the ethos of the age – the need to redesign the city centre, cater for motor vehicles and rigidly zone land uses. On the other hand, at least some of the planning proposals were implemented, especially with regard to zoning. Fundamentally, however, the plans had two weaknesses: first, the lack of local resources tended to reduce them to the level of indicative plans; and secondly, they were dealing only with the artificially defined municipal areas which contained less than half the populations of the metropolitan areas.

Partly as a reaction to these problems, a new Planning Act was passed in 1971 (embodied in Decree Laws 560/71 and 561/71), which defined a three-tier hierarchy of plans. Municipalities were to prepare *planos geraes de urbanização* (general urbanization plans) for the main settlements within their boundaries, with the procedure for this being simplified and made more flexible, and the plans to be revised every five years. The limitation of the plans to the immediate areas of the towns meant that they still did not include the surrounding rural-urban fringe areas which were under the greatest pressure. The obligation to revise the plans every five years also seems rather derisory, given the delays experienced in processing the initial plans. The lowest tier of the hierarchy were the *planos de pormenor* (detailed land-use plans) essentially for areas of expansion. Of course, detailed land-use plans already existed in practice, but the 1971 Act formalized their role. Finally, the Acts brought into being a new tier of urban planning at the supra-municipality level: *planos de áreas territoriais* (territorial plans) were to be prepared for areas covering more than one municipality where the environment was under particularly acute pressure, or where there were especially complex inter-urban relationships. The responsibility for the preparation of these plans rested with the General Directorate of Urban Planning (Ministry of Public Works) and not with the municipalities. By 1980 work had commenced on thirteen of the territorial plans and these included many of the larger urban areas, such as Coimbra, Aveiro, Leiria, Setúbal and Guarda, as well as the entire Algarve region[64]. While the creation of larger-scale planning units was welcomed as an acknowledgement of the realities of contemporary urbanization, the competency of these territorial plans *vis-à-vis* the municipalities was not clear, and it also represented a further case of the centralization of planning powers[65].

Since the early 1950s another innovation in urban planning has been the development of Metropolitan Planning Agencies for the Lisbon and Oporto sub-regions. They are subordinate to the Ministry of Housing and Public Works (created in 1978 as an enlargement of the old Ministry of Public Works) and have two functions: indicative planning for the entire metropolitan region (for example, a metropolitan plan for Lisbon was prepared in 1964) and the preparation of partial urbanization plans, subject to approval by the Ministry. The most important of these was the *Plano da Urbanização da Costa da Sol* which paved the way for the development of the tourist area around Estoril[66].

Thus it can be said of this period that there were two main changes in urban planning. First, there was an attempt to clarify the existing urban planning legislation and to develop a more comprehensive framework for different types of planning activities. Secondly, the reality of decision-making in the planning process was quite different: municipalities still lacked the resources to prepare urban plans, and most plans were prepared by the General Directorate of Urban Planning (which, in turn, placed contracts with private planning agencies for the prepartion of most of the plans). These plans were constantly subject to long delays in approval, and many of the general urbanization plans for the more important cities, such as that for Coimbra in 1974, received only partial approval. This procedure meant that all important planning decisions had to be referred to Lisbon for approval, and this was part of the continuing process of the centralization of decision-making. At the same time, real decision-making powers seem, by default, to have passed to private sector developers.

One direct outcome of these shifts in planning power was the growth of *bairros clandestinos*, or illegal housing, which may range in quality from being *bairros de lata* (shanty towns) to luxurious developments (see figures 4.13 and 4.14). This is housing which has been developed without municipal permission (as required by the 1951 General Regulation of Urban Buildings Act), either to short-circuit long planning delays, or to maximize profits through developing land which has been zoned as 'green space', reserved for agriculture or recreation. Although the municipalities have the powers to order the demolition of such dwellings, they have invariably chosen to ignore them, both because they have lacked the technical means to enforce the law, and because, in the absence of adequate housing policies, there has been no alternative housing for the populations of the expanding cities[67]. The wish of many emigrants to invest their savings in land and property had also contributed to the growth of the *clandestinos*. The most reliable estimates suggest that there were between 80,000 and 150,000 illegal dwellings in the late 1970s[68] and that over 80 per cent of these are located in metropolitan areas of Lisbon and Oporto, with other important nuclei existing in urban centres such as Coimbra and Évora, or tourist areas such as the Algarve. These, of course, are the areas where the demand for housing is greatest. The distribution of the *clandestinos* at a more local level also has a distinctive pattern; the shanty towns are located on the poorest land (for example, adjacent to railways and motorways), and are usually quite close to the city centres while the more solidly built commuter homes of the working and middle classes are located in the rural-urban fringe, away from the main roads.

The importance of clandestine development is that although most of the dwellings have been quite solidly built (and sometimes are luxurious, with their own tennis courts), being illegal they lack publicly supplied services. A study of the Quinta de Conde area, near Lisbon, has shown that most dwellings lack sewers, piped water and mains electricity[69]. As it is far more expensive to install such facilities after the houses have been built, this creates additional problems for any plans to remedy the deficiencies of these areas. The devel-

FIGURE 4.13. A *bairro do lata* in Lisbon.

FIGURE 4.14. A luxurious clandestine development in Lagoa de Albufeira, near Lisbon.

opment of the *bairros clandestinos* has also created other problems for urban planning. There is a lack of social and commercial facilities, which results in unduly long journeys to shopping, educational and health facilities. In the larger zones of illegal development, such as Quinta do Conde, entire townships may be created with no more facilities than are usually to be found in a village. Furthermore, these *bairros* are usually developed at very low densities and they absorb large tracts of land, frequently of the better agricultural quality. This, of course, makes a mockery of any attempt to develop an orderly approach to the zoning of land in the metropolitan areas. It is also storing up enormous future problems for planners who will have to integrate these areas more effectively into overall urban structures.

The *bairros clandestinos* are not simply a result of the inadequacies of urban planning, for their growth also reflects the failure of the conventional housing industry to respond adequately to need in the urban areas. The most potent symbol of this failure is the growth of shanty towns, especially in the Lisbon metropolitan area, where some of the shanty towns are enormous; that at Brandoa de Figueira, for example, had more than 12,000 dwellings constructed of timber and metal sheets[70]. The private sector has been unable to meet the demand for dwellings, especially as resources have been diverted into luxury housing and tourist developments. The public sector also has had a limited impact, and investment in public housing in Portugal is one of the lowest recorded in Europe[71]. Even by the mid-1970s there were less than 100,000 publicly owned dwellings; and although some of these, such as the *Casas Desmontaveis* (Relocation Dwellings), were designed for rehousing the inhabitants of slums or shanty towns, others were designed for civil servants. Therefore the level of state provision for the lower-income groups was far less even than the official figures suggest. Nevertheless, state housing programmes were concentrated in the metropolitan areas, where 70 per cent of new local authority houses were built in the early 1970s.

Public sector housing was, thus, quantitatively of no great magnitude, but it did have an important influence on urban form. Most of the major cities now have peripheral public housing estates which dominate their skylines. Although the early state housing schemes were of low-rise, single-family units, a fundamental architectural change occurred in this period. An important turning point was the 1948 Congress of Architects which led to a survey of vernacular architecture which, in turn, led to the discrediting of the myth of the typical Portuguese house[72]. The time was ripe for the re-emergence of Modernist architecture, and in 1955 high-rise designs were accepted for the Olivais-Norte scheme in Lisbon, comprising 1900 dwellings. Then, in rapid succession, high-rise designs were also accepted for a number of other schemes such as Olivais Sul and Chelas in Lisbon and Aleixo in Oporto[73].

POST-1974: AFTER THE REVOLUTION

The failure of the Salazarist regime to end the colonial wars and to reform the political system led to a military coup in Portugal in April 1974, when a group of young officers seized power. At first they had no specific political programme beyond ending the military struggle in Africa, but gradually a number of distinctive groups emerged within the military, and some of these affiliated themselves to the fledgling political parties. During the next twenty months there was a constant struggle for power, and in November 1975 this culminated in troops loyal to the government blocking what was arguably an attempted coup by the far left[74]. Subsequently, there has been a move to a system of parliamentary democracy, but this has not resulted in a stable system of government. Until recently power has been held by a succession of uneasy coalition governments, some of which have been at odds with the elected President, Antonio Ramalho Eanes. These internal political events, allied with the world recession and the disruption of production in Portugal following the revolution, have led to reduced growth in the economy. There have also been rising unemployment and high inflation rates since 1974[75]. Growth has continued to be spatially uneven, and the concentration of production and population in the littoral region has increased. This has been encouraged by the recent rersurgence of the tourist industry, and by the renewed interest of foreign investors such as Renault and Ford, most of whose investments are located in the littoral region[76].

The level of urbanization has also increased, especially in the littoral region, and the 1981 census shows that growth has been sustained around the major metropolitan areas. Although there were only modest population increases in the cities of Lisbon and Oporto, there were very high rates of increase in their surrounding satellite towns (see figure 4.15). For example, in the Lisbon metropolitan area there were population increases of over 100 per cent in Seixal and Oeiras, and increases of 50 per cent in Vila Franca de Xira, Sintra and Loures. In the Oporto metropolitan area there were also high growth rates, although these did not achieve the spectacular levels observed in Lisbon; the largest increase was 53 per cent in Valango. These remarkably high rates of growth are a reflection of internal migration, returned emigration from Europe, and the arrival of almost a million *retornados* from the African colonies in 1975[77]. The pattern revealed in figure 4.15 also shows that growth in the Lisbon region continues to be more polarized than in the northern region, where it is more spatially diffuse.

These population shifts have compounded the pressures which already existed in the urban system before this period, so that the inadequacies of the existing planning framework have been even more clearly indicated, and the need to reform urban planning has become more urgent. In addition, popular demands have also increased the pressure to reform the planning system. After the 1974 Revolution, there was an upsurge of urban political movements demanding various types of reform in the administration of urban life. The most important of these movements was the *commissões dos moradores* or residents associations. The *commissões* were mostly formed in the areas of public

Population changes for concelhos, 1970-81

FIGURE. 4.15. Population changes 1970–81 in the north-west and south-west regions of Portugal.

housing or the shanty towns in Lisbon, Oporto and Setúbal, and their demands were either for reform in the administration of state housing or for provision of public housing for those living in urban slums[78]. There was a need, then, both to improve the efficiency of, and to democratize the approach to, urban planning, but there have been limited responses to these needs from the public administration. What response there has been falls within one of five categories, each of which will now be treated in turn: reform of the general context for planning; reform of the planning machinery itself; urban conservation measures; large-scale public housing schemes; and initiatives in the private sector.

The general context for urban planning has been reformed through an increase in the financial autonomy of the municipalities and there has also been a reform of the laws relating to land and expropriation. Local authorities were given a measure of financial autonomy by the Local Finance Act of 1979 which gave them direct control over 15 per cent of state expenditure. The municipalities were to receive their funds from direct taxes, a share of some national taxes, and a direct subsidy from central government (calculated in relation to the size of population and the level of social need in the area)[79]. This restored to the local administrations some of the autonomy that they had lost during the early years of the Salazarist regime. The Act was complemented by the Local Government Act (the *Lei de Atribuições das Autarquias e Competências das Respectivos Orgãos*) of 1977, which defined the competency of the municipalities in relation to the role of central government. As a result of this Act, local authorities obtained greater powers in the fields of housing and urban planning, especially with respect to the provision of infrastructure and services, public health, cultural activities and the management of housing[80]. However, in practice their dependence on central government is still considerable, because of their lack of resources and the delays in fully implementing the Acts.

The other change in the general context of urban planning stems from the Land Act (Decree Law 794) and the Expropriation Code (Decree Law 845), both dating from 1976. The former is a wide ranging Act which covers the activities of municipalities with respect to land and sets out preventative measures, means of control, rights of preference of the administration in the purchase of land, restrictions to demolition, and the declaration of critical areas for recovery. It therefore defines a very wide scope for intervention by the municipalities in a number of aspects of urban development. The municipalities also acquired powers to expropriate land where there were particular problems involved in its development, especially where there were speculative pressures or widespread illegal building. The actual procedures for expropriation were regulated and simplified by the 1976 Expropriation Code, and include publication of the reasons for expropriation, approval by the Ministry, methods for calculating the level of compensation, and recourse to tribunals in cases of disagreement on land values. The powers of expropriation have been important in conservation work as, for example, in the Ribeira-Barredo area in Oporto. Furthermore, the existence of these powers has been used effectively by some authorities, as in Évora, to deter speculation and illegal development. However, there seems to be disappointment amongst most commentators that the Act has not been used more widely to control urban development[81].

There have also been some limited changes in the machinery of urban planning. The major change has been the decision taken in 1976 to establish special planning units, *Gabinetes de Apoio Técnico* (GATs), to assist the planning work of the municipalities. For this purpose the 274 municipalities have been grouped together to form forty-nine sub-regions, the classifications being based on their socio-economic characteristics. The GATs then prepare physical plans for these areas which are supposed to provide a framework for the preparation of general urbanization plans as well as a means of identifying the main investment projects to be undertaken by the individual authorities. In turn, the activities of the GATs are co-ordinated by the regional planning commissions, the *Commissões de Coordenação do Planeamento*. The GATs are, therefore, an important innovation because they provide the means of integrating the rather disjointed set of plans which would otherwise result from the fragmented nature of local government. They also provide invaluable technical support to help overcome the deficiencies of the municipalities in terms of this resource. The GATs however have not provided an answer to the problems of co-ordinating planning in the metropolitan areas of Lisbon and Oporto. Here, jurisdictional fragmentation continues to cause a number of problems in the fields of urban planning, water supplies, infrastructural provision and industrial planning[82].

In terms of actual planning activities, probably the most important achievements have been in the field of urban conservation. Work has begun on conservation of the historic centres of both Évora and Coimbra, but the most substantial progress has been in Oporto, in the Ribeira-Barredo zone[83]. Growth of the riverside zone dates from the medieval period and the area lies just inside the Muralha Fernandina (the medieval walls) of the city. It used to be the commercial heart and the high-status residential area of Oporto. However, with the changes in urban structure which occurred in the nineteenth century (described earlier), it increasingly became an overcrowded, physically degraded area, which functioned as a residential zone for poor rural immigrants. By the middle of the twentieth century some houses in the zone had already been demolished, there had been proposals to demolish further parts to make way for car-parking and public open spaces, and the whole area was in a very advanced stage of decay. Following April 1974, two of the earliest residents associations in Oporto were established in the Ribeira-Barredo, and they demanded both improvements in the area and access to rehousing in new public housing schemes. In response to the first demand, the Commission for the Urban Renovation of the Ribeira-Barredo Area (CRUARB) was established in 1974, funded by Housing Development Agency (FFM) which itself is an arm of the Ministry of Housing. The plan which it prepared for the improvement of the area is shown in figure 4.16. The overall achievements of the

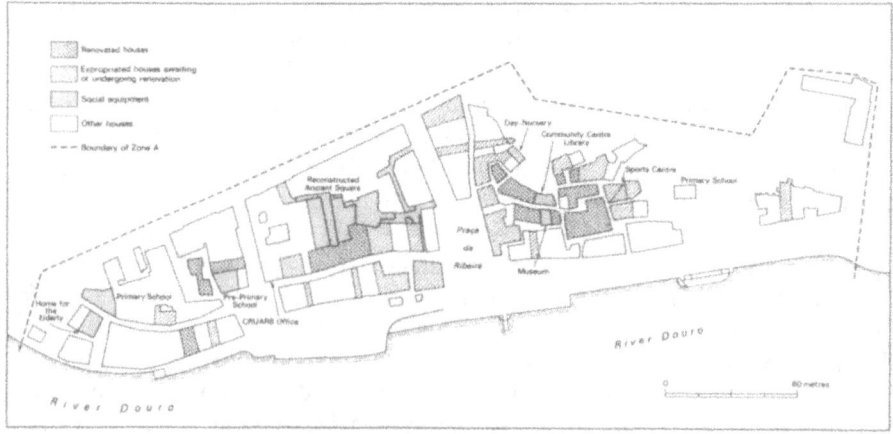

FIGURE 4.16. The CRUARB plan for conservation in the Ribeira-Barredo zone in Oporto.

FIGURE 4.17. Improved dwellings in the interior of the Ribeira-Barredo conservation zone in Oporto.

CRUARB planning team have been threefold: first, through comprehensive internal rebuilding they have substantially improved the quality of housing in the area; secondly, by a policy of facadism in rebuilding and sensitive replacement of already demolished buildings, the architectural character of the area has been conserved (see figure 4.17); and, finally, the provision of improved social and communal facilities, combined with measures (such as subsidized rents) to retain the existing population in the area, have contributed to the 'cultural renovation' of the Ribeira-Barredo. The work of CRUARB might well provide a model for future urban conservation schemes.

The other important innovation in conservation came from the short-lived experiment of the Serviço Ambulatório de Apoio Local (SAAL), a self-help agency which was established soon after the Revolution. The concept of SAAL was that small technical brigades should be established to help local residents to improve their areas or to build new housing. The state provided only limited funds for these schemes, and most of the resources were to be found from within the local communities using, for example, self-help labour-intensive methods[84]. An example of the work of the SAAL teams can be seen in the São Victor area of Oporto, which is a zone of *ilhas*. The SAAL technical brigade for this area was formed in November 1974, in response to the local residents' demands for better living conditions. The plans prepared by the

SAAL team suggested a shift in emphasis from demolition to improvements, which included the addition of second floors to the existing houses, and the linking of the *ilhas* to each other by the construction of new passageways. New houses were also to be built on some cleared land in the zone, and some semi-ruined dwellings were to be rebuilt. Delays in the building programme and dissatisfaction with the allocations procedures tended to dampen enthusiasm for the project, but it did show that there were alternatives to the usual approach to urban renewal (involving replacement with new blocks of flats) adopted by the municipality under the *Plano de Melhoramento*[85]. However, the SAAL process, both in Oporto and elsewhere, became increasingly politicized, and towards the end of 1976 it was brought to a close. As a result, it is remembered today more for its approach than for its achievements.

In contrast to the innovation in urban conservation, there have not been any significant changes in the direct role of the state in new urban developments. State housing policies have continued on broadly the same lines as existed previously, with fairly large-scale medium- and high-rise schemes being dominant. The one development which is important to note is the scheme for the new town of San André, which is being built as part of the larger plan for the Sines industrial growth centre. The aims of the Sines project are to develop a port, oil-refining, petro-chemicals and iron and steel complex in a relatively undeveloped part of the Alentejo region in the south of Portugal. In order to house the workforce for this complex, it was proposed to develop a new town – Portugal's first – at nearby San André. The initial target for the new town is 5000 dwellings, but this is to be increased ultimately to 20,000. Neighbourhood areas (see figure 4.18) based on local schools, are being developed, and these are linked by two major roads (with a network of

FIGURE 4.18. Housing in San André new towns.

FIGURE 4.19. The plan for San André new town.

secondary routes) to the commercial centre of the town and to the zone of light industry (see figure 4.19). Pedestrian routes are also being provided within and between the neighbourhoods. This scheme, which is now well underway, probably represents the best example to date of an integrated urban development scheme in Portugal.

The final area of innovation in urban planning has been with respect to the *bairros clandestinos*. Immediately following April 1974 there was an enormous increase in the level of clandestine construction. The response of central government was to establish *comissariados* (commissariats) in the areas of most intense activity, such as Lisbon and the Algarve. The *comissariados* were to record the extent of illegal development, prepare plans to legalize these, and provide technical support for the municipalities which had to implement the plans. The co-ordinating role of the *comissariados* was critical as many of the *bairros clandestinos* were located astride one or more municipal boundaries[86]. The basic approach to legalization has included three elements – prevention

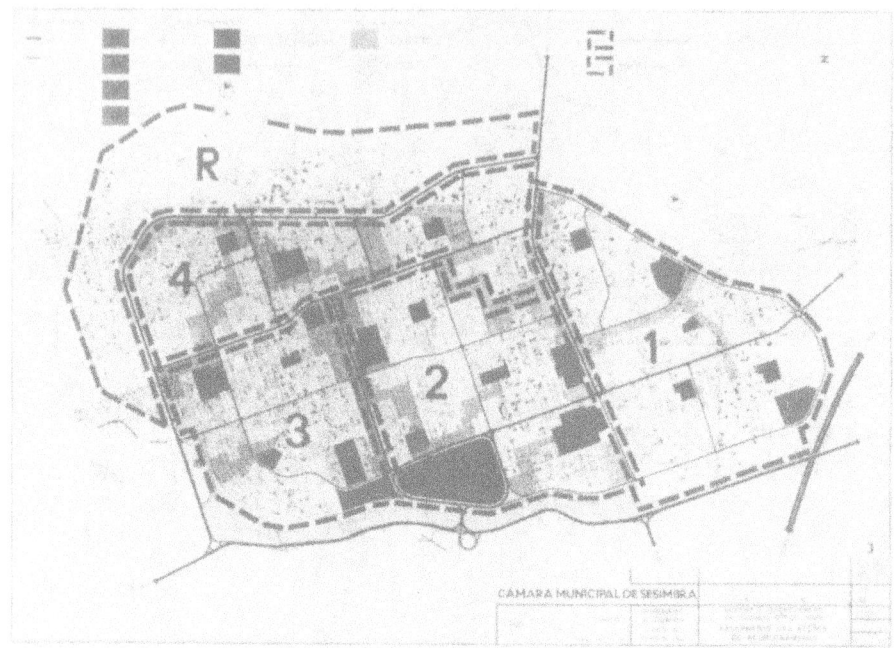

FIGURE 4.20. Plan for the improvement and legalisation of a *bairro clandestino* in Sesimbra.

of further development; legalization of illegal dwellings which are then provided with basic services in return for a fee; and planning for a more orderly use of space. It is the last element which has caused most controversy, because the owners of some *lotes* (building plots) have had to give up or exchange their development claims to these so that land can be obtained for communal facilities or recreation zones. The plan prepared for one such *bairro clandestino* in the municipality of Sesimbra, which is to be implemented in four phases, is shown in figure 4.20. Areas around the *bairro* are to be reserved as 'green' zones, primary and secondary roads are to be developed within the *bairro*, and sites are set aside for schools, commercial facilities and other services. This has been one of the more controversial plans, for the owners of *lotes* which have been earmarked for communal facilities have in exchange only been offered the right to an appartment in medium-rise housing elsewhere.

## Urban Development and Planning in Retrospect

The process of urban development in Portugal has been profoundly influenced by the nature of political and economic changes. Economic development has been spatially selective, especially during the two periods of rapid industrialization in the late nineteenth century and post-1950. Towns in the interior have stagnated while those in the littoral have expanded fairly rapidly. However, urban growth has really been dominated by only two cities, the quite distinctive metropolitan areas of Lisbon and Oporto. In European terms, most of the other towns could only be considered small or, at best, medium sized.

The planning response to the many problems associated with urban growth has been fairly limited. The most important planning schemes have been in Lisbon, notably the redevelopment of the *baixa* in the eighteenth century and the *avenidas* extension plans of the late nineteenth century. Elsewhere, urban planning has been fairly piecemeal and, indeed, only in the mid-twentieth century did a legislative framework for urban planning emerge. The Acts of 1934, 1944 and 1971 have provided the main elements of this framework and they have evolved a system of obligatory urban planning at the municipal level, with plans being essentially concerned with land use.

However, planning has suffered from a number of deficiencies. The process of plan preparation and approval has been very slow, planning powers have been centralized in Lisbon to a very high degree, and the real initiative in urban development has usually rested with legal or illegal privately-sponsored schemes. The result has been the accumulation of enormous problems in urban areas, especially in Lisbon and Oporto. There are extensive areas of shanties, degraded older housing and clandestine developments, and there are also poorly developed systems of urban transport and inadequate provision of infrastructure.

Since 1974 a start has been made in tackling some of these problems, and there have been innovations in urban conservation, in the legalization of *bairros clandestinos* and in the devolution of autonomy to the municipalities. However, there are still a number of critical areas in urban planning which require reform. A recent report has listed some of these[87]: there is a need for better training of those involved in planning; the hierarchy of national, regional and urban plans needs to be better integrated; effective metropolitan planning is required in Lisbon and Oporto; public participation in planning needs to be improved; and greater local autonomy for the municipalities should be encouraged. These issues all pose challenges for the reform of urban planning in the 1980s which will be critical in influencing the form of urban development in Portugal during the remainder of the twentieth century and beyond.

NOTES

1. Gabinete de Planeamento e Contrôle do ex MHUC (1979) *Documento de trabalho preliminar do plano de longo prazo do sector urbanismo e habitação*. Lisbon: Ministério de Habitação.
2. This definition of 'urban' included all places with population larger than 2000.
3. Lewis, J. R. and Williams, A. M. (1981) Regional uneven development on the European periphery: the case of Portugal, 1950–1978. *Tijdschrift voor Economische en Social Geografie*, 72(2), pp. 81–98.
4. See Hugo-Brunt, M. (1972) *The History of City Planning: A Survey*. Montreal: Harvest House, pp. 114–17. Also see Kubler, G. and Soria, M. (1959) *Art and Architecture in Spain and Portugal and their American Dominions 1500 to 1800*.

Harmondsworth: Penguin. Kubler considers that Brazilian artistic ties with the mother country were closer than those of Spanish America and that '... the community of interest is most clearly reflected in architecture' (p. 116).
5. *Bairros clandestinos* are areas of illegal housing constructed without a building licence, and often contravening land-use zonings.
6. Gaspar, J. (1969) A morfologia urbana de padrão geométrico na idade média. *Finisterra*, 4(8), pp. 198–215.
7. França, J. A. (1980) *Lisbon: urbanismo e arquitectura*. Lisbon: Biblioteca Breve.
8. de Oliveira, J. M. P. (1973) *O espaço urbano do Porto*. Coimbra: Instituto de Alta Cultura.
9. França, J. A. (1977) *Lisboa pombalina e o iluminismo*. Lisbon: Livraria Bertrand.
10. See Kubler and Soria (1959) *op. cit.*, p. 115 (see note 4).
11. França, J. A. (1978) *A reconstrução de Lisboa e a arquitectura pombalina*. Lisbon: Biblioteca Breve.
12. Gutkind, E. A. (1967) *Urban Development in Southern Europe: Spain and Portugal*. New York: The Free Press, p. 75.
13. França (1980) *op. cit.*, p. 46 (see note 7).
14. de Oliveira (1973) *op. cit.* (see note 8).
15. Taylor, R. (1961) The architecture of port wine. *The Architectural Review*, pp. 389–99.
16. Bairoch, P. (1976) Europe's gross national product. *Journal of European Economic History*, 5, pp. 273–340.
17. Pereira, M. H. (1971) *Livre Câmbio e desenvolvimento economico: Portugal na segunda metade do século XIX*. Lisbon: Edições Cosmos, p. 399.
18. Pollard, S. (1981) *Peaceful conquest: the industrialization of Europe 1760–1970*. Oxford: Oxford University Press.
19. da Costa, R. (1976) *O desenvolvimento do capitalismo em Portugal*. Lisbon: Assiro and Alvim.
20. Pereira (1971) *op. cit.*, p. 398 (see note 17).
21. The definition of *cidade* is a very broad one and includes all cities which are capitals of *distritos* as well as those with populations which are larger than 2000.
22. Pereira (1971) *op. cit.*, p. 43 (see note 17).
23. França (1980) *op. cit.* (see note 7).
24. Gonçalves, F. (1978) A mitologia da habitação social: o caso Português. *Cidade Campo*, 1, pp. 21–83.
25. Salgueiro, T. B. (1981) Habitação operária em Lisboa. *Arquitectura*, No. 143, pp. 74–77.
26. Costa, A. A., Siza, A., Guimarães, C., Moura, E. S. and Fernandes, M. C. (1979) SAAL/Norte, *Cidade Campo*, 2, p. 20.
27. de Oliveira (1973) *op. cit.* (see note 8).
28. Williams, A. M. (1980) Conservation planning in Oporto: an integrated approach in the Ribeira-Barredo. *Town Planning Review*, 51, pp. 177–94.
29. The questions are given in Gonçalves (1978) *op. cit.*, p. 22 (see note 24) and are drawn from Fuschini, A. (1884) *Construção de casas económicas e salubres para habitação das classes pobres*. Lisbon.
30. França (1980) *op. cit.* (see note 7).
31. Rodrigues, M. J. M. (1980) O plano de extensão de Lisboa no último quartel do século XIX. *Arquitectura*, No. 138, pp. 28–38.

32. Fernandes, J. M. (1980) Alguns apartamentos sobre urbanismo alfacinha. *Arquitectura*, No. 138, pp. 40–49.
33. França (1980) *op. cit.*, p. 70 (see note 7).
34. de Oliveira (1973) *op. cit.* (see note 8).
35. For example, see Robinson, R. (1979) *Contemporary Portugal: A History*. London: Allen and Unwin.
36. Wiarda, H. J. (1977) *Corporatism and Development: the Portuguese Experience*. Amherst, Mass: University of Massachusetts Press.
37. Baklanoff, E. N. (1978) *The Economic Transformation of Spain and Portugal*. New York: Praeger.
38. de Alarcão, A. (1969) *Mobilidade geográfica da população de Portugal (Continente e Ilhas Adjacentes): Migrações internas: 1921–1960*. Lisbon: Fundação Calouste Gulbenkian, Centro de Estudos de Economia Agrária.
39. Ministério das Obras Públicas (1953) *25 anos de administração públicas*. Lisbon.
40. For a fuller discussion of public housing, see Gonçalves (1978) *op. cit.* (see note 24).
41. França, J. A. (1976) 1930/1948: Le fascisme pur et dur. *L'Architecture d'Aujourd'hui*, No. 185, pp. 2–4.
42. Callado, J. (1978) A casa portuguesa. *Cidade Campo*, 1, pp. 84–100.
43. Discussed briefly in Stilwell B. (1980) S.A.A.L. Slum rehabilitation policy in post-coup Portugal, B.Arch dissertation, University of Liverpool. For a fuller treatment see França J. A. (1966) *A arte em Portugal no século XIX*. Lisbon: Livraria Bertrand.
44. The best general discussion of the urban planning acts is provided by Gonçalves, F. (1977) *Comentários sobre a prática urbanística sueca em confronto com a experiência potugesa*. Lisbon: Laboratório Nacional de Engenharia Civil, Lisbon.
45. Gonçalves (1977) *op. cit.* (see note 44).
46. Gonçalves, F. (1979) Formação e qualificação dos urbanistas em Portugal. *Cidade Campo*, 2, pp. 156–81.
47. Estudos de urbanização (1954) *Boletim de Direcção-General dos Serviços de Urbanização*. 1, pp. 95–104.
48. Gonçalves (1979) *op. cit.* (see note 46).
49. Gonçalves, F. (1979) *Plano director do município: seu lugar entre os planos de urbanização e os planos de ordenamento do território*. Lisbon: Laboratório Nacional de Engenharia Civil, p. 4.
50. Gonçalves (1977) *op. cit.*, p. 35 (see note 44).
51. França (1980) *op. cit.* (see note 7).
52. de Oliveira (1973) *op. cit.* (see note 8).
53. de Costa (1976) *op. cit.* (see note 19).
54. Charbrier, P. and Rosenblatt, J. (1966) Recent economic developments in Portugal. *I.M.F. Staff Papers*, 13, pp. 283–343.
55. Gaspar, J. (1979) *Portugal em mapas e em números*. Lisbon: Livros Horizonte.
56. Lewis and Williams (1981) *op. cit.* (see note 3).
57. Gaspar, J. (1980) Urban Growth in Mediterranean Countries in the 1980s: Portugal. Unpublished report prepared for the OECD.
58. Economic Commission for Europe (1978) *Present Trends and Policies in the Fields of Housing, Building and Planning*. Lisbon.
59. Lewis and Williams (1981) *op. cit.* (see note 3).
60. Gonçalves (1977) *op. cit.* (see note 44).

61. Gonçalves (1979) *op. cit.* (see note 49).
62. Gonçalves (1979) *op. cit.* (see note 49).
63. Information provided by Maria de Fatima Silva, of the Gabinete de Planeamento a Estudos do M.H.O.P.
64. *Ibid.*
65. Gonçalves (1979) *op. cit.* (see note 49).
66. Information provided by Arqto. Margarida Sousa Lobo.
67. Salgueiro, T. B. (1979) Bairros clandestinos na periferia de Lisboa. *Finisterra*, 12(23), pp. 28–55; Williams, A. M. (1981) Bairros clandestinos: illegal housing in Portugal. *Geografisch Tijdschrift* 15, pp. 24–34.
68. Gabinete de Planeamento e Contrôle (1978) *O Sistema informal de habitações: situação da construção clandestina,* Estudos diversos 3/78. Lisbon: Ministério da Habitação e Obras Públicas.
69. See Williams A. M. (1981) Portugal's illegal housing. *Planning Outlook,* 23, pp. 110–14, for an illustration of these problems. The full study of Quinta do Conde is contained in: Comissariado do Governo para a Região de Lisboa: Recuperação de Zonas Clandestinas e Degradadas (1977) *Quinta do Conde: Relatorio – Guia,* Volume 13 (including 'anexos'). Lisbon.
70. de Carvalho, M. (1978) Brandoa Falagueira: área crítica. *Poder Local,* No. 6, pp. 50–54.
71. Lewis, J. R. and Williams, A. M. (1984) Housing in Portugal, in Wynn, M. (ed.), *Housing in Europe.* London: Croom Helm.
72. Stilwell (1980) *op. cit.* (see note 43).
73. Duarte, C. (1976) 1961/1974: L'ouverture néo-capitaliste. *L'Architecture d'Aujourd'hui,* No. 185, pp. 22–26.
74. Porch, D. (1977) *The Portuguese Armed Forces and the Revolution.* London: Croom Helm.
75. Harvey, R. (1978) *Portugal: Birth of a Democracy.* London: Macmillan.
76. Lewis, J. R. and Williams, A. M. (1982) Desenvolvimento regional desequilibrado em Portugal: situação actual e impacto provável da adesâo à C.E.E. *Desenvolvimento Regional,* nos 14/15, pp. 79–140.
77. *Ibid.*
78. Downs, C. (1980) Comissões de moradores and urban struggles in revolutionary Portugal. *International Journal of Urban and Regional Research,* **4,** pp. 267–94.
79. de Almeida, L. (1979) Lei de finanças locais e ordenamento do território. *Poder Local,* No. 13, pp. 33–37.
80. Simões, J. (1982) Decentralization in Portugal. *Planning and Administration,* 9(1), pp. 60–65.
81. Almeida (1979) *op. cit.* (see note 79).
82. Gaspar (1980) *op. cit.* (see note 57).
83. Williams (1980) *op. cit.* (see note 28).
84. Oliveira, P. and Marconi, F. (1978) *Politica y projecto.* Barcelona: Editorial Gustavo Gili.
85. Stillwell (1980) *op. cit.* (see note 43).
86. Williams (1981) *op. cit.* (see note 67).
87. Gabinete de Estudos e Planeamento (1980) *Relatório sobre a actividade do grupo da traballho da lei-quadro do planeamento urbano e territorial.* Lisbon: Ministério da Habitação e Obras Públicas.

# 5

# Spain

## MARTIN WYNN

This chapter examines the development of urban planning and city growth in Spain in a roughly chronological fashion, from the early eighteenth-century attempts at planned development up to the 1980s. For several reasons, Madrid and Barcelona feature as the major illustrative examples throughout the chapter. They have been Spain's two foremost cities since medieval times and have today populations three and four times greater, respectively, than Bilbao, the next largest city[1]. Further they have been the major arenas within the country for the development and application of new planning concepts and they have exhibited, more than any other city, the problems associated with rapid urban growth. Concentration on Madrid and Barcelona has also facilitated a certain degree of continuity which would not otherwise have been possible if examples from other cities such as Valencia and Bilbao[2] had been included.

### TOWN PLANNING ORIGINS

Until the mid-nineteenth century, Spain's cities were by and large confined within their medieval walls. It was only then that the Madrid government decreed that the walls were no longer necessary for defence purposes, and permitted city expansion beyond the old medieval quarters. The subsequent plans of expansion (*ensanche*) marked the first attempts at city-wide planning in the country, but the origins of town planning in Spain are to be found in the earlier plans for reform and development within the old medieval cities, above all those of Madrid and Barcelona.

Madrid and Barcelona grew around early Greek, Roman, and Visgoth settlements, and by the Middle Ages, comprised walled enclosures of several hundred hectares. It was in the eighteenth century, however, with the advent

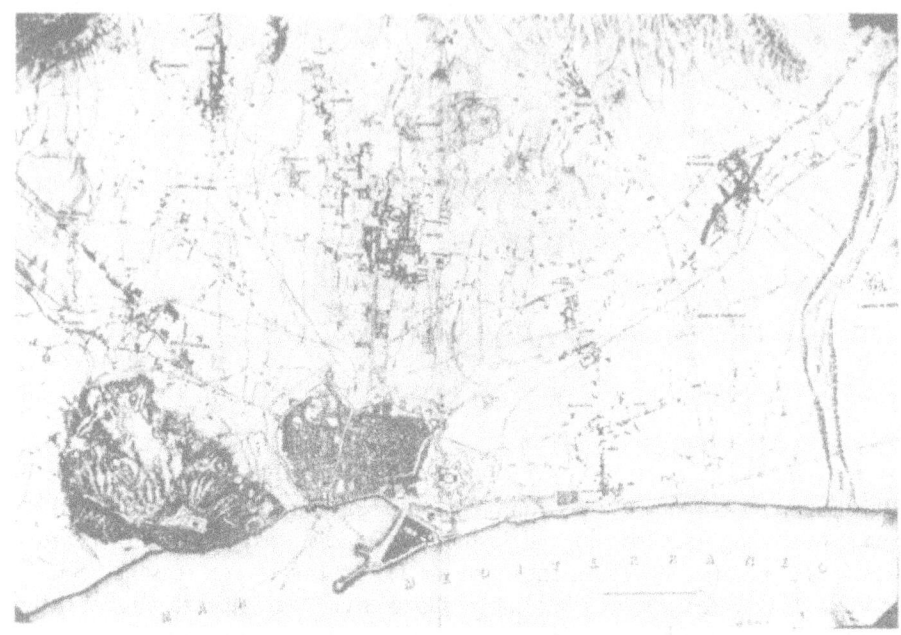

FIGURE 5.1. Cerdà's Topographical Plan of Barcelona, 1855.
The citadel and Barcelona are to the right of the old city, and the outlying settlements inland. The foothills of the Tibadabo mountain run across the top of the plan.
*Source:* Archivo Historico Municipal de Barcelona.

of Bourbon rule, that the first significant attempts at urban planning were made. In Barcelona, this was precipitated by the destruction of over 1300 dwellings in 1717 to make way for the citadel ordered by Felipe V. According to Bruguera[3] over 6300 people (out of a total population of 35,000) were made homeless, but there seems to have been little attempt at planned resettlement in the years immediately after the construction of the citadel. By 1740, haphazard development of wooden huts (*barracas* – to act as both living quarters and store), which housed the local fisherfolk, had taken place on the spit just south of the citadel. It is likely that the fisherfolk had formerly lived in the Ribera, the area of the old city destroyed to make way for the citadel. In 1753, however, the military governor ordered the planned construction of a new settlement on this sand-spit to accommodate those living there. This new *barrio* – named Barceloneta (little Barcelona) – was the first extramural expansion of the city, and well illustrates the main features of Baroque architecture which dominated planning under the early Bourbons – straight streets intersecting at right angles, uniformity in building styles and dominance of the military square and barracks (figure 5.1).

In the 1760s limited reform within the old cities of Madrid and Barcelona was undertaken by the military authorities, against a background of agricultural crises, increasing country-city migration and a general air of corruption

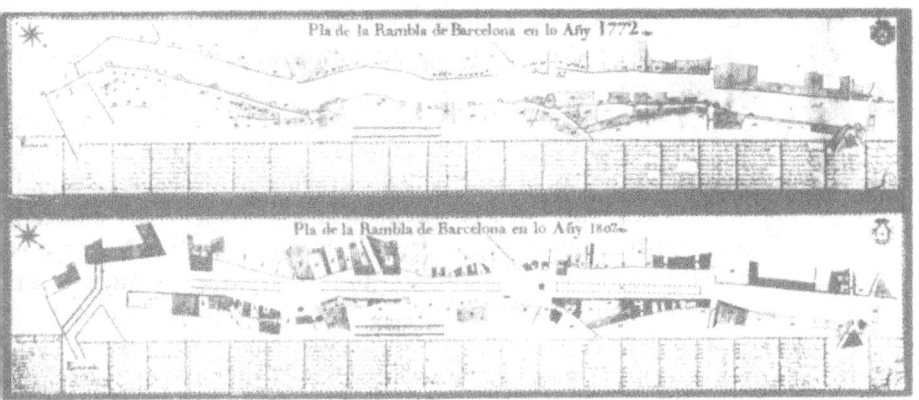

FIGURE 5.2. The Ramblas, Barcelona, in 1772 and 1807.
The straightening of the Ramblas in 1779 was accompanied by the destruction of the medieval wall running along its eastern (lower) side and the construction of a central walkway.
*Source:* Archivo Historico Municipal de Barcelona.

within the old local administrations in face of rapidly deteriorating urban conditions. Mesonero Romanos provides a graphic description of the living conditions in Madrid at the time: 'In the streets of Madrid . . . think nothing of the misalignment or uneven heights of buildings, nothing of the narrow width or tortuous nature of streets and nothing of the lack of public facilities . . . The streets are inundated by beggars in the day and by pickpockets at night'[4]. In an attempt to confront such problems, King Carlos III, on the advice of his military staff, implemented a reform programme in Madrid which was matched by similar developments in Barcelona. Major streets were widened and straightened (figure 5.2), new *paseos* were opened up, and new public buildings – including the Prado Museum in Madrid – were erected. Administrative changes brought the introduction of the *serenos* (nightwatchman) service to keep law and order at night; and the building permit cession procedure was tightened up in an attempt to stamp out corrupt practices.

The last thirty years of the eighteenth century saw a construction boom in the major towns and cities as the incipient industrial bourgeoisie flourished in a period of economic liberalism. Madrid and Barcelona, having expanded horizontally to their walled limits, now grew upwards, with new floors and extensions being added to existing buildings to completely fill their accompanying medieval land parcels. Capmany i Montpalau, writing of Barcelona in the 1790s, noted that the 'rising up of new buildings constructed to house the ever increasing population in small spaces' had meant that 'the old plots with spacious yards have been reduced, and with the narrowness of its streets, the city has come to be like a pine forest of houses, towers, domes, balconies and roofs'[5]. Although existing building regulations did attempt to limit the upward growth of buildings and room subdivision, property speculators, with the acquiescence of sections of the council, found loopholes in, or ways around, them – a pattern that was to be repeated in later eras. In particular, the upper floors, often technically outside the scope of building regulations, were built with low ceilings and minimal room dimensions. According to Lopez[6], a house of 15 metres height built in or before 1771 would have four floors in total, whereas in 1791 a new or extended dwelling of this height would have six floors. This reduction in average floor height usually only affected the upper floors, whilst the lower floors, frequently the living quarters of the landlord, remained the same height as before. In this way, the classic contrast between high and low which existed in the medieval house was accentuated, but changed from a functional difference within the family house to a class difference within rented property – what Bohigas[7] has called the 'eighteenth century urban house'.

The second half of the eighteenth century saw the first stages of the Industrial Revolution in Spain, and the consequent expansion of industrial activity had direct effects on the urban morphology of Spain's major cities. The larger manufacturers needed new types and sizes of buildings for factories and workshops, and houses for their workers, and thus the medieval parcels of land often had to be regrouped to form frontages of 20 metres or more. Indeed, at the end of the century, the industrialists Camps and Bastero drew up plans to build seventy to ninety dwellings respectively, in Barcelona, to house their workforces. Although there is no record of these estates having been built, they represent early attempts at planned development which, according to Grau[8], acted as models for nineteenth century industrialists.

From 1793 until 1814 Spain was involved in the French Revolutionary and Napoleonic Wars, and there then followed a period of repressive government under Ferdinand VII, culminating in the first Carlist Wars in the 1830s. During this era, and following the initiative of Jose I (Josef Bonaparte), many new *plazas* were created in the country's major urban areas. Lack of space and overcrowding, however, remained constant features of urban life, and following cholera epidemics in the 1830s, large areas of monastery and convent land in Madrid and Barcelona were annexed by the municipal authorities for building purposes. The populations of these two cities continued to expand rapidly, Madrid's increasing from 167,000 in 1797 to 275,000 in 1853, and Barcelona's from 111,000 in 1787 to 216,000 in 1857, with population densities as high as 1500 inhabitants per hectare in some zones. The need for a spatial expansion of these cities beyond their medieval walls was greater than ever.

### THE PLANS OF ENSANCHE:
### PLANNED EXPANSION BEYOND THE MEDIEVAL WALLS

In 1854, the new Madrid government declared that the walls which constrained the country's major cities were no longer necessary for security purposes, and thereby authorized their destruction. Since the 1840s, the military authorities in Madrid and Barcelona had drawn up a series of plans for piecemeal development beyond the medieval walls (which were never implemented), but now far more ambitious plans of expansion became feasible. These early plans of *ensanche* represented a conceptual advance in the evolution of planning thought in Spain; new homogenous, well-defined cities could be planned and built around the old medieval centres. This type of planning was seen as a global solution to the problems of urban growth, in which every element of city life was accounted for in the new planned development. Nowhere was this more apparent than in Ildefonso Cerdà's 1859 *Plano de reforma y ensanche* for Barcelona, usually referred to as the Plan Cerdà.

Cerdà's plan was officially approved by the Madrid government in 1859, despite the fact that the Barcelona Council had held its own competition and selected an alternative plan – that of Rovira i Trias (figure 5.3). Cerdà was a civil engineer who had meticulously studied Barcelona and the surrounding plain, and only in the past decade has the significance of his contribution to planning thought been studied in depth. His 1855 Topographical Plan of Barcelona (figure 5.1) laid the groundwork for the 1859 plan (figure 5.4) which attempted to link the old city with the ring of outlying settlements inland. The new city comprised some 900 octagonal blocks of development (*manzanas*), and a great deal of recent research has concentrated on identifying the underlying idealized model in which all services are distributed in a polycentric hierarchy of zones, districts, and sectors (figure 5.5). The *manzanas* were to

FIGURE 5.3. The plan of *ensanche* for Barcelona of Antonio Rovira i Trias, 1859.
*Source:* Archivo Historico Municipal de Barcelona.

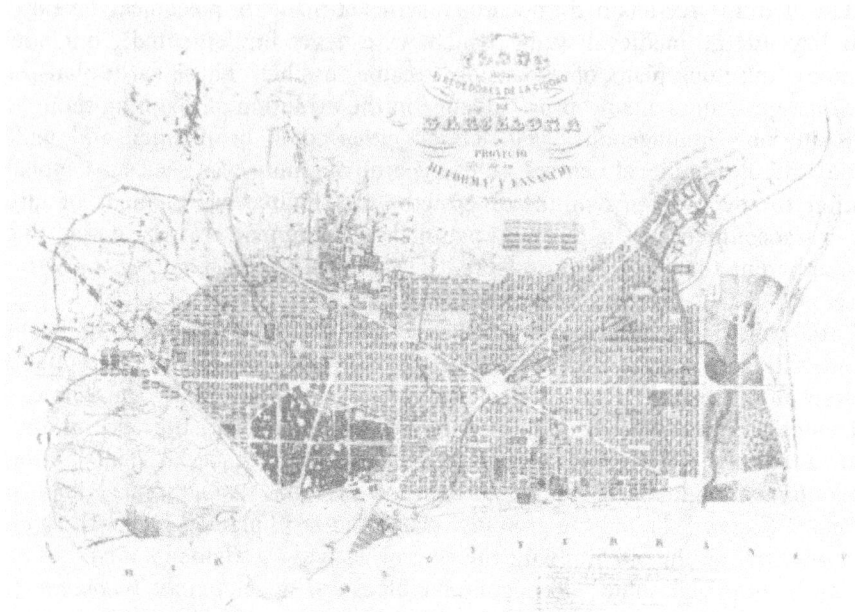

FIGURE 5.4. The Plan Cerdà, 1860.
*Source:* Archivo Historico Municipal de Barcelona.

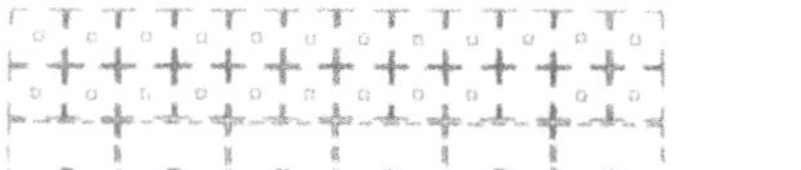

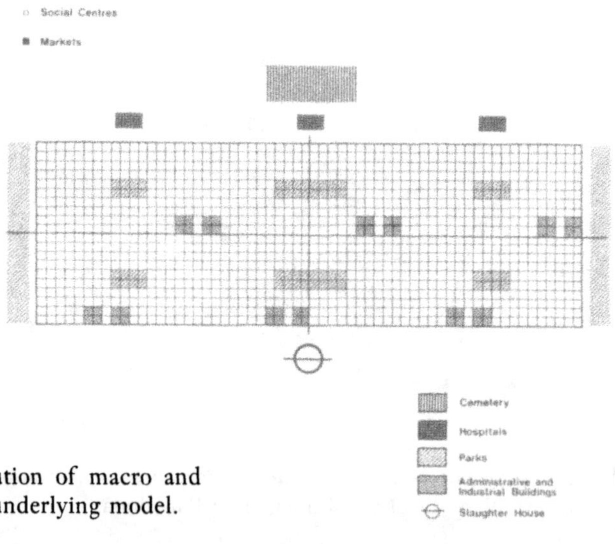

FIGURE 5.5. The distribution of macro and micro services in Cerdà's underlying model.

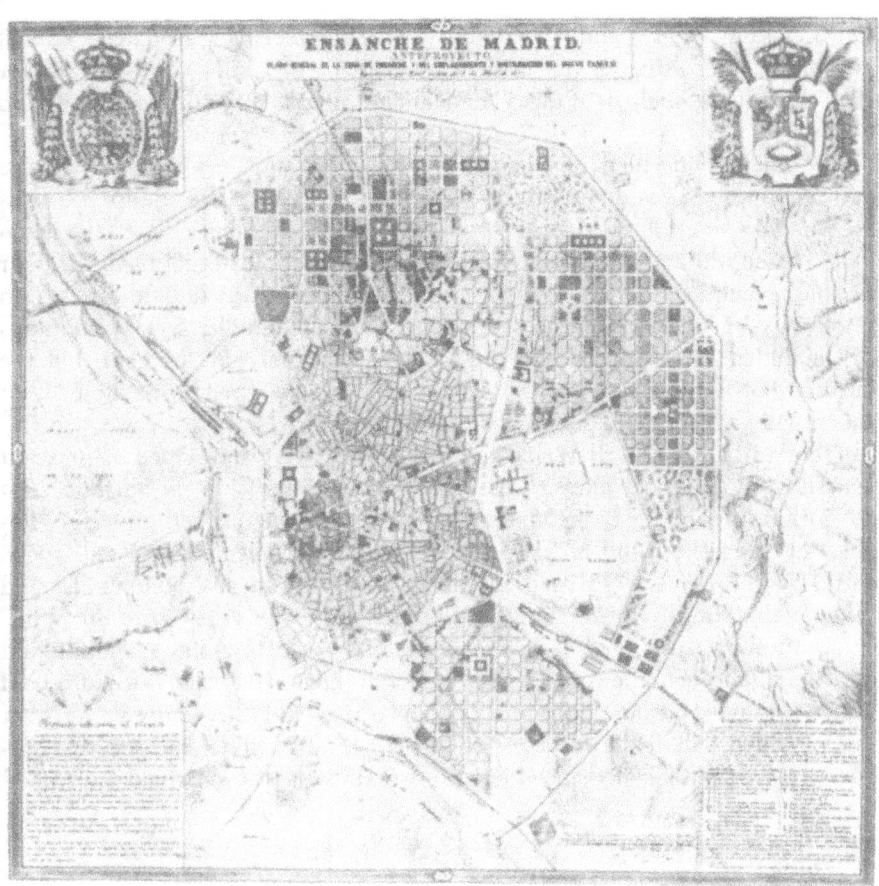

FIGURE 5.6. The Plan Castro, 1860.
The streets, 15 or 30 metres wide, are orientated N-S and E-W to avoid acting as wind tunnels. There are a significant number of green space areas and blocks demarcated for public buildings. The Plan Report includes a land zoning not shown on the plan itself, with the upper classes living to the north, the middle classes in the northeast, and the working classes to the east and south.
*Source:* de Teran, F. (1978) *Planeamiento Urbano en la Espana Contemporanea.* Barcelona: Gustavo Gili.

be built-up on two sides only, to a depth of 20 metres and with a maximum height of 16 metres. Despite certain ambiguities in the plan which Grau[9], for example, has drawn attention to, there seems much to support Garrut's assertion that 'Barcelona lost the opportunity of becoming a city that, even today, would be one of the most modern and most beautiful in Europe'[10]; and when one takes into account the depth and rigour of Cerdà's major works[11], then Domingo's view that 'in many ways he was the founder of an urban science preceding Baumeister (1876), Stubben (1893), Unwin

(1908), Triggs (1909) and Haverfield (1913)'[12] seems reasonable. This is particularly interesting, given critical assessment of Cerdà's work by earlier urban historians such as Puig i Cadafalch[13] inside Spain, and Gutkind outside[14].

The other major plan of *ensanche* drawn up in this era was that of the engineer Carlos Maria de Castro for Madrid. The Plan Castro (figure 5.6) was based on an extension of Madrid to the east, south and, above all, to the north of the old city in a series of *ensanches* delimited by the external *rondas* (rather like the French *boulevards*), and by a series of major roads radiating out from the old city. A number of large green spaces and community service buildings were included within the regular grid pattern of block development, but the plan was not as all-embracing as Cerdà's nor was there such a technically or conceptually advanced underlying model.

In both Madrid and Barcelona, the *ensanches* were developed with scant regard to the approved plans. The *manzanas* were built up on all four sides and within (figure 5.7), parks and gardens were encroached upon or disappeared altogether, and *manzanas* destined for schools, markets and social centres in the plans were used for house construction and commercial and industrial buildings. Speculative development saw the cities grow in radiocentric form (see figure 5.8) in fits and starts, reflecting the economic and political climate of the time. The first rail links (Barcelona–Mataro and Madrid–Aranjuez) were built in 1860. As these and the tramway network were extended within the *ensanches* (figure 5.8), a functional and social segregation[15] was established in which the working classes remained encamped

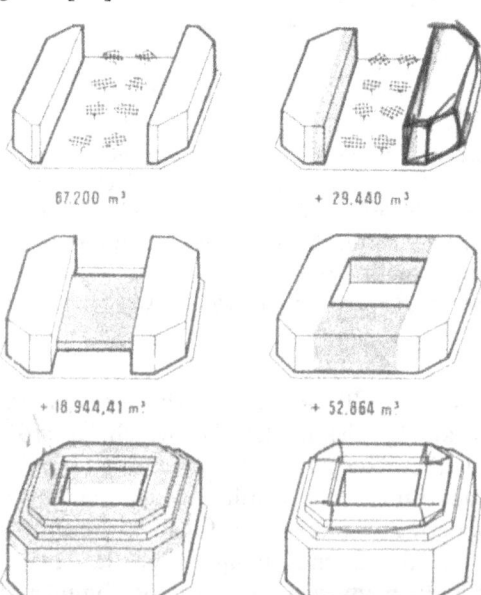

FIGURE 5.7. The infilling of Cerdà's *manzana* (block). The built-up space in the average *manzana* increased from 67,200 m³ in the Plan Cerdà (top left) to almost 295,000 m³ in 1972 (bottom right).
*Source: Construcción de la Ciudad,* 1972.

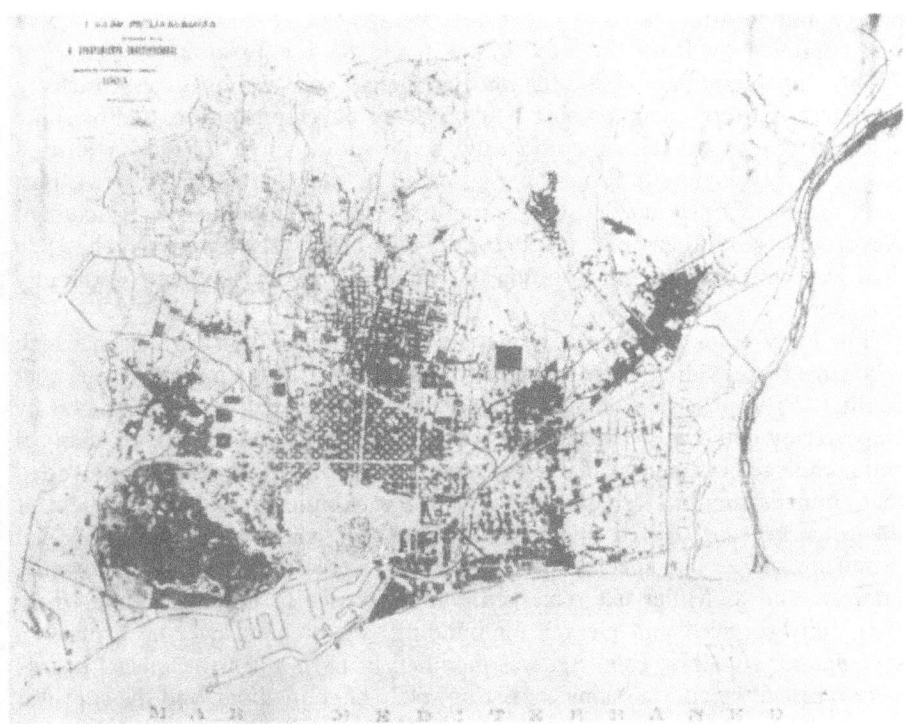

FIGURE 5.8. Barcelona, 1903.
Expansion out from the old city has been in radiocentric form whilst the old settlements on the plain have grown in anarchical fashion with scant regard to the dictates of the Plan Cerdà.
*Source:* Archivo Historico Municipal de Barcelona.

in the old city centres or in the 'mixed zones' (residential/industrial) of the *ensanche*, while certain areas – around the Paseo de Gracia in Barcelona and in Salamanca in Madrid – became the main residential areas of the moneyed classes. The population growth of the two cities continued apace with Barcelona reaching the half million mark by the turn of the century, at which time Madrid had a population of 576,000.

The plans of *ensanche* in the smaller towns and cities of Spain in the nineteenth and early twentieth centuries were generally less ambitious in scale and content than those of Madrid and Barcelona. In San Sebastian, following the opening of the Madrid–Paris railway in 1864, the medieval walls were demolished and the architect Cortazar's plan won the ensuing municipal competition to find a plan for the city. His plan comprised some fifty new 'blocks' of development similar to those contained in the Plan Castro for Madrid, but much of the detail of the plan was lost in subsequent modifications made by the municipal authorities. Meanwhile, in Bilbao, the multiplicity of municipalities bordering the old city led to inter-council disputes on the nature and location of town expansion. Finally, in 1876, the council's plan was approved by Royal Decree. It was based on a population projection of 70,000 inhabitants (cf. 600,000 for Barcelona) and was again essentially a grid street pattern encompassing new blocks of development, crossed by some diagonal roads, and also incorporating some rather more irregularly shaped blocks of development. Provision was made in the plan for park areas, but, as in the San Sebastian Plan, few community service buildings were included. Nevertheless, between 1876 and 1926, the bulk of the area covered by the 1876 plan was built-up with the addition of some isolated development on the city periphery.

The early plans of *ensanche* brought with them a body of legislation which was aimed at guiding their implementation. The 1864 City Expansion Act facilitated the provision of road and service infrastructure in the *ensanches* by empowering councils to expropriate the necessary land and by making financial and technical assistance available to carry these works out. It also recommended that councils should establish special boards to administer the development of the *ensanches* and offered financial incentives for landowners who developed their land there. The special boards, however, were dominated by landowning interests and as Miller has remarked with reference to Barcelona, 'the whole area, fully serviced and cleared for building, was handed over on a plate to speculators'[16]. The 1864 Act was modified in 1876 when the special boards were replaced by commissions consisting solely of councillors; and the approval of new building regulations to govern development in the *ensanches* was also authorized. Finally, in 1892, a special Act was passed clarifying the legal framework for development in the *ensanches* of Madrid and Barcelona; this Act was later also applied to other cities.

In summary, then, the plans of *ensanche*, and above all the Plan Cerdà, represented a landmark in the conceptual development of urban planning in Spain. By the end of the nineteenth century they were seen as providing the master solution to the problems of city growth, and other cities followed suit in adopting such plans (Zaragoza 1894, Valencia 1907, Pamplona 1915 and Murcia 1920). But gradually, as new and old problems were encountered in the development of the *ensanches*, so new theoretical developments appeared, leading to more open-ended, heterogenous concepts and providing pluriform answers to the different demands of city formation. It is to these, then, that we now turn.

### Advances in Planning Thought and Practice 1890–1931

Around the turn of the century, a series of new planning concepts were beginning to find expression in the urban plans of the day, as overcrowding and congestion in Spain's old city centres remained, and powerful external influences came to bear on planning ideology and practice.

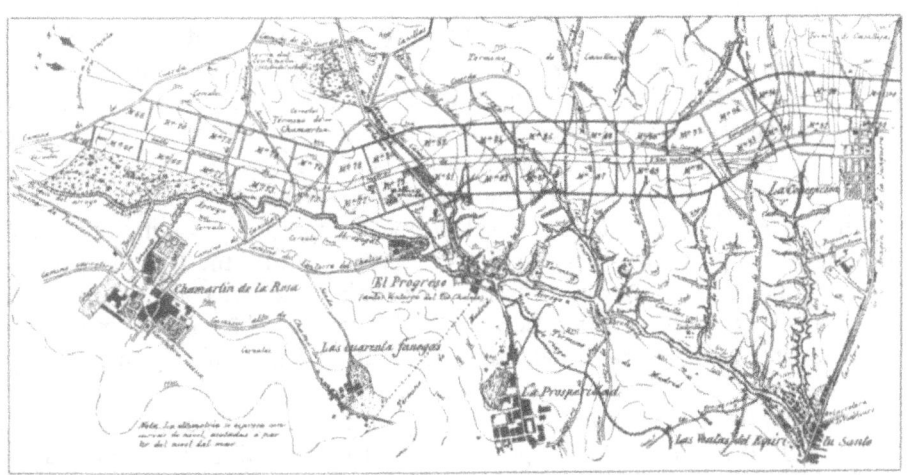

FIGURE 5.9. The Linear City (*Ciudad Lineal*) of Arturo Soria y Mata, built outside Madrid in the 1890s.
Source: *Ciudad Lineal,* No. 120, 1902.

Ironically, however, Arturo Soria's 'Linear City', which subsequently received widespread acclaim overseas, found only lukewarm support in Madrid. Indeed, writing in 1901, Soria reflected that 'the architects of Madrid have, as a rule, shown no enthusiasm at all for our linear city, and some have opposed it ferociously'[17]. The fundamentals of his linear city were relatively simple: city growth was to be developed in linear fashion, around an axis of high-speed, high-intensity transportation; and such development, ideally only several hundred metres deep on either side of the main communications line, was to be separated from the countryside beyond by belts of woodland or green areas. He suggested that the major cities of Europe could be joined by such linear growth and proposed an initial link between Cadiz in Spain and Leningrad in Russia. In fact only a short stretch of a few kilometeres was ever built – outside Madrid in the period 1892–1930 – and it is difficult to recognize this today because it has been enveloped by the peripheral expansion of the city.

In 1892, the Madrid government approved Soria's project to construct a new rail line circling the city and linking up the outlying settlements. In 1894 the Compañia Madrileña de Urbanización (Madrid Development Company) was founded, with Soria as director, to construct a 'linear city' around this transportation axis. By 1906, 18 km of rail line had been laid (used at first for horse drawn carriages) to the north-east of the capital, and 300 houses built; by 1913, 4000 people were living in 680 dwellings, mainly in the Chamartin–El Progreso section (figure 5.9). In the 1920s, the linear city concept was further developed by Soria's followers, the most notable of whom was probably Hilarion Gonzalez de Castillo. He viewed the linear city as a form of garden city and was much influenced by the Garden Cities and Town Planning Association in Britain. He also modified some of the extremes of

Soria's ideas in answer to criticisms from Garden City proponents outside Spain.

Gonzalez de Castillo's work included plans for major cities both inside and outside Spain. In 1919, at the Brussels Reconstruction Exhibition, his plans for a Belgian 'Linear City' were limited to a maximum length of 10 km and were of greater depth than in Soria's earlier plans. A civic centre was planned at the crossing-point of the longitudinal and transverse axes of the city with parellel zones of urban, industrial, agricultural and forest land around the major lines of communication. Proposals for city growth within the London Region were also put forward, in which linear cities linked the city core with satellite cities beyond the green belt. The plan, which thus combined the Linear and Garden City concepts, was published by the Garden Cities and Town Planning Association in 1931[18].

Proposals for the new application of the linear growth concept to planning in Madrid[19] and Barcelona appeared in the 1920s and 1930s, and Gonzalez de Castillo continued to work assiduously up until the Civil War. The linear concept appeared in the work of several renowned planners and theorists outside Spain, including Le Corbusier, Miliutin and Hilberseimer[20], and in the 1943 Mars Group Plan for London and in the 1965 *Schema Directeur* for Paris, amongst others. It was a concept of genuinely Spanish origin which had surprisingly little impact on the content of urban plans or patterns of urban growth within the country, remaining a largely theoretical formulation in need of refinement and further development, but which received more recognition outside Spain than within.

By the later stages of the nineteenth century, it had become clear that new measures were needed to attack the urban problems of the day. The plans of *ensanche* were blueprint plans – in some cases exceptionally advanced and well thought out – that failed to get to grips with the processes involved in implementing development. Thus, although the basic road networks in these plans provided a physical framework for development, the development which took place often differed drastically from that specified in the respective plans; and away from the *ensanches*, in the old medieval cities and beyond in the outer periphery, redevelopment and continued growth brought a new set of old problems.

In Barcelona, Baixeras's 1881 plan had attempted to open up three major new roads running across the old city, but the ensuing battle between reformist elements in the council and property-owning interests (both inside and outside the council) thwarted its implementation, despite the approval in 1895 of the Inner Areas Reform Act which gave councils greater power to expropriate the land necessary for such intervention. It was only, in fact, in 1916, when the socialist reforming elements for once overcame the landowning interests in the council, that one of Baixera's new roads – the Via Layetana – was constructed, cutting through one of the most densely populated areas of the old city (figure 5.10). At the same time, in Barcelona, an international competition was held in 1903 to find a plan to link the *ensanche* with newly

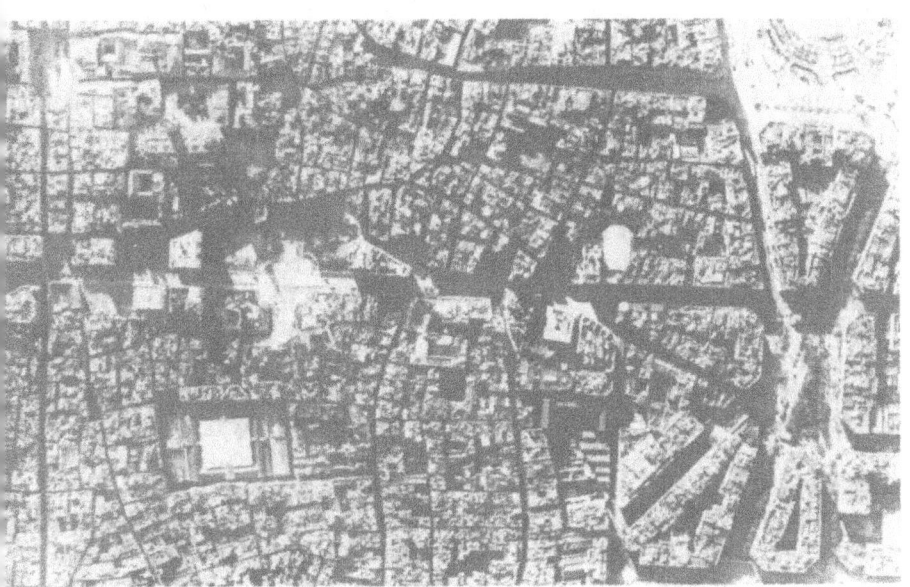

FIGURE 5.10. A section of Barcelona's old city at the end of the 1920s. Via Layetana, opened in 1916, is running right to left across the photo.
*Source:* Archivo Historico Municipal de Barcelona.

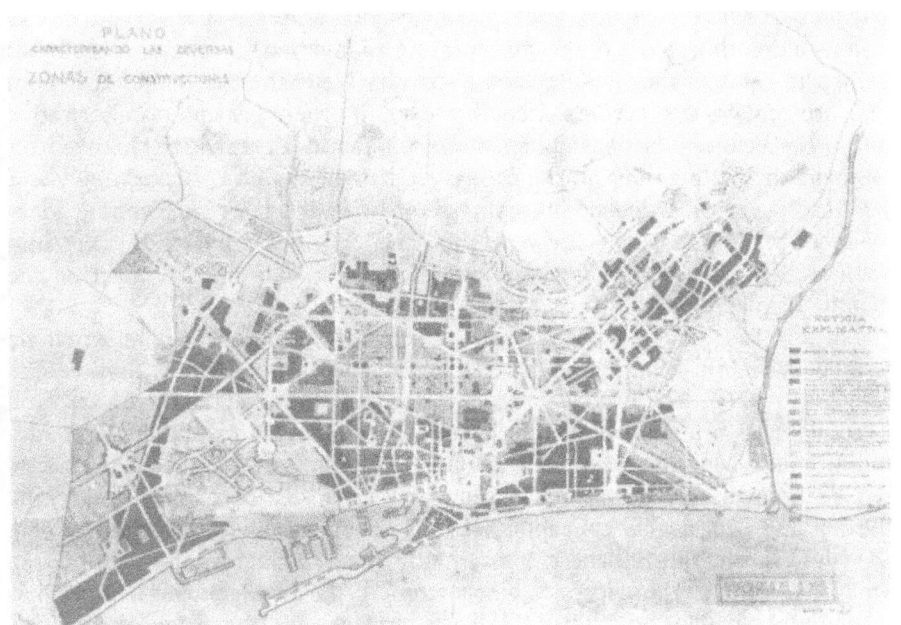

FIGURE 5.11. The Plan Jaussely, 1907.
*Source:* Archivo Historico Municipal de Barcelona.

annexed suburbs which remained outside the ambit of the Plan Cerdà. The winning entry by the French architect Leon Jaussely (figure 5.11) also attempted to transform Cerdà's quadricle street pattern by the incorporation of geometric layouts (diagonals, radials, curves and right angles) that epitomized the French *belles artes* school at the time. Jaussely's proposals were hardly realistic, and only a much watered down version of the plan was approved in 1917 (known as the Plan Romeu-Porcel after the two municipal architects who modified it). Jaussely's proposals for the *ensanche* were dropped and only the peripheral roads linking the city with the outlying settlements were included.

Meanwhile, in Madrid, the rapid growth of unplanned construction beyond the limits of the *ensanche* produced a ring of new settlements cut off from the city centre and generally deficient in basic service infrastructure. This peripheral zone, which became known as the *extraradio*, lay outside the control of the Madrid Council, and outlying councils often tended towards a *laissez-faire* attitude as regards development within their municipal limits.

In 1908, the Madrid Council commissioned the civil engineer Nunez Granes to draw up a plan to link the city with the outlying settlements, and in his accompanying report he noted that the only legal obligation on developers in these municipalities was that they submit plans of alignment and gradient to the local council. Indeed, in 1910, only 5210 of Spain's 9266 municipalities had approved building regulations.

Nunez Granes's 1910 project (figure 5.12) proposed to extend the radial roads of the Madrid *ensanche* and the construction of new ring roads and blocks of housing on three sides of the city, forming an inverted 'C' around it in similar fashion to some of the late-nineteenth-century German projects of expansion. The project was not accompanied, however, by the legal and administrative measures necessary for its implementation, but it did emphasize the need for supra-municipal planning in the capital. It was, in any case, conceptually and technically poor, particularly in comparison with the body of planning ideas produced by the Garden City movement which was beginning to filter into Spain at this time, and which was eventually to have a major impact on the shaping of plans for Madrid.

The Garden City movement was introduced into Spain[21] almost single handed by Cebriu Montoliu in Barcelona, where he founded the 'Garden City Society' in 1912. The new theoretical vision of a city integrated with its rural surrounds was propounded at a series of conferences and exhibitions in Spain, and although Montoliu went into voluntary exile in 1920, the seeds of change had been sown. We have already seen how Gonzalez de Castillo linked the Garden and Linear City concepts; and in 1924 the architects Aranda, Garcia, Cascales, Lorite and Sallaberry presented a report to the Madrid Council, in which they stated the necessity of overcoming the blinkered peripheral view of planning evident in Nunez Granes's project, and suggested a land-use zoning of the Madrid built-up area and the location of satellite cities beyond its central nucleus[22]. In 1929 the Madrid Council employed Aranda and

FIGURE 5.12. Nunez Granes's project for the extension of Madrid, 1910.
*Source:* de Teran, F. (1978) *Planeamiento Urbano en la España Contemporanea.* Barcelona: Gustavo Gili.

Garcia Cascales as a team to draw up the brief for an international competition to find the definitive urban plan for the capital. The winning *Plan de Extensión* of 1929 by the Spanish architect Zuazo and German planner Jansen (figure 5.13) was an adaptation of the radiocentric decentralizing model that stemmed from Howard's work. It consisted of radial and ring roads enclosing the central urban core, surrounded by a green zone beyond which were situated satellite cities linked by a peripheral ring road. The plan also included proposals for the reform of the old city, principally aimed at easing traffic congestion. This plan was subsequently approved during the Second Republic (1931–36), and provided the basis for the planning of Madrid up until the 1960s.

This influx of new planning ideas emphasized the need for the revision of existing planning legislation, which remained anchored in the disparate Acts of the previous century. The Municipal Statute of 1924 synthesized, re-ordered and consolidated previous planning legislation, but failed to introduce new measures to facilitate supra-municipal planning. The Statute did, however, establish that urban planning was the responsibility of individual councils, in accordance with the general spirit of municipal autonomy that characterized its text, and specified that councils of municipalities which had experienced a population increase of 20 per cent or more in the decade 1910–20 were legally

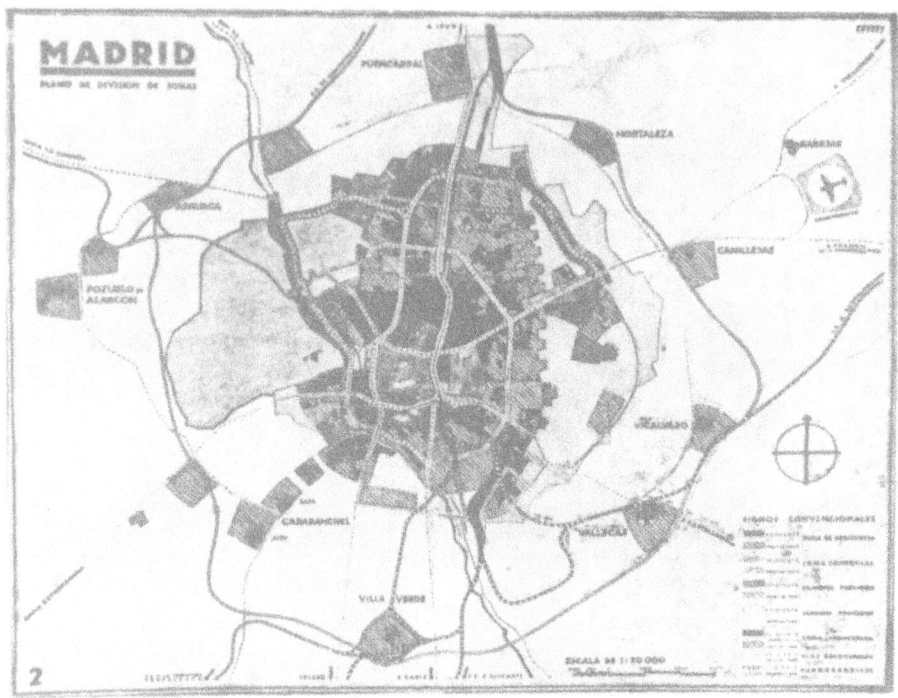

FIGURE 5.13. The *plan de extensión* for Madrid, 1929.
The plan, drawn up by Zuazo and Jansen, won the international competition held to find a new plan for the city. A greenbelt isolates the central core from the planned satellite cities beyond.
*Source:* de Teran, F. (1976) Notas para la Historia del Planaemiento de Madrid. *Ciudad y Territorio,* No. 2/3, Madrid: IEAL.

obliged to draw up a plan of *ensanche* or *extensión* within the following four years. Here then, a new type of plan was recognized. Whilst plans of *ensanche* (expansion) were to accommodate city growth beyond the old city walls, plans of *extensión* (extension) were to cover the areas between the *ensanches* and the territorial limits of the municipality, precisely the area where the *extraradio* settlements had sprung up in Madrid. However, as Bassols[23] has pointed out, the concept of one development plan encompassing the entire municipality was not evident in the Municipal Statute, which rather recognized a series of different plan types — expansion, extension, and inner-city reform — to be used according to the needs and individual circumstances of each municipality.

The Municipal Statute was severely criticized at the Eleventh National Architects' Congress in Madrid in 1926 at which Nicolau Rubio, Secretary of Montoliu's Garden City Society of Barcelona, introduced the theme of regional planning into Spain, probably for the first time, taking largely from British and French developments that had been set out at the International Federation of Garden Cities' Congresses in Amsterdam (1924) and New York

(1925). The principal conclusion of the Madrid congress was that there was an urgent need for a General Planning Law to recognize the modern concepts in urban and regional planning, which continued to appear in the urban plans of the 1920s and 1930s entered in competitions held by the councils of major cities to find new plans of *extensión*. These competitions attracted entrants from abroad; Stubben, for example, entered the Bilbao competition in 1926; Zuazo y Jansen, as we have seen, won the 1929 competition for Madrid (figure 5.13); and Le Corbusier's Plan Macia won the 1932 Barcelona competition, in a period of intensive urban planning activity and citizen participation under the Second Republic.

## The Second Republic And After

With the fall of the monarchy in 1931 and the advent of the Second Republic, a period of intense but short-lived urban activity was inaugurated, led by GATEPAC[24] a radical Spanish architect/planning group, in collaboration with similar bodies from outside Spain (CIAM and CIRPAC). Nevertheless, as Teran[25] has pointed out, there is a certain degree of continuity in the evolution of planning in Spain from the pre-republican era through to the postwar era, even if the pace of change was heightened during the Republic; and, as before, planning remained strongly influenced by developments in the international planning arena.

The new council in Madrid drew up a further plan for the city in 1931, based very much on Zuazo and Jansen's 1929 plan. The accompanying plan report also recommended the extension of the Madrid municipal boundaries and stressed the importance of the necessary expropriation powers for such plans to be implemented effectively. The *plan de extensión* was finally approved by the central government in 1933, but only that part of the plan falling within the confines of the Madrid municipality. The stern opposition of the outlying municipal councils meant that enlargement of the Madrid municipality had to wait until after the war (when it was extended to encompass the surrounding fourteen municipalities), and the prospect of effective supra-municipal planning in the capital was again thwarted.

Nevertheless progress towards supra-municipal planning was made in other ways, and here again the influence of outside ideas played its part. Following the publication of the second report of the Greater London Regional Planning Committee in 1932, the Madrid Council began preliminary studies for a *Plan Regional* for Madrid. Fernando Mercadal, founder of GATEPAC and Spanish delegate to CIRPAC, who had done much to bring European planning ideas and influences to bear on the planning of Madrid since the 1920s, was again a key figure, as was Julian Beisteiro, president of the Comite de Reforma, Reconstrucción y Saneamiento de Madrid that drew up and finally published the plan in 1939. From the references and terminology used in the accompany-

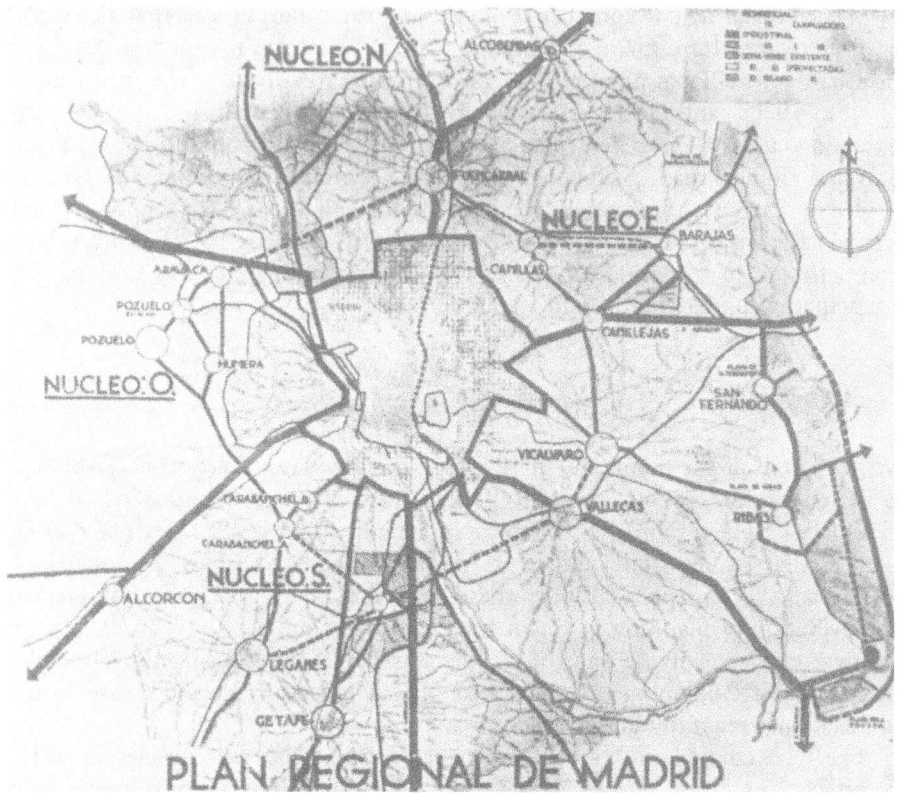

FIGURE 5.14. The Regional Plan for Madrid, 1939.
Source: de Teran, F. (1978) *Planeamiento en la España Contemporanea*. Barcelona: Gustavo Gili.

ing report, it seems that the Comite collaborated with the Greater London Planning Committee throughout the 1930s. The report justifies the regional approach because of the need to 'embrace the extensive zone of influence of Madrid and improve living conditions in the already existing satellite cities, and to create new ones in areas specially chosen because of their natural conditions'[26]. In the plan, the growth of the city was limited by a green ring beyond which satellite cities of essentially industrial/residential nature were situated, there being four new nuclei (figure 5.14). The whole region was served by a functional network of radial and ring roads, and land-use classifications were extended to cover the entire region. The plan also included proposals for the protection and utilization of the large recreational areas outside Madrid – the Sierra de Gredos, Sierra de Guadarrama, and the Jarama River Valley – and finally the report stressed the need for a management body – Comite de Plan – with the necessary authority and capacity to control and manage subsequent development in the region, in accordance with the plan.

In Barcelona, GATCPAC, the Catalan wing of GATEPAC, which included such international figures as J. Lluis Sert and J. Torres Clave, worked with Le Corbusier on trying to provide a new planning framework for the resolution of the city's appalling problems of overcrowding, old decaying housing and abject poverty, above all in the old city. The population density remained over 1000 per hectare in 1932 in the infamous Distrito V of the old city (figure 5.15), with a mortality rate in some streets as high as 20 per cent a year[27].

Both the population density and mortality figures were the highest among the thirty-one cities studied at the 1932 CIRPAC conference in Barcelona. Outside the old city, the central section of the *ensanche* consisted almost entirely of luxury and middle-class housing, but to the east and west lay the so-called 'mixed zones' of working-class housing and industry, which had grown almost without control since Cerdà's time, albeit within the road pattern of his plan (figure 5.16). And beyond these, a ring of *barracas* – a term used two centuries before to describe the wooden huts on the sandspit overlooking the port – had sprung up to form the zones of *autoconstrucción*, the slum dwellings built by

FIGURE 5.15. Barcelona's old city from over Mont Jüich, in the late 1920s. Distrito V is in the middle third of the photograph between the two major roads – the Ramblas and Marques Duero – running left to right. Note also the very straight roads running the other way, opened by the military authorities in the late eighteenth and early nineteenth centuries.
*Source:* Archivo Historico Municipal de Barcelona.

FIGURE 5.16. A section of the outlying *ensanche* of Barcelona in the late 1920s. Nearly all the *manzanas* are fully built-up in this mixed zone of housing and industry. Some of the buildings pre-date the Plan Cerdà as suggested by their alignment.
*Source:* Archivo Historico Municipal de Barcelona.

their inhabitants, which still exist in some parts of the city today. This form of accommodation was the spontaneous response of the 100,000 migrants that arrived in Barcelona between 1924 and 1930. In 1931, Barcelona's population reached 1 million (c.f. Madrid 950,000 in 1930), and migration into the city continued to increase throughout the 1930s.

GATCPAC's response to the rapidly declining urban situation was its 1932 five-point Reform Programme (table 5.1) which was embodied in the 1934 Plan Macia (figure 5.17). This plan included proposals for radical renewal in the old city, a functional zoning of the existing built-up area and new segregated

TABLE 5.1. The five-point plan of reform proposed by GATCPAC in 1932.

| | |
|---|---|
| 1. | The sanitation of the old city. |
| 2. | Immediate cessation of the growth of *Ensanche* (i.e. Cerdà's *manzanas*) and the determination of a new lay-out, more in accordance with the needs of the city. |
| 3. | Classification of the city into functional zones – housing, industry etc. – and immediate limitation of the so-called 'mixed zones'. |
| 4. | The linking of the city, via an extension of the Gran via, with the coastal area of Castelldefels, to be used as a large maritime zone for recreation and relaxation. |
| 5. | The modification of municipal regulations in whatever way necessary to achieve the above. |

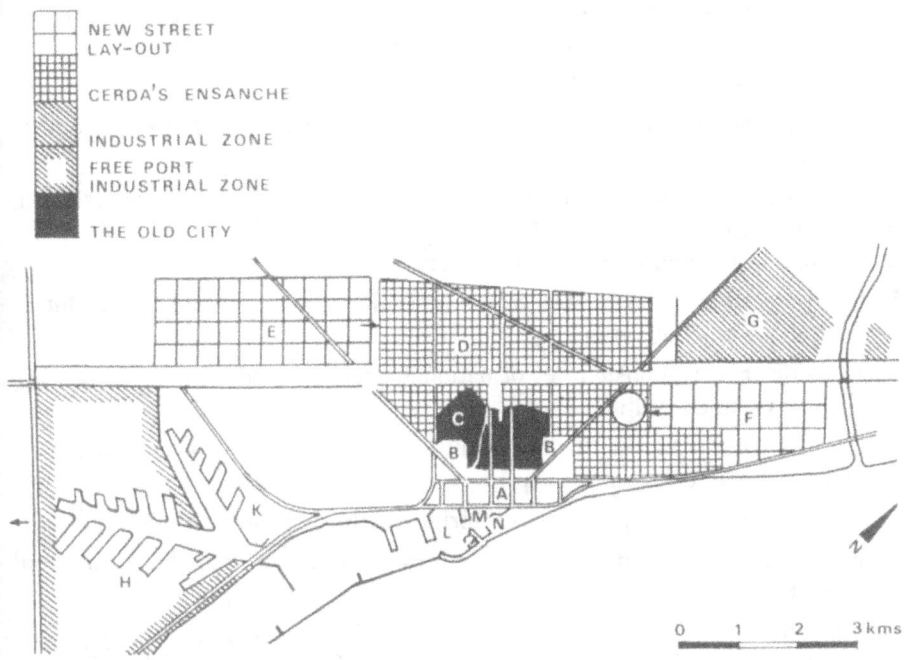

FIGURE 5.17. The Plan Macia, 1934.
*Source:* Wynn, M. (1979) Barcelona: planning and change 1854–1977. *Town Planning Review,* 50(2) (drawn by J. Harvey).

zones of industry and housing to the east and west. Although the Plan Macia found increasing support amongst the general public, the Reform Programme was disrupted by the onset of Civil War (1936–39) and very little of the Plan Macia was carried out.

It is also worth noting the publication of Rubio i Tuduri's 'Regional Plan for Catalonia' in 1932, in which many of GATCPAC's proposals were recognized. The plan gave macro-zonings to an area that encompassed the lower Llobregat Valley and the Tibidabo mountains inland, and attempted to limit the sprawling growth of the city. The most radical proposal of the plan was perhaps the creation of a new decentralized tertiary and industrial centre inland beyond Tibidabo. Although the plan never became executive, it was generally regarded as the first example of a regional plan in Spain, and also provided the basis for subsequent planning at this level in postwar Barcelona.

The Republican era closed with considerable progress in the development of ideas concerning what reforms were needed in the institutional framework of urban planning. These were expressed in the major reports[28] which followed the Municipal Congress held at Gijon in 1934, and are of particular interest because of their recurrence in the postwar era. The major recommendations of the Gijon Congress may be summarized as follows.

1. Legal obligation of all municipalities to draw up development plans to cover the entire municipal area, with state subrogation in case of default.

2. Urban plans to be revised after 15 years in force.

3. Regional plans to be drawn up to provide guidelines for the development of the country's major city regions.

4. Land-use classifications to be used in all plans; each classification to specify land use and maximum building volume, and to have clear and precise regulations to be binding on all developers.

5. Land re-division procedure to be revised and standardized to facilitate smooth plan implementation.

6. Activities and responsibilities of national, regional, and municipal planning authorities to be co-ordinated.

7. Creation of a Central Planning Authority to work in conjunction with a National Economic Planning Board.

8. Creation of regional planning authorities with their own planning offices.

9. Formulation of municipal land values indices, as guidelines for land expropriation by municipal councils.

10. Introduction of legislation to give municipal councils the necessary powers for expropriation of any land deemed necessary for the successful implementation of municipal development plans; alternatively 'collective associations' could be formed to act as development agencies, in which landowners would be represented according to the value of their property.

In April, 1939, the Civil War ended; Madrid lay in ruins, and under the new Fascist regime, planning was initially concerned with reconstructing the Capital de Imperio along the lines of Hitler's Berlin and Mussolini's Rome, with long wide avenues for triumphal marches and processions, large assembly areas for military gatherings and symbolic representations of Religion, Culture and the National Party. Elements of the 'falangist city' were evident in the Plan General de Urbanización de Madrid of 1941 (for example the Fachada de Manzanares consisting of the Cathedral, Royal Palace and new Falange headquarters, and the great avenues of Via de Europa, Via de Victoria and Via del Imperio), but the plan was essentially a continuation of the 1929 and 1931 plans for the capital. The 1941 Plan was approved in 1946 (figure 5.18) with the central core of the city enclosed by a green ring with satellite settlements beyond. Some industrial zones were added to the south of the city and an attempt was made to divide the central core into individual units separated by open spaces. The outline of the 1946 Plan is reminiscent of many of Eliel Saarinen's proposals for 'organic decentralization' in the inter-war era[29] and at the same time has much in common with Abercrombie's London Plan of 1944. There was, however, one new theoretical undercurrent that stemmed more directly from within the Fascist regime – that of segregation

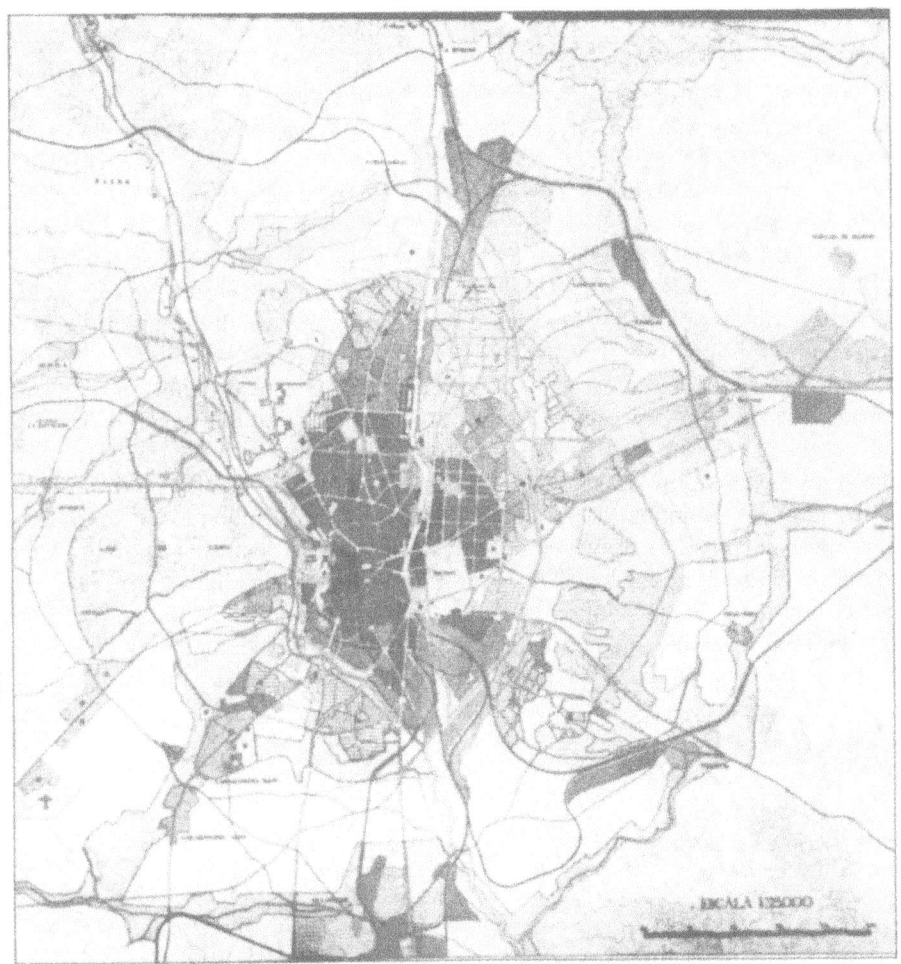

FIGURE 5.18. The Madrid 'Plan General' of 1941, approved in 1946.

and division of the working class. For example, a member of the planning team explained that 'the distribution of industrial zones has responded to the need to localize the working classes in satellite settlements that constitute true defensive nuclei against the invasion by the inactive masses encamped in the periphery, forming the suburban belts of misery against which we fight with difficulty'[30].

The 1946 Plan for Madrid drew the distinction between the *general* (municipal or sub-regional) plan and the *local* plan. The general plan was to provide the structure for urban growth of the city, providing land-use classifications for the entire plan area; local plans were to 'be in accordance with the outline structure of the General Plan, and must specify the design, volume and use characteristics for all buildings and free space zones within the area covered by the Local Plan'[31]. As we shall see, this distinction was subsequently included in the National Planning Act and became of paramount importance in planning and development in Spain in the postwar era.

The first postwar decade (1940–50) also saw significant advances in the establishment of upper-tier planning authorities in Spain. The General Directorate of Architecture was created in 1939 as part of the Home Office, with the specific task of directing the reconstruction of settlements destroyed or damaged in the war, as well as co-ordinating and regulating architectural practice in the country. The National Reconstruction Plan revived prewar initiatives to draw up a National Urban Plan, and to this end, an Urban Planning Division was established in 1949, to function within the General Directorate of Architecture. It was empowered to direct all urban planning matters in the country and to carry out preliminary studies for the drawing up of a National Urban Plan. This process had already been put in motion through the creation of provincial planning commissions[32] in the 1940s. These were to function as part of the provincial governments (*Diputaciones*), and were not only to draw up outline development plans for each Province to act as a guideline for lower tier (municipal or sub-regional) planning authorities, but also to contribute towards the formulation of planning policy at the national level and the configuration of the National Urban Plan.

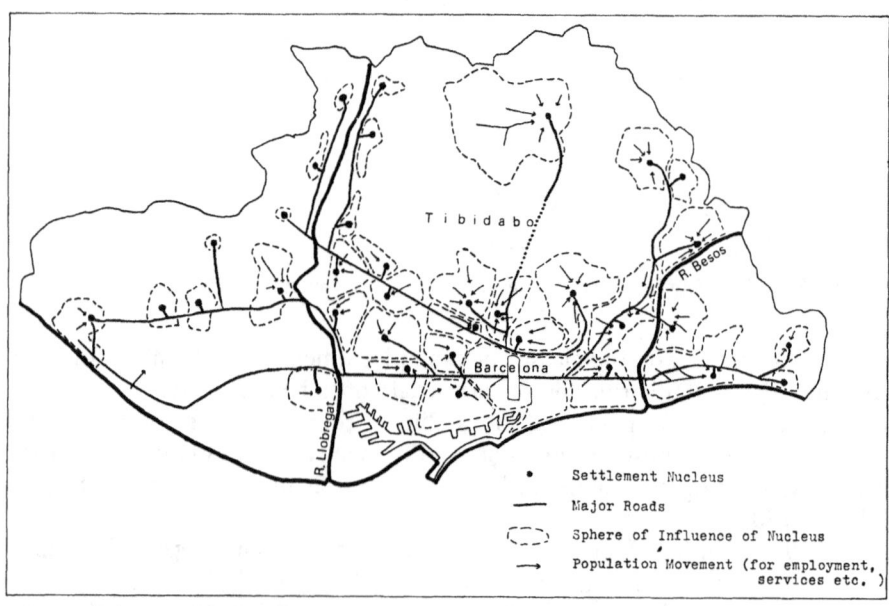

FIGURE 5.19. The 1953 Barcelona sub-regional plan.
The sub-region of twenty-eight municipalities was viewed as a collection of individual nuclei, rather than one urban continuum; and land-use classifications were introduced for the entire area, there being thirty such classifications in all.

# SPAIN

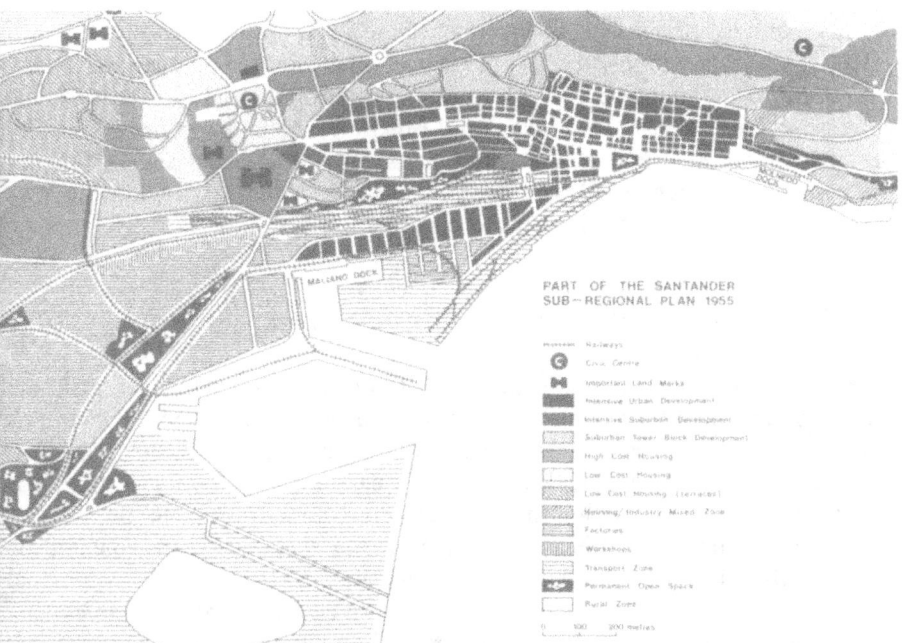

FIGURE 5.20. Part of the 1955 Santander sub-regional plan. Land-use classifications were normally accompanied by regulations governing building type, use and volume.

In the housing field, the National Institute of Housing was founded (as an arm of the Ministry of Labour) in 1939 to instigate and regulate state-subsidized house construction within the framework of the National Reconstruction Plan, and the 1939 and 1944 Housing Acts made central government monies available for state housing. During the 1940s over half a million new houses were built, over 120,000 of them by central state authorities; but nearly all were located in the 'devastated regions' of the south and west, where whole villages had been destroyed in the war. In Barcelona, for example, only 15,000 houses were constructed in the 1940s of which 13,500 were financed by the private sector. In 1950 the housing deficit was estimated at 80,000 in Barcelona and 30,000 in Madrid, while, according to Teran[33], by 1955 the deficit for the country as a whole was 1.5 million.

In the major urban areas, public order and political control were seen as all important and the effervescent spirit of urban reform, public participation and democratic citizen politics of the Republican era became things of the past. An anti-urban ideology was preached by certain state or state-controlled institutions – the Church, the press, and schools – in which the city was portrayed as the centre of vice and evil (communism, separation, prostitution, crime) and the rural base of the country was exalted as being the essence of Spanish civilization. A series of urban problems was tolerated or ignored by the central authorities, despite the continuation of planning activity and the approval of new urban plans for many of Spain's major cities including Madrid (1946), Valencia (1946), Bilbao (1946), Barcelona (1953–figure 5.19) and Santander (1955–figure 5.20). The deterioration of the old city centres, the increasingly high densities in the central *ensanches*, the mixed zones on the city peripheries, the housing and service deficits and the growing areas of shanty development throughout the country's major urban centres, all contributed to the grim legacy bequeathed to future planners.

## The 1956 Land and Urban Planning Act

The 1956 Land and Urban Planning Act was the cornerstone of planning legislation in Spain for the next two decades, during which time the country's major cities experienced a construction boom unparalleled since the immediate post-*ensanche* period. Although the Act was passed in 1956, a committee was set up as early as 1949, within the General Directorate of Architecture, to work on the Act, which established a planning system that was clearly inspired by many of the ideas and aspirations contained in the reports of the Municipal Congress held at Gijon in 1934. It was described by Pedro Bidagor as 'one of the most complete and up-to-date of all the planning acts in Europe'[34], and was based on the Italian, French and Belgian models[35]. We shall return in the subsequent section to review the overall functioning of the Act in the years following its approval; first, however, let us look in some detail at the planning system embodied in the Act itself.

### PLANS AND PLANNING AUTHORITIES

The Act made provision for a tiered hierarchy of urban plans and planning authorities at the national, provincial, sub-regional, municipal and local levels. The National Urban Planning Council (NUPC), was to be set up within the Home Office as the 'upper level planning authority in the country ... to co-ordinate the plans and projects of the different Ministries that intervene in urban planning'[36]. It was made responsible for the overall direction of a National Urban Plan, which was to set out the 'major guidelines for urban development'[37] in all Spain. Within the NUPC, a Central Urban Planning Commission (CUPC) was to be created to 'act as a Standing Committee for the NUPC, to implement and administer the NUPC's policy directives'[38]. Within the General Directorate of Architecture, the Urban Planning Division was expanded and the Directorate was renamed the General Directorate of Architecture and Urban Planning (GDAUP), to act 'as a permanent authority charged with the preparation, management and implementation of the directives of both the NUPC and the CUPC'[39].

At provincial level, provincial planning commissions, some of which already existed, were empowered to draw up provincial plans 'to provide the basic structure for urban planning in the Province'[40], whilst at the level of the municipality, the larger councils[41] were made responsible for producing general development plans, giving land-use classifications to the entire municipality, to be binding on all developers and development. Councils could combine together to form sub-regional planning authorities, and draw up sub-regional general development plans, some of which, as we have seen, preceded the 1956 Act.

TABLE 5.2. The plan approval process established in the 1956 Planning Act.

| Plan-making Authority | Initial Approval | Public Information Stage | Audience of Local Corporations Stage | Provisional Approval | Definitive Approval |
|---|---|---|---|---|---|
| 1. Local council or private enterprise | By the local council | Opened by the local council, to last one month, during which time members of the public and affected development agencies may put their case either for or against the plan | —— | By the local council | By the sub-regional or provincial planning authority |
| 2. Other planning authority or state agency | By the plan-making authority | As above but opened by the plan-making authority | Opened by the plan-making authority, to last one month, during which time the local council (and other public agencies) may put their case either for or against the plan | By the plan-making authority | By the sub-regional, provincial or other upper-tier planning authority (e.g. General Directorate of Urban Planning) |

At the local level, plans were seen as an instrument for the implementation of general plans. They were 'for the development of General Plans'[42] and were to contain the detailed design and lay-out of new development, and building regulations based on density and volume limits set in the land-zone classifications of the general plan. Similarly, roads and service projects were to design, programme, and cost out the provision of road and service infrastructure (roads, drainage, sewerage system, street lighting) in the local plan areas. Local plans and roads and service projects could be drawn up by any planning authority, and 'along with municipal plans, these can be drawn up by private individuals'[43]. The four-stage plan *approval* process (table 5.2), however, gave planning authorities the responsibility for giving definitive approval to urban plans, without which they were not executive.

LAND-USE CLASSIFICATION

The land-use classification system was based on three broad types of division of land into which all classifications were to fall – 'urban land', 'urban reserve' and 'rural land'. As a rule, all land within the existing built-up area at the time of plan approval was given 'urban land' status, 'urban reserve' comprised those areas earmarked for the possible future expansion of the built-up area, and all other terrain was classified as 'rural land'.

Through this classification system, the Act attempted to impose strict conditions on development. On 'rural land' all development was prohibited except that which conformed with the particular rural land use (e.g. farm houses, forestry administration buildings etc.). For development to take place on 'urban reserve', a local plan would first have to be drawn up and approved, providing detailed plans of the proposed development, and changing the land-use classification(s) as necessary, thereby giving the area the generic status of 'urban land'. Even then, however, development could not take place until the necessary services infrastructure had been provided, which was stipulated as 'road surfacing and pavementing, and water, sewage and street lighting systems'[44]. This meant, then, that any development on green-field sites would have to follow a strictly regulated procedural course in which local council and sub-regional or provincial planning authorities could exert a planning and development control role at the local plan, roads and service project, and building permit cession stages (figure 5.21). It is worth noting here that sub-regional plans for most of the country's major cities pre-dated the 1956 Act and that in these plans more complex land-use classification systems had been used (figure 5.20). Whilst the 1956 Act recognized these plans and their land classification systems, it left each municipality within the sub-region to superimpose the three-way generic division of land onto the established classifications, subject to approval by the sub-regional authority. In practice, this became a mere technicality, as the rural classifications were self-evident, and in these zones non-conforming development was prohibited; if basic service infrastructure did not exist in areas classified for development, then by definition these were

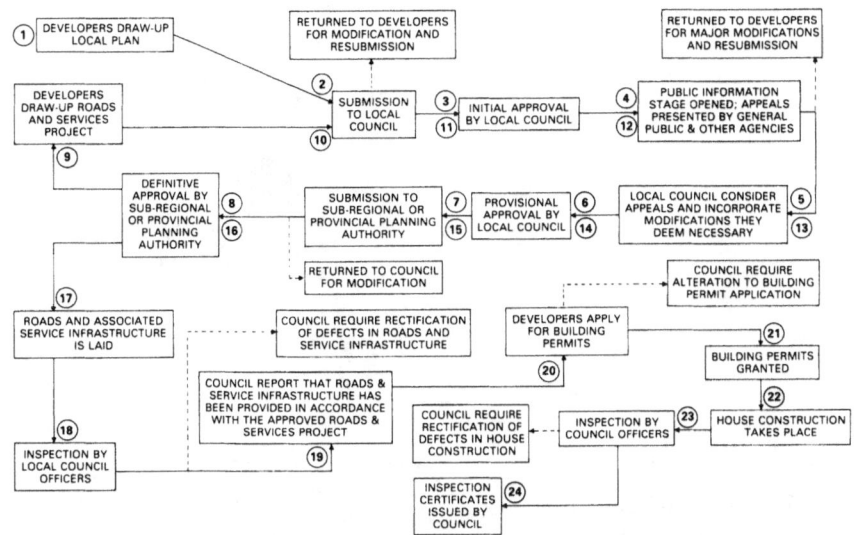

FIGURE 5.21. Plan approval and control procedure in the residential development of a green-field site by a private sector developer.

'urban reserve', and a local plan and roads and service project had first to be drawn up and approved before development could proceed.

THE IMPLEMENTATION OF PLANS AND DEVELOPMENT

The 1956 Act emphasized that urban growth should proceed through the controlled development of new estates (*poligonos*):

> For the implementation of General Plans, the plan area may be divided into so many estates, to attend the necessities of urban development. These estates will normally comprise several blocks (*manzanas*) of development and will be planned for one or more of the following reasons:
> 
> –To create an integrated nucleus of buildings and services.
> 
> – To create a homogenous area of development in a zone characterized by a predominantly different type of development.
> 
> – To facilitate the development of an area by public or private enterprise[45].

The legislators, then, envisaged a model of urban growth in which the sprawl of the central core was arrested, and new development, carefully planned and controlled through the local plan mechanism, would take place in the 'urban reserve' areas surrounding the central core (figure 5.22).

The Act also devised four 'systems of intervention' in which landowners and local authorities could combine to finance and manage the implementation of new development. Under the *co-operative system*, owners of land to be developed

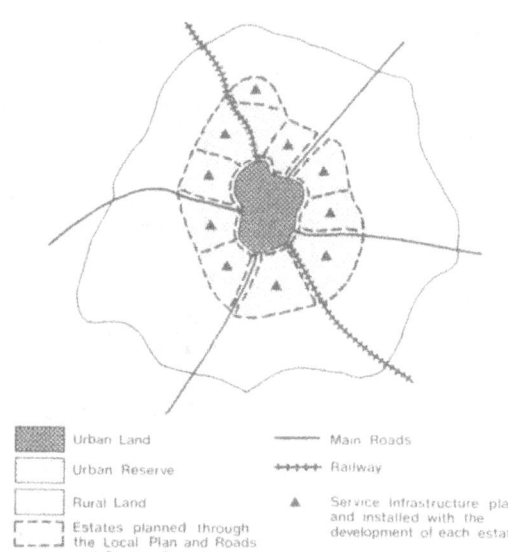

FIGURE 5.22. The model of urban growth envisaged in the 1956 Planning Act (after Teran).

had to cede, without payment of compensation, the land on which roads, public parks and gardens were to be built, and also '*finance* and *manage* the provision of roads, pavementing, drainage, sewage, streetlighting, water, gas, and electricity networks, and such tree, shrub and flower planting as there may be...'[46]. Councils and other public bodies were empowered to declare development to be of 'immediate importance' and bring the co-operative system into effect, or alternatively, proceed by compulsory purchase through the *expropriation system* and undertake development themselves. Landowners could also join together to form development boards to finance and manage the plan-making for, and development of, their land. Members of the council and other local corporations could be co-opted onto the board, which became responsible for working out compensation payments for landowners affected by the proposed development. For this reason, this form of management, which allowed for the planning and development of completely private estates, was called the *compensation system*. Finally, the *cession of roads system* was similar to the co-operative system, except that the local authority, rather than the developers, took responsibility for financing and managing the provision of service infrastructure (roads, pavements, sewage system, drainage, street lighting etc.), once land had been ceded to them. The local authority, however, could then charge landowners benefiting from the infrastructure 'special contributions' to cover 80 per cent of the capital expenditure.

In practice, the two most common forms of intervention have been the 'co-operative' and 'cession of roads' systems and we shall examine below just how this has affected the urban growth process. As regards the other two systems, local authorities have, as a rule, been limited by lack of finances from using the expropriation system, although development by central state authorities has often involved expropriation on a large scale. The compensation system has been used for financing and promoting private estates, but these have constituted a relatively minor component in the growth of Spain's cities.

SUMMARY

There are many other aspects of this Act that could be discussed, and this brief account has attempted to cover the fundamental components only. We can summarize the most significant features of the Act as follows:

1. The Act established a tiered hierarchy of urban plans and planning authorities at the national, provincial, sub-regional, municipal and local levels.

2. It established the distinction between general (municipal or sub-regional) plan and local plan. Local planning authorities were made responsible for drawing-up and approving general development plans. Local plans were to be used for the detailed planning of 'estates', which constituted the major physical form of urban growth.

3. A land-use classification system was to be used in general plans, as a means of controlling development. New 'estate' development was to take place in the areas of 'urban reserve', but a local plan had first to be drawn up and approved. Systems of intervention were set out to provide further guidelines for co-operation between the various agencies involved in the development process.

4. The Act accepted that private enterprise could play a leading role in the plan-making and development processes, although plan approval remained in the hands of planning authorities within the Public Administration.

Let us now turn to examine how this machinery functioned in practice.

## STATE HOUSING POLICY AND THE APPLICATION OF THE 1956 PLANNING ACT

There seems little doubt that the creation of the Ministry of Housing in 1957 and the government pre-occupation with housing policies and programmes in the 1950s and 1960s contributed significantly to the rupture of the tiered hierarchy of planning authorities which was central to the functioning of the planning system laid down in the 1956 Act. As already noted, the shortage of houses in the major urban centres led to the rapid spread of shanty towns in the city peripheries, constituting something of a crisis situation. The masses encamped in the shanty areas represented an ever present threat to law and order, and the General Strike in 1951 in Barcelona was repeated elsewhere in the early 1950s; the *resistencia de la población* more or less forced the central government to intervene more directly in the housing sector.

From the early 1950s onwards, the General Directorate of Architecture (then part of the Home Office) worked in conjunction with the Ministry of Labour and the sub-regional planning authorities on the planning and development of the early housing estates in the major cities. In 1954, the Limited Cost Housing Act introduced new subsidies[47] for private and public promotors of limited-cost housing, and the majority of housing estates constructed in Madrid and Barcelona over the next twenty-five years drew on the state aid and subsidies made available in this Act, and its 1957 Amendment Act[48]. The first National Housing Plan was launched in 1955 with the objective of constructing 550,000 houses between 1956 and 1960, and was followed in 1961 by a more ambitious Housing Plan with a target figure of 3.7 million houses in the period 1961–76, a figure passed in 1975.

The provision of housing, then, through direct intervention by state housing authorities, but above all through subsidies made available to the private sector, was a major concern of successive Franco governments from the early 1950s onwards. This tended to divert attention within the Cabinet away from creating the upper-tier planning authorities which featured in the 1956 Planning Act, which in turn resulted in a general lack of control, co-ordination and direction of urban planning practice and machinery in the country as a whole. In October 1956, just five months after the passing of the 1956 Act, a Decree was issued setting out the guidelines for collaboration between the National Institute of Housing and the General Directorate of Architecture and Urban Planning (GDAUP) on the acquisition and preparation of urban land to be used for the construction of state housing estates. This role was reinforced with the creation of the Ministry of Housing in 1957 and the removal of the GDAUP from the Home Office to function within the new Ministry as two new separate Directorates – the General Directorate of Architecture and the General Directorate of Urban Planning (GDUP). Similarly the National Institute of Housing was taken from the Ministry of Labour to become part of the General Directorate of Housing within the new Ministry (figure 5.23).

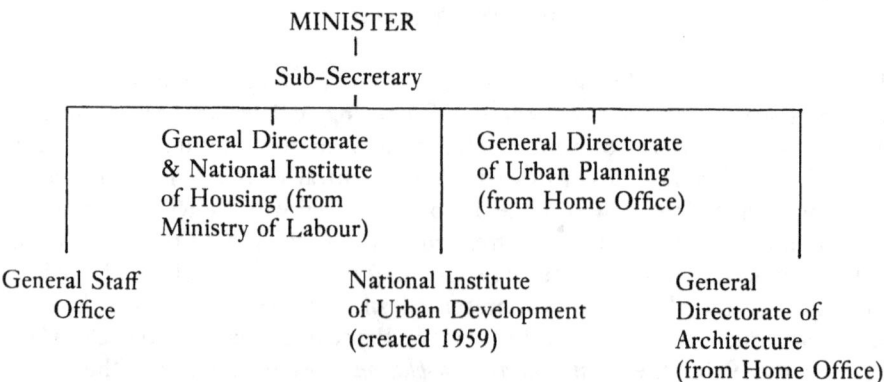

FIGURE 5.23. Internal structure of the Ministry of Housing, 1957.

This reorientation of the GDUP meant that little attention was given to creating the other upper-tier planning authorities referred to in the 1956 Act. Neither the National Urban Planning Council nor the Central Urban Planning Commission were ever created, with the GDUP theoretically taking on all upper-tier responsibilities assigned to these two bodies in the 1956 Act. But in fact, the ministerial reorganization destroyed the coherency of the country's planning machinery with the GDUP functioning within the Ministry of Housing and the local councils still directly answerable to the Home Office. The GDUP became increasingly concerned with the acquisition of land for the construction of state-financed (and subsidized) housing estates, acting independently of the local councils, often without consultation, in the programming of state housing estates. Work on the National Urban Plan did not start until the early 1960s, following the creation of the National Institute of Urban Development in 1959 (within the Ministry of Housing) to take on some of the land acquisition responsibilities of the GDUP[49]; but even then, only preparatory studies were undertaken before the whole project was shelved after the World Bank report of 1962 recommended the adoption of four-yearly national (regional-economic) development plans[50], three of which were subsequently drawn up and approved for the periods 1964–66, 1968–71, 1972–75, based very much on the French growth poles model.

In this changing political-economic and planning context, the provincial planning commissions which, as noted above, were supposed to have played a crucial role in strategic and regional planning as a link mechanism between the National Urban Plan and the general plans, found themselves overshadowed by Ministerial investment programmes and central state intervention that by-passed the provincial governments, or at most, used them as rubber stamp authorities. At the same time they received 'increasingly less economic support from the Local Corporations, which had previously felt under some obligation to co-operate when the General Directorate of Urban Planning was part of the Home Office,'[51]. Only two provinicial plans (Barcelona 1963, Guipuzcoa 1964) were ever approved, both drawn up by Doxiadis Associates, the international consultants, and both plans soon became obsolete because of changes in the economic policies to which they were closely tied. At the national and provincial levels, then, neither the planning authorities nor the plans for which provision had been made in the 1956 Act fulfilled their attributed responsibilities and roles.

At the general (sub-regional and municipal) plan level, however, the story is not so bleak. In a study published in 1974, Capel[52] noted that there existed 1116 general plans in all Spain (the vast majority of which had been drawn up since 1956), 738 having been definitively approved and 378 being in various stages of preparation. Although these general plans collectively encompassed only 1389 municipalities out of a national total of over 9000, nearly all the country's major urban areas were covered. Teran[53] has pointed out how, in the drawing up of these plans, the ministerial schism between the GDUP and the local councils, alluded to above, resulted in councils adopting a much more autonomous line than would otherwise have been the case, with the procedural and technical demands of the 1956 Act often being misunderstood or even deliberately ignored.

As regards the local plan level, we have already noted that the 1956 Act laid particular emphasis on the 'estate' as the major morphological form of peripheral growth and that planning law demanded that a local plan and a roads and services project be drawn up and approved before estate development could take place. This, then, would enable planning authorities to exercise a development control role at this level, as well as at the building permit level. Studies undertaken on the role of local plans in the expansion of metropolitan areas (Ferrer[54], Herrero[55], Ribas Piera[56]) reveal that the local plan mechanism was indeed a key element in the planning and development of peripheral growth, even though these plans were not always definitively approved by the planning authorities. At the same time, studies such as those of Montero[57] and Wynn[58] in Barcelona show that local plans were often used to bring about changes in land-use classifications established in general plans, usually with resultant increases in residential and/or building densities compared with those specified in the general plan. Additionally, the desire of municipal councils 'not to appear a village' (*no parecer un pueblo*) and inter-municipal rivalry tended to favour high-rise construction by private developers, and a recent study of Can Serra[59] reveals how local level planning instruments and regulations were often circumvented or used in the bargaining process between developer and council. As Teran has said 'a rivalry between Councils and cities sparked off a chain reaction benefiting the innoble career of so many developers that in this era exploited to the full their El Dorado. How many prestigious avenues did they create in this way, with the ensuing congestion from which those same cities suffer today?'[60].

The resultant poverty of the urban environment can also be explained by the fact that development has not always been carried out in accordance with the dictates of the local plan for a specific zone, as is witnessed by the lack of made-up roads, green spaces, schools and other facilities in many of Spain's peripherally-located housing estates. Teran[61] has suggested a model for city growth in Spain in which housing and industrial estates (with or without local plan approval) and haphazard shanty development have been built on land classified as 'urban reserve' and 'rural land' in the general plan, and increased building densities in the centre ('urban land') have resulted in congestion and overcrowding (figure 5.24).

There are a number of interconnected factors which have contributed to these forms of development. The local level planning machinery established in the 1956 Act had certain inherent weaknesses. The Act was extremely vague on the local plan–general plan relationship, stating that local plans were for 'the development of'[62] general plans but not specifying to what extent land-use classifications might be changed. This loophole in the Act was made all

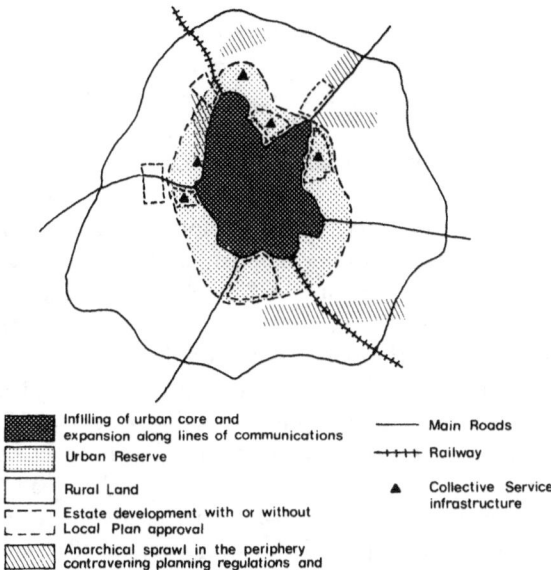

FIGURE 5.24. Teran's model of urban growth in Spain since 1956.

Legend:
- Infilling of urban core and expansion along lines of communications
- Urban Reserve
- Rural Land
- Estate development with or without Local Plan approval
- Anarchical sprawl in the periphery contravening planning regulations and land use classifications
- Main Roads
- Railway
- Collective Service infrastructure

the worse because of the rigid system of checks and controls which the Act introduced for the regulation of estate development proved to be unworkable in practice. It is often unrealistic to expect all road and associated service infrastructure to be completed in an entire zone prior to all construction, given the fragmentation of property boundaries, the speculationary retention of land[63] by some landowners, and the impotence of financially-weak local councils to intervene as effective development agencies. The inadequacy of the local level planning instruments in practice reflects the fact that planning law in Spain, in the Franco era, was ill-equipped to deal effectively with the wide range of political and economic variables that play such an important part in conditioning the functioning of the development process. The 'cession of roads' and 'co-operative' systems of intervention were often hamstrung in practice by the interplay of a number of factors – lack of local authority finances and loan facilities; multiplicity of private sector development agencies; local authority-private sector corruption and collusion; and non-co-ordination and general inadequacy of macro-service provision (schools, hospitals etc.) by government ministries.

This combination of circumstances meant that the provision of road and service infrastructure through the 'co-operative' and 'cession of roads' systems was unlikely to take place, if it took place at all, prior to house and factory development, and that the statutory planning machinery was unlikely to play a major role in the regulation and co-ordination of development. Once local plans had been approved, the local council and private sector developers embarked on the *ad hoc* implementation of development, in which behind-the-scenes collaboration played a major part in directing the course of change.

At the same time, the by-passing of plan procedure by central state housing authorities[64] has only added to the lack of credibility given to the formalized planning system, and reinforced a *status quo* in which the local planning authorities openly collaborated with private sector agencies in the 'bending' or open contravention of planning procedure.

The resultant urban growth process has been one of piecemeal anarchic sprawl in the city periphery and increasing building densities in the old city centres and central *ensanches,* as tertiary activities have replaced residential properties[65] (figure 5.25). Above all, however, it is the deficit in basic services which have constituted the major problem with which the new administrations in the post-Franco era have had to grapple. Some impression of the magnitude of the problem is given by the Financial Economic Survey[66] undertaken as a preliminary study for the revision of the 1953 Barcelona Sub-Regional Plan. The survey found that to meet *existing* deficits in schools, water supply, drainage and sewerage networks, road infrastructure, health centres, markets etc., in the sub-region, the public administration would have to find 64,000 pesetas (£420) for every person (3.2 million) living in the sub-region. To comply with the minimum service standards set by statute and incorporated into the 1976 Sub-Regional Plan, the local councils alone would have to buy 1500 hectares for urban parks, 450 hectares for collective service buildings (schools, hospitals, libraries etc.) and 1800 hectares for roads. It is worth noting

FIGURE 5.25. Part of the Princess Triangle in the Pozos neighbourhood of Madrid, where office and commercial development replaced old city residences in the 1970s.

also that 16,500 hectares in the sub-region have been affected by local plans, almost one-third of the entire area, and Sabater Cheliz[67] has shown that this raised the population potential of the sub-region to $7\frac{1}{2}$ million in 1974, compared with a 4.1 million estimate in the 1953 Sub-Regional Plan.

Finally, it is interesting to note that in the 1960s attempts were made to draw up and approve metropolitan area plans for Madrid and Barcelona, a level of planning for which provision had *not* been made in the 1956 Act. In Madrid, five industrial/residential decongestion estates had been designated outside the city in 1959 and these were reinforced in the Madrid Metropolitan Area Plan, drawn up in 1963, which was a further extension of the decentralization theme embodied in the 1933 and 1946 plans. The growth of the centre was to be contained by a forested green belt and new industrial growth centres in the Tajo and Henares valleys were to transform the capital into a 'pole of impulsion' for the future growth of the central region. New out-of-town commercial, social and cultural centres were to be created to serve the city periphery and counterbalance the pull of the established centre. The plan was approved in 1964 and a new urban management body – COPLACO – was established to manage and supervise plan implementation and the co-ordination of sectoral investment in the metropolitan area. In practice, however, the autonomous intervention of different ministries has prevented COPLACO playing any effective co-ordinating role and at the same time has failed to provide the basic service infrastructure included in the plan. The urban management role of COPLACO has in effect been reduced to a weak development control function in which a wide range of modifications to the plan's zonings have been accepted, as the private sector has been left to play the dominant role in the development process. As such the 1963 Metropolitan Plan soon became outdated and lost credibility as a framework for the growth of the capital.

Meanwhile, in Barcelona, the Sub-Regional Planning Authority (created in 1953), whilst undertaking the revision of the 1953 Sub-Regional Plan in the early 1960s, suggested that the effective planning of the Barcelona conurbation demanded planning at metropolitan area level. The resultant *Plan Director* (figure 5.26), covering half the province (193 municipalities), was technically more advanced than its Madrid counterpart but was in fact a compromise between two main decentralist schools of thought. Where the conflict was clearest was in the location of commercial, service, and administrative centres. On the one hand, the diverse components of these activities, belonging to spheres of influence of different magnitude which generally centre on Barcelona, suggested their concentration in one centre. On the other hand, the interdependence of such activities suggested comprehensive decentralization of all activities. The first option, which led to criticism on the grounds of resultant congestion of the centre and high costs of renewal, was in many ways an extension of the decentralization model that formed the basis of the plans for Madrid in the 1920s, 1930s and 1940s: the metropolitan fabric, composed of a series of satellites, needs a 'core' body of distinct and superior character.

FIGURE 5.26. The *Plano Director* for the metropolitan area of Barcelona.

In the final version of the *Plan Director,* the *centro direcciónal,* located not in Barcelona, but beyond the mountain mass of Tibidabo between San Cugat and Sardanyola, fulfilled this purpose. On the whole, however, the plan was closer to the city-territory structural model based on the decentralization of all activities. It aimed principally at stimulating secondary poles in the metropolitan system, by means of the retention of higher levels of 'directional' and tertiary activities in each centre, some of which were clearly to function as 'propulsion' nuclei for their surrounding sub-regions, some as 'rehabilitation' centres, aimed at bringing about a restructuring and improvement of ill-equipped peripheral areas, whilst others had certain characteristic functional specializations (transport, commerce, administration). It was this more radical form of decentralization, based on the city-territory model, and catering more for social-equity goals, that characterized the Metropolitan Area Plan for Barcelona which was finally approved by the central government in 1968 as a partial modification to the 1963 Provincial Plan. In the early 1970s support for the plan was subsequently withdrawn by the Madrid government, whilst it gained increasing support amongst industrialists and economists as the diseconomies of agglomeration, particularly congestion in and around the city, began to outweigh the external economies. It remains an interesting technical document that might well yet be resurrected as the basis for subsequent planning at this level in the near future.

## DEVELOPMENTS IN THE 1970s

By the end of the 1960s, the urban situation in Spain's major cities was reaching a crisis point. Migration into Madrid and Barcelona (table 5.3) continued on such a scale (in the early 1970s the growth of Madrid and Barcelona each averaged over 100,000 a year, constituting almost half the national annual demographic growth) that new measures were clearly needed to plan and control their growth effectively. This was all the more so because the planning machinery embodied in the 1956 Planning Act had failed to function efficiently at all levels, and the development of new planning concepts abroad only served to emphasize the need for alternative planning forms and solutions in Spain. Such change, which occurred in different ways throughout the 1970s, brought about the introduction of new planning concepts in a revised National Planning Act, in individual plans for different cities, and in *ad hoc* initiatives at both the macro and micro levels.

TABLE 5.3. Inter-regional migration 1900–1970. (The figures strikingly reveal the increasing dominance of the north east and Madrid as the main migration 'gainers' in the country this century.)

| Region | Net Migration ('000) | | |
|---|---|---|---|
| | 1901–30 | 1951–60 average per decade | 1961–70 |
| Galica | −109 | −227 | −229 |
| Cantabrico (centring on Bilbao) | −12 | 121 | 168 |
| Western Duero | −103 | −196 | −276 |
| Eastern Duero | −70 | −153 | −190 |
| Madrid | 150 | 412 | 687 |
| Western Tajo-Guadiana | −32 | −302 | −618 |
| Eastern Tajo-Guadiana | −30 | −167 | −217 |
| Western Ebro | −41 | −35 | 48 |
| Eastern Ebro | −51 | −79 | −46 |
| North East (centring on Barcelona) | 190 | 484 | 806 |
| Levante | −66 | 5 | 201 |
| Western Andalusia | 32 | −156 | −435 |
| Eastern Andalusia | −106 | −413 | −409 |
| Canaries | 10 | −6 | 19 |
| Whole country | −238 | −712 | −491 |

*Source:* Richardson, H. W. (1975) *Regional Development Policy and Planning in Spain,* Farnborough: Saxon House.

The most dramatic of these initiatives was the New Towns policy introduced in 1970 by Antonio Linares, the new Director of Urban Planning in the Ministry of Housing. The Urgent Development (ACTURS) Act of 1970 gave the Ministry of Housing new powers to expropriate land to develop green-field new towns and short-cut statutory planning procedure in the plan approval and implementation stages. Eight new towns (or 'integrated urban units') were designated, 10–30 kilometres outside Barcelona (three projects), Madrid, Valencia, Seville, Zaragoza and Cadiz, covering more than 11,000 hectares in all with a total population projection of 800,000. It was in many ways an implicit recognition by the central government that they had little time for a planning system that demanded forms of co-ordination and management that they could not provide. Instead, they were substituting an autonomous, heavy handed, intervention which cut right across existing statutory plans (but which ironically coincided to some degree with the *Plan Director* in Barcelona which the central government had shelved) and which attempted to provide a rapid solution to the urgent need for new housing, new land and decongestion in Spain's urban centres.

The new town designations met opposition from several quarters. Planners attacked the ACTURS as anti-planning because of the scant regard paid to statutory procedure and the general absence of an overall planning framework. Noguera, for example, wrote that 'it needs great ingenuity to see how a vast estate of housing and industry, created autonomously by those who choose to ignore the basics of the urban growth process, has anything to do with planning or the strategy of development'[68]. The 1970 Act also provided for private enterprise to play a leading part in planning, financing, and managing the new towns once the state had expropriated the land, and many were concerned at trusting the large capital promoters with these responsibilities: the form and content of the programme led many to believe it would only encourage peripheral sprawl on an even larger scale than before.

Affected landowners, including the councils, fought the expropriation orders tooth and nail, taking their case to the supreme appeal courts, which invariably upheld the order but often increased compensation payments. The court hearings so held things up that the momentum of the ACTURS programme in general was lost, and by the mid-1970s only in Gallecs (1472 hectares), near Barcelona, and Tres Cantos (1690 hectares), outside Madrid, had much progress been made in acquiring the land, and in none of the new towns had building been started.

This loss of momentum was compounded by political changes in the Ministry of Housing in Madrid and a general weakening of support for the ACTURS policy in the Cabinet, following strong opposition from the property-owning lobbies of Madrid and Barcelona. In 1975, however, in the first government of King Juan Carlos, the new Minister of Housing (Lozano Vicente) revived the ACTURS projects, and the following year two 'mixed companies', founded with public and private capital, were created by decree, one in Madrid to manage Tres Cantos, the other in Barcelona to try to revive the flagging Gallecs project. Since then, however, the protracted devolution of power to the Catalan Parliament has left the Gallecs issue somewhat in limbo[69] and only in Tres Cantos is construction going ahead. Thus, over a decade after the approval of the Urgent Development Act, not one of the eight new towns is yet built and the future of all except Tres Cantos must remain in doubt.

Long before Linares had embarked upon the ACTURS new towns initiative, the GDUP had started work on a series of studies to provide the basis for the revision of the 1956 Planning Act. At the upper-tier levels, the provincial plans had failed to provide the necessary link between national economic planning and 'general' urban planning, and the Third National (Regional-Economic) Development Plan (1972–75) called for a new type of regional plan to fulfil this role. At the general plan level, there was a general feeling amongst the planning profession that the 1956 Act was inadequate, in that it was too rigid to accommodate new planning concepts and techniques, with its emphasis on blue-print, land-zone classification plans. In the general plans of Logroño, Elche, Santiago and the revision of the Barcelona plan (figure 5.27), planners

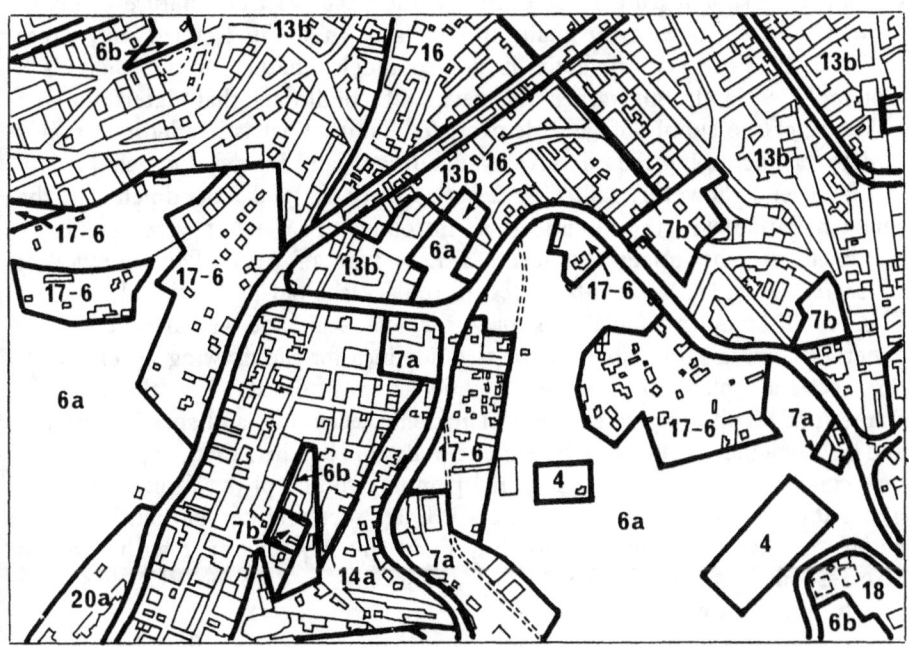

FIGURE 5.27. A section of the Barcelona 'Plan General Metropolitano' of 1976.
These land-use classifications in and around the Tres Turons hill area, north of the city are an area of shanty and 'marginal' dwellings. Of particular significance are classifications 6b (new park areas), 14a (public remodelling), 16 (urban renovation/rehabilitation) and 17–6 (urban renovation: change of use)
*Source:* Wynn, M. (1979) Barcelona: Planning and Change 1854–1977. *Town Planning Review,* 50(2) (drawn by J. Harvey).

were incorporating new techniques that were contradictory to the planning concepts underlying the 1956 Act. General criticism of the Act was only reinforced by comparison with the new planning ideas and concepts introduced in the 1968 Town and Country Planning Act in Great Britain and the 1967 *Loi d'orientation foncière* in France.

It was, however, at the local plan level that many planners felt the law should be tightened up. The vagueness of the 1956 Act on the local plan–general plan relationship and the freedom given private enterprise in the plan-making process had meant, as we have seen, that in some cities private and public developers had been permitted to make radical changes in land-use classifications in general plans, through the local plan mechanism. At the same time, direct intervention by state housing authorities in the construction of housing estates had not always followed 'local plan' regulations and procedure, only compounding the 'credibility problem', with the GDUP finding it increasingly difficult to enforce planning law at the local level when other state authorities were known to have contravened planning procedure themselves.

Land speculation, as part cause, part effect, of the failure of the 1956 Act, remained a major feature in determining the pace, cost and nature of urban growth. Lasuen, one of the main architects of the 1976 Reform Act, wrote in 1972 that 'the critical factor is not so much whether or not there is a monopoly of land, but rather the series of conditions that determine the elasticity of the supply of, and demand for, land. What is needed is a policy directed at increasing the effective availability of land for development'[70].

In the end, however, following a series of drafts and amendments in the Spanish Parliament, the modifications introduced in the Act were essentially technical. At the upper-tier level, a new type of plan – *Plan Director de Co-ordinación* (PDC) was introduced to replace the old provincial plans. The PDC could be on provincial or supra-provincial scale and was intended to set general planning regulations to act as guidelines for the drawing up of lower-tier (general) plans. At the same time, it was to establish 'the physical framework for the implementation of national, economic and social planning, and in particular regional development policy'[71]. This, then, represented a new conception of the role of regional planning to link physical planning with national economic planning, and to co-ordinate sectoral intervention. Unfortunately, however, the Act did not introduce any new planning authorities to take responsibility for this level of planning, and, to date, no PDC has been drawn up in Spain.

As regards general plans, the Act gave them a more open, flexible role that did not have to be so closely tied to strictly defined land-use zonings. Nevertheless, general plans had to 'classify the plan area to establish the corresponding legal framework for development; define the fundamental elements of the general structure for the ordering of the area; and establish a programme for its development and implementation'[72]. On the crucial issue of local plans, the Act stated that 'they [local plans] cannot be drawn up unless there is an existing General Plan, and in no case can they modify the specifications of the General Plan'[73]. At the same time, minimum standards for green zones and service provision were established for local plans, and a general prohibition on all buildings of more than three floors high, unless special provision was made for such in plans and planning regulations, was introduced. The Act also introduced the concept of 'Special Plan of Interior Reform' (SPIR) to be used for the 'improvement of the urban and rural environment and the city suburbs'[74], at local level. More specifically, they could be drawn up and approved with the 'objective of carrying out operations in urban areas aimed at the decongestion of crowded zones, the clearing and improvement of unhealthy areas, improving traffic circulation, environmental conditions or public services, or achieving similar objectives'[75]. The concept of special plan had, in fact, been introduced in the 1956 Act, but had been scarcely used in the urban areas, and the emphasis on improvement and renewal, a concept poorly developed in Spanish planning history, was new to the 1976 Act.

In summary, the 1976 Reform Act undoubtedly had its limitations, and should perhaps best be seen as an attempt to rationalize and control the urban growth process, which those who worked on the Act generally accepted as being necessarily linked to the evolution of Spanish capitalism at the time. As Ribas Piera has said:

> Clearly one law cannot stand-out as being radically different from the general legal system of the country, which is a faithful reflection of the social-political structure which it attempts to regulate[76].

In comparison with the 1956 Act, the 1976 Reform introduced certain new positive measures to improve and update the potential functioning of the planning and control system, but today, in a changed political climate, a more radical reform of the law may soon be required. This is particularly the case with regard to the machinery for incorporating resident opinion into the planning process in an era when conservation, rehabilitation and renewal are emerging as major new themes in both local and national politics.

The residents association movement in Spain is one of the most advanced in Europe in terms of organization and political activity. The widespread 'mobilization' of residents associations is nevertheless a relatively recent phenomenon, and Borja in fact identifies the mid-1960s as the turning point in the history of the movement:

> The relative passivity of the working classes up until the mid-1960s manifested itself in a general acceptance of the disorderly growth of the city and the scant publicity given to the role of Local Plans in the development process. But from the mid-sixties onwards, the working classes and certain elements of the press adopted more active stances, as witnessed in recent years in increasingly successful campaigns against the lack of collective service installations[77].

FIGURE 5.28. Resident protest in San Cosme outside Barcelona.
This was one of several marches organized by the Residents Association in a state housing area infamous for its poor quality construction.
(Photo: M. Wynn, see: Wynn, M. (1980) San Cosme, Spain: planning and renewal of a state housing area. *Journal of the American Planning Association,* January.)

By the mid-1970s, the political and academic left were hailing a number of victories by residents associations in their fight against housing agencies, local authorities and developers. In many of the public housing areas, residents demanded house repairs (figure 5.28), the provision of missing schools, roads and green areas, and the drawing up of missing tenancy agreements[78], but the protest campaigns were not only limited to the public housing estates. Castells notes that:

> In recent years, new social classes have become involved in these disputes, especially those in the residential complexes in the immediate suburbs, which were constructed by private promoters for skilled workers, officials and technicians. Their main concerns are with urban facilities and services, particularly schooling, where there is an insufficient number of places. In other cases, demands concern the quality of the environment, proposed increases in population density and the preservation of park areas[79].

Berriatua[80] has recently published his survey of resident association campaigns in Bilbao, and he notes how the association moved from an essentially defensive stance in the early 1970s to a more positive involvement in the planning and development processes in the post-Franco era, formulating (often with the help of consultants) its own proposals for renewal and improvement, and this impression is borne out by the accounts of Castells[81] and Borja[82] referring to Madrid and Barcelona. Nevertheless, as Wynn's studies[83] in Barcelona reveal, existing legislation makes no adequate provision for the incorporation of resident preferences into the decision-making process in an era when the demand for new housing and development has begun to slacken, and improvement and renewal of existing peripheral estates have increasingly become major aspects of housing management. The legislative frameworks for planning, and above all, for financing such schemes were largely non-existent in the Franco era, and although the 'special plan of interior reform', introduced in the 1976 Planning Reform Act, has been used to good effect in some instances, such schemes generally rely heavily on the *ad hoc* co-operation and collaboration of varying central state agencies.

In Madrid, COPLACO produced a number of interesting studies relating to the revision of the 1964 Metropolitan Plan[84], including the Madrid-Gudalajara corridor (figure 5.29) in the 1970s, but rapid political change and divergent non-co-ordinated ministerial and local council policies have thwarted its attempts to secure any new executive planning framework for the Madrid

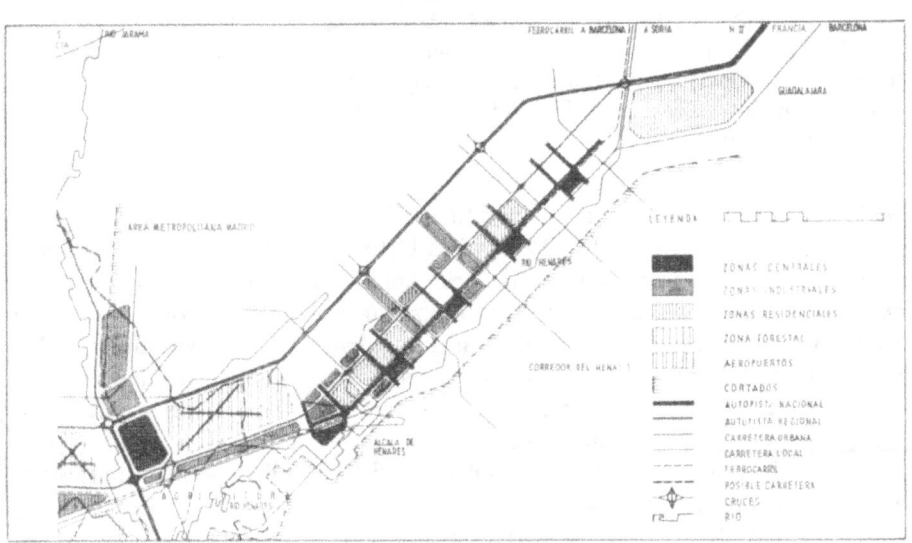

FIGURE 5.29. The Madrid-Guadalajara Corridor, 1972.
This development of Soria's Linear City concept arose from post-doctoral research undertaken at Cornell University in the early 1970s. Whilst it stimulated a great deal of interest in Madrid, it was never accepted as a formalized plan.
*Source:* Menendez de Luarca, J. (1976) El Corredor Madrid-Guadalajara. *Ciudad y Territorio,* No. 2/3.

FIGURE 5.30. La Corrala in the Lavapies district of Madrid.
These two buildings comprise sixty-five houses in which over 500 people live. Made of adobe brick and based on a wooden structure, the buildings were declared a ruin (thus facilitating demolition) by the owner in 1975 and only saved after a long campaign by the residents and the Madrid College of Architecture.
(*Photo:* M. Wynn).

region (despite the merging of the Ministeries of Housing and Public Works to form the Ministry of Public Works and Urban Affairs in 1977). At the local level, however, conservation of historic buildings in the old city and the *ensanche* (figure 5.30) has become an important issue in local politics[85], and COPLACO has also initiated a series of Immediate Action Programmes (PAI) aimed at providing short-term service provision in the capital to coincide with, and contribute to, the drawing-up of a *Plan Director de Co-ordinación* at regional level[86]. It must be said, however, that the planning of Madrid at this upper-tier level poses enormous problems and that radical political initiatives and administrative reform will be required if any real change in current trends is to be achieved. This was borne out by the subsequent devolution of planning powers to the Madrid municipalities in 1980, following a series of disagreements between the local and central administrations in Madrid, and the drawing up of a new series of general plans, by the Madrid municipalities in 1981–82. Time will tell if these new plans, reflecting a firm new initiative by the democratically-elected local governments, prove any more successful in controlling the growth of the capital than their numerous predecessors.

## Concluding Remarks

In conclusion, it is perhaps worth some re-emphasis of the plans and events which emerge as being of particular significance in the evolution of planning and urban growth in Spain in modern times. The expansion of the old medieval cities beyond their walls in the middle of the last century ushered in a new era in planning and urban growth in the country, centring on the planning and development of the *ensanches*. Of the plans of *ensanche*, the Plan Cerdà stands out as technically and conceptually far in advance of the equivalent plans of other Spanish cities. Following recent research by Domingo[87] and Tarrago and Soria[88], little doubt now remains about the scientific rigour with which Cerdà approached the urban problems of his time and the importance of the idealized model, involving a functional specialization and an egalitarian hierarchy space, on which he based his plan.

In the early years of this century, the speculative development of the *ensanches* and the periphery beyond, and the ever present old city problems (overcrowding, congestion, poor sanitary conditions) saw the adoption and adaptation of a range of new planning ideas in the plans and projects of the time, Of these, Arturo Soria's Linear City has received widespread acclaim as the first formalized expression of a concept which has reappeared in a welter of plans and planning documents ever since, although ironically it has had relatively little impact on planning within Spain. And the Garden City concept features strongly in the plans for Madrid from the 1920s onwards, during an era straddling the second Republic, in which the exchange of ideas and experiences between European planners and their Spanish counterparts had a marked impact on the development of planning thought in the country.

The development of a body of national legislation to regulate the functioning of the country's planning machinery lagged behind advances made in individual plans. The 1924 Municipal Statute *did* make local authorities responsible for urban planning but was conceptually and technically of little consequence. Not until the approval of the 1956 Planning Act were all the disparate pieces of legislation affecting planning and development in the country drawn together in one Act. The failure of this Act to regulate urban growth effectively in the country was, as already discussed, the result of the interplay of a number of factors. The Act itself was vague and open to interpretation on certain critical issues, and the planning machinery was inflexible and inadequate in certain aspects. Ministerial schisms and rivalries, non-co-ordinated state intervention that often contravened approved plans, local political rivalry, corruption and collusion – all contributed to the malfunctioning of an Act which was drawn up in the late 1940s and early 1950s when the massive country-city migration, the increase in personal mobility and the urban and coastal construction boom of the 1960s and early 1970s were not foreseen.

A further factor, and an issue of utmost importance today, concerns the devolution of political power to the local level and the financial, human and

TABLE 5.4. The council budget – the four major elements.

| 1. | Staff salaries | 30–50% |
| 2. | Municipal services: maintenance and provision | 30–40% |
| 3. | Annual interest payments and repayments on loans | 10–20% |
| 4. | Investment ('special budgets') | 10–20% |

technical resources available to local government. The financial weakness of most councils has meant they have had to rely almost entirely on the private sector or central state agencies to finance new development. Clusa[89] has pointed out that council budgets in Spain have rarely totalled 10 per cent of the gross public sector budget over the past forty years, compared with average figures of 18 per cent for West Germany, 27 per cent for Great Britain and 38 per cent for Holland. Furthermore, gross public sector expenditure in Spain has averaged about 25 per cent of the GNP, compared with figures of around 50 per cent for these other countries. Clusa also notes that staff salaries alone account for up to 50 per cent of a typical council budget and that investment in new development and infrastructure is generally limited to 10–20 per cent of the budget (table 5.4).

It is clear that for local authorities to exercise, effectively, a planning and management function appropriate to today's urban problems, both their financial and administrative structure, and the planning and legislative framework within which they operate, will require substantial reform. Many councils' resources remain woefully inadequate to plan and manage the operational intervention necessary to ensure the provision and maintenance of an acceptable range and standard of services and infrastructure. Technically multi-disciplinary, as well as politically pluri-ideological, local governments are needed, far removed from the air of corruption, collusion and dependency in which the two or three-man committee and elementary technical services sections carried out their planning and management functions in the 1960s and early 1970s.

New legislative machinery is also required both to make greater finances more systematically available to local authorities[90], and to enable the general public to play a more participatory role in the planning process at local level, without having to resort to the pressured confrontation strategies and *ad hoc* collaborative channels that still epitomize resident association activity in local planning. Only then, when Spain's planning machinery is seen to operate effectively at the local and municipal levels, will effective planning at the upper tier levels become feasible. To this end, Spain's legislators and professionals must attempt constructive adaptation and amendment of the current machinery in the light of experience gained in recent years, to offset the lack of credibility from which planning in Spain now suffers – a reflection of the general failure of urban planning to channel and control city growth effectively in recent times.

# SPAIN

### NOTES

 1. During the nineteenth century, both Madrid and Barcelona expanded from less than 200,000 each in 1800 to over half a million each in 1900, whilst the population of the country as a whole increased from 10.5 million to 18.5 million. In 1975, the Barcelona Metropolitan Area contained a population of over 4 million, that of Madrid 3.3 million. The Metropolitan Area of Bilbao, the next largest city, contained 1 million people in 1976.
 2. de Teran, F. (1978) *Planeamiento Urbano en la España Contemporanea*. Barcelona: Gustavo Gili.
 3. Bruguera, M. (1862) *Historia del Memorable Sitio y Bloque de Barcelona*, Volume II. Barcelona.
 4. Mesonero Romanos, R. (1860) *Nuevo Manual Historico-Topografico Estadistico de Madrid*. Madrid.
 5. Capmany i Montpalau, A. (1961) *Memorias Historicas sobre la Marina, Comercio y Artes de la Antigua Ciudad de Barcelona*, Volume I. Barcelona.
 6. Lopez, M. (1975) Vivienda y segregación social en Barcelona 1772–91. *Construcción, Arquitectura y Urbanismo*, No. 19, May/June.
 7. Bohigas, O. (1963) *Barcelona entre el Plá Cerda i el Barriquisme*. Barcelona.
 8. Grau, R. (1973) La manufactura algodonera y la ciudad. *Construcción Arquitectura y Urbanismo*, No. 19., May/June.
 9. Grau, R. (1974) La Barcelona industrial en la obra de Cerdà. *Cuadernos de Arquitectura y Urbanismo*, No. 100, January/February.
10. Garrut, J. M. (1963) Ildefonso Cerdà, su ensanche y la satira de ambos. *San Jorge*, No. 51, July.
11. Cerdà's known works include:
    *Statistical Information on Barcelona* (1855)
    *Topographical Plan of Barcelona and its Suburbs* (1855)
    *Statistical Monograph of the Working Class in Barcelona* (1856)
    *General Theory of Construction of Cities, applied to the Project of Reform and Expansion of Barcelona* (1859)
    *Theory of Urban Movement and its Application to Inner City Reform in Madrid* (1862)
    *Theory of Linkages between Land and Sea Communications and its Application to the Port of Barcelona* (1865)
    *General Theory of Urbanization* (1867)
    *Project of Regionalization and Provincial Communications Network of Barcelona* (1873)
    Of these works, large sections of many remain undiscovered. In addition, much of Cerda's unpublished work has not yet been found.
    For a more in-depth examination of his work see Wynn, M. (1980) Ildefonsa Cerdà, his 1859 Plan for Barcelona and Egalitarian Urban Science. *Trent Papers in Planning*, No. 16, Department of Town and Country Planning, Trent Polytechnic. See also Wynn, M. (1979) Barcelona, Planning and Change 1854–1977. *Town Planning Review*, 50, (20).
12. Domingo, M. (1973) Consideraciones sobre el plan Cerdà. *Construcción, Arquitectura y Urbanismo*, No. 19, May/June.
13. Puig y Cadafalch, J. (1927) *La placa de Catalunya*. Barcelona: Llibreria Catalonia.
14. Gutkind, E. A. (1967) *Urban Development in Southern Europe: Spain and Portugal*. New York: The Free Press.

15. A social and functional segregation was envisaged in the plan report of Castro's Plan for Madrid. It notes that the factory area would be Chamberi, and the upper classes would live to the north on both sides of the Paseo Castellana, the middle classes in Salamanca, and the working classes to the south and to the side of the Retiro park. As for the Plan Cerdà, there is some disagreement amongst urban historians about Cerdà's intentions. Some, like Grau (see above, note 9.), consider that Cerdà intended the working classes to live to the east in and around the old pre-*ensanche* settlement nuclei and to remain in the old city, with the monied classes occupying the central *ensanche* and Gracia.
16. Miller, B. (1977) Ildefonso Cerdà: an introduction. *Architectural Association Quarterly,* **9,** (1).
17. Soria y Mata, A. (1901) Un triunfo de la Ciudad Lineal. *Ciudad Lineal.*
18. Gonzalez de Castillo, H. (1931) A Spanish view of London's future. *Garden Cities and Town Planning,* London, December.
19. See, for example, Gonzalez de Castillo, H. (1933) Urbanismo, planes regionales: el plan regional de Madrid. *La Construcción Moderna,* Madrid, September.
20. See Ortiz, A. (1976) Perspectiva y prospectiva desde Cerda: una linea de tendencia. *2C Construcción de la Ciudad,* No. 6/7.
21. See Wynn, M. and Smith, R. J. (1978) Spain: urban decentralization. *Built Environment,* March.
22. Sallaberry, J., Aranda, P., Lorite, J., and Garcia Cascales, J. (1924) *Plan General de Extensión de Madrid y su distribución en zonas.* Madrid.
23. Bassols, M. (1973) *Genesis y Evolución del Derecho Urbanistico Español: 1812–1956.* Madrid: Editorial Montecorvo, pp. 85–90.
24. 'GATEPAC' – The vanguard Spanish architect/planner group – stands for 'Grupo de Arquitectos y Tecnicos Españoles para el progreso de la Arquitectura Contemporanea'.
25. de Teran, F. (1976) Notas para la historia del planeamiento de Madrid. *Ciudad y Territorio,* No. 2/3.
26. Comite de Reforma, Reconstrucción y Saneamiento de Madrid (1939) *Esquema y bases para el desarrollo del Plan Regional de Madrid.* Madrid.
27. 'In the streets of Amalia, Arco de Teatro, Berenguer, Cadena, Carretas, Cera, Cid and Conde de Asalto, there exist dwellings with a 20 per cent annual mortality rate'. Public lecture by Dr. Aguade, Mayor of Barcelona, quoted in *A/C* (GATEPAC's official journal), No. 6, 1932.
28. Congreso municipalista (1934) Ponencias. *Tiempos Nuevos,* No. 10/11, Madrid.
29. Saarinen, E. (1943) *The City, Its Growth, Its Decay, Its Future.* Cambridge, Mass: M.I.T. Press.
30. Martinez de la Madrid, A. (1948) La creación de zonas industriales en Madrid. *Gran Madrid,* No. 3.
31. Presidencia del Gobierno (1946) Decreto Ley sobre el Plan General de Ordenación Urbana de Madrid. *Boletin Oficial del Estado,* July, Article 3.
32. A provincial planning commission sat under the presidency of the civil governor of the province and was made up by representatives of the Ministries of Public Works, Industry and Agriculture, plus specialist planners, engineers, architects and surveyors drawn from local authorities, consultancies, and elsewhere.

33. Teran (1978) *op. cit.*, p. 342 (see note 2).
34. Bidagor, P. (1967) Situación general de urbanismo en Espana. *Revista de Derecho Urbanistico*, No. 4, Madrid.
35. According to private conversations between F. de Teran and P. Bidagor. See Teran (1978) *op. cit.*, p. 334 (see note 2).
36. Presidencia del Gobierno (1956) Ley de Regimen del Suelo y Ordenación Urbana. *Boletin Oficial del Estado*, May, Article 198.
37. *Idem*, article 7.
38. *Idem*, article 199.
39. *Idem*, article 200.
40. *Idem*, article 8.
41. Only those councils of municipalities with a 50,000 population, and councils of provincial capital cities, were made legally responsible for drawing up development plans. In other municipalities it was the overall responsibility of the provincial or sub-regional planning commissions to do so.
42. Presidencia del Gobierno (1956) *op. cit.*, article 10 (see note 36).
43. *Idem*, article 40.
44. *Idem*, article 63.
45. *Idem*, article 104.
46. *Idem*, articles 115–117.
47. The 1954 Limited Cost Housing Act introduced two categories of state aid. For 'Group 1 houses' no direct state subsidy was given, but constructors were conceded low-interest loans and exemptions from local rates. In addition to these benefits the constructors of 'Group 2 houses' (for which construction costs were regulated) could claim 20 per cent grants from the state for their construction, but the sale or rent return to the promotor was strictly limited. This limitation on profits restricted the uptake of grants by house promotors in comparison with the 'fixed subsidy' system introduced in the 1957 Amendment Act. For more detail, see Wynn, M. (1984) Spain, in Wynn, (ed.) *Housing in Europe.* London: Croom Helm.
48. The 1957 Housing Act introduced the category of 'fixed subsidy dwellings', for which a 30,000 peseta per house direct state grant was made available. Loans from the Construction Credit Bank were also made available at low interest rates with fiscal exemptions. In 1963 certain incongruities between the 1954 and 1957 Acts were smoothed out in a further amendment Act.
49. By 1976, the National Institute of Urban Development (INUR) had 128 residential and 46 industrial estates throughout the country, occupying over 7000 hectares, with a further 7000 hectares under construction. See: INUR (1977) *La creación de suelo urbanizado-informe.* Madrid: Arce & Potti S.A.
50. For the history of national development in Spain in the 1960s and 1970s see: Richardson, H. W. (1975) *Regional Development Policy and Planning in Spain.* Farnborough: Saxon House; Naylon, J. (1975) Iberia, in Clout, H. (ed.) *Regional Development in Western Europe.* New York: Wiley; and Alonso, L. and Hebbert, M. (1982) Regional planning in Spain and the transition to democracy, in Hudson, R. and Carney, J. (eds.) *Regional Planning in Europe.* London: Pion.
51. Bidagor (1967) *op. cit.* (see note 34).
52. Capel, H. (1974) Agentes y estrategias en la producción del espacio urbano español. *Revista de Geografia*, (1–2), University of Barcelona, pp. 19–56.

53. Teran (1977) *op. cit.*, p. 506 (see note 2).
54. Ferrer, A. (1974) *Presentación y Estadistica de los Planes Parciales de la Provincia de Barcelona*. Barcelona: COACB.
55. Herrero, A. (1972) El desarrollo de nuestras ciudades después de la ley de suelo: Huelva. *Ciudad y Territorio*, No. 4, IEAL, Madrid, pp. 15–34.
56. Ribas Piera, M. (1976) Ante el nuevo plan de ordenación de Murcia. *Ciudad y Territorio*, No. 1, IEAL, Madrid, pp. 29–62.
57. Montero, J. (1972) El planificación parcial en la Comarca de Barcelona. *Cuadernos de Arquitectura y Urbanismo*, No. 87, January/February.
58. Wynn, M. (1980) The Planning and Implementation of Development in the Barcelona Periphery (A Case Study Approach). Ph.D. Thesis, CNAA/Department of Town and Country Planning, Trent Polytechnic.
59. Wynn, M. (1981) The residential development process in Spain – A case study. *Planning Outlook*, 24(1).
60. Teran (1978) *op. cit.*, p. 507 (see note 2).
61. *Idem*, p. 569.
62. Presidencia del Gobierno (1956) *op. cit.*, article 10 (see note 36).
63. Every piece of planning legislation since the Civil War has made some reference to the need to combat the viscious circle of speculation, but none has succeeded in doing so. Maragall's study of land prices in the Barcelona Sub-Region shows that the real price of land increased an average 6.13 per cent per year during the period 1951–78, or a forty times increase over the period as a whole. See Maragall, P. (1978) *Els preus del sol (el cas de Barcelona)*. Doctoral thesis, Barcelona University.
64. See, for example, Wynn, M. (1980) San Cosme, Spain: Planning and renewal of a state housing area. *Journal of the American Planning Association*, January; and Wynn, M. (1979) Peripheral urban growth of Barcelona in the Franco era. *Iberian Studies* (University of Keele), Spring.
65. For an examination of the increase of tertiary activities in the centre of Madrid, see Alvarez Mora, A. (1979) *Madrid, las transformaciones del centro-ciudad en el modo de produción capitalista*. Madrid: COAM.
66. Corporación Metropolitana de Barcelona (1976) *Estudio-Economico-Financiero del Plan General Metropolitano*. Barcelona: CMB.
67. Sabater Cheliz, S. (1977) Proceso de urbanización en Barcelona y su traspais. *Ciudad y Territorio*, No. 3, IEAL, Madrid.
68. Noguera, J. (1972) Nueva ciudad de Riera de Caldes. *Cuadernos de Arquitectura y Urbanismo*, No. 87, January/February.
69. See: Wynn, M. (1980) Gallecs New Town, Spain. *Town and Country Planning*, November.
70. Lasuen, J. R. (1972) La politica de suelo urbano. *Arquitectura*, No. 162, COAM, Madrid.
71. Ministerio de la Vivienda (1972) *Proyecto de Ley de Reforma de la Ley sobre Regimen del Suelo y Ordenación Urbana*. Madrid.
72. Presidencia del Gobierno (1976) Ley Sobre Regimen del Suelo y Ordenación Urbana. *Beletin Oficial del Estado*, April, Article 11.
73. *Idem*, Article 13.
74. *Idem*, Article 22.
75. *Idem*, Article 23.

76. Ribas Piera, M. (1976) La practica del planeamiento urbanistico y la reciente ley de reforma de la del suelo. *Cercha,* No. 18, p.48.
77. Borja J. (1977) Urban social movements in Spain, in Harloe, M. (ed.) *Captive Cities.* Chichester: Wiley.
78. The 1954 and 1957 Housing Acts made possible both the sale and renting out of state subsidized housing. In the 1960s there was a general tendency towards sale and away from renting-out by both public and private sectors alike. In the public housing estates, most residents associations demanded that they paid fixed rents (at no more than 10 per cent of average salary), rather than long-term mortgage payments. Acceptance of a sale contract would invariably mean accepting responsibility for the repair of what were often poor quality dwellings.
79. Castells, M. (1978) Urban social movements and the struggle for democracy. *International Journal of Urban and Regional Research,* 2(1), p. 139.
80. Berriatua, J. M. (1977) *Las Asociaciones de Vecinos.* Madrid: IEAL.
81. Castells, M. (1978) *op. cit.* (see note 79).
82. Borja (1977) *op. cit.* (see note 77)
83. Wynn, M., *op. cit.* (see notes 58, 59 and 64).
84. COPLACO (1977–78) *Colección: Analisis de problemas y oportunidades,* Documentos Monograficos, Nos. 1–12. Madrid: Coplaco.
85. See: Wynn, M. (1980) Conserving Madrid. *Town and Country Planning,* February.
86. See: *Ciudad y Territorio,* No. 1, 1981, which focuses on recent planning initiatives in Madrid.
87. Domingo (1973) *op. cit.* (see note 12).
88. Soria y Piug, A. and Tarrago Cid, S. (1976) *Ildefonso Cerdà (1815–1876) Catálogo de la Exposición Comemorativa del Centenario de su Muerta.* Barcelona: Colegio de Ingenieros.
89. Clusa, J. (1978) Algunos problemas economicos y administrativos de la gestión publica urbana. *Butlleti,* No. 5, CEUMT, pp. 4–9.
90. During the Franco era, purely local sources of revenue, collected by local authorities, were gradually replaced by taxes collected by the Finance Ministry, which thus assumed the role of paymaster, dictating to the local authorities how monies should be spent rather than leaving them free to raise and spend money in accordance with their own perception of local needs.

# 6

# Turkey

## RUŞEN KELEŞ and GEOFFREY PAYNE

This chapter describes the evolution of town and planning and housing policies in Turkey during a period of fundamental social and economic change. It traces the origins of urban administration under the Ottoman Empire and the ways in which Republican strategies prepared the way for subsequent developments.

A detailed case study is given of Ankara, which replaced Istanbul as the national capital in 1923. Its role as a new strategic centre, free from the physical and psychological links with the past reflects the ambitions and aspirations of urban planners of the time and highlights some of the issues facing modern Turkey.

### TOWN PLANNING ORIGINS IN OTTOMAN TIMES

The history of Republican Turkey is completely different from that of the Ottoman Empire in terms of social and economic development, settlement patterns, external political relationships and world outlook. However, there are some continuities in the socio-cultural and economic structures of both societies, and it may thus be useful to describe briefly the socio-political characteristics of the Ottoman Empire, which lasted from 1453 until 1920.

In the prosperous periods of the Empire, the settlement pattern and distribution of cultural, industrial and commercial activities was relatively well balanced. Most regions benefited equally from the national wealth and welfare. Villagers were discouraged from leaving the land, partly because it was given to them by the state to cultivate, and also because migration from their village obliged them to pay compensatory state taxes.

Modern Turkey inherited from the Ottoman Empire a highly rural and semi-feudal society with only one city – Istanbul – having a population of over a million inhabitants. All medieval towns and cities of the Empire throughout the Arabic-speaking Near East, Anatolia and the Balkan Peninsula preserved their character until the end of the nineteenth century, with only minor modifications. There was no specific provision in Ottoman law relating to the planned growth of urban settlements or the renovation of central urban areas, although such things as street widths and building heights were covered by national legislation.

The typical Ottoman city consisted of a gridiron street pattern interspersed with a series of narrow, winding lanes (figure 6.1). The mosque and other important buildings were located at the centre, but as there were no formal zoning patterns for different land uses throughout the city, commercial activity developed freely within residential areas. Increasing contact with the West, however, gradually began to alter this traditional pattern; from the late nineteenth century onwards, new towns were built alongside the older ones, a process accelerated by rapid population growth and a pre-occupation with monumentalist city planning concepts from Germany and other parts of Europe[1]. At the same time, such new development was frequently complemented by piecemeal growth on the fringes of the existing built-up areas.

Social organization in the Ottoman city was shaped by the neighbourhood

FIGURE 6.1. A narrow street typical of Ottoman towns.
*Photo:* G. K. Payne.

unit or *mahalle*, the residents of which usually shared the same ethnic, religious, employment and regional background. The trade guilds also played a large part in influencing *mahalle* life and providing facilities for their members.

The Ottoman land tenure system did not make provision for private ownership in either rural or urban areas until the Land Law of 1858 was passed. Before this time, all land officially belonged to either the state (*miri* land), religious foundations (the *waqf*), or tribes (*musha* land), and the acquisition of land for public purposes posed few problems. The declining power of the sultans, however, led to administrators responsible for collecting land taxes (based upon use-rights on state land) effectively acting as landlords and exploiting the weakness of central government for their own benefit. The 1858 Land Law, by permitting state land to be passed on by an occupant to his successors (*mülk* tenure), thereby formalized a land market process which had already become current practice. By the end of the nineteenth century, the extent of *mülk* lands under the control of ağas (feudal barons or leaders) or other powerful families was sufficient to cause a collapse of the traditional Ottoman pattern of urban development, and subsequent growth became haphazard and difficult to control. The *waqf* foundations also exerted considerable political influence in both rural and urban areas through their extensive land holdings[2].

Another characteristic of nineteenth-century Ottoman planning was a tendency of government agencies to deal with development problems in an *ad hoc* fashion, rather than treating cities as organic entities that required comprehensive planning. Regulations were made to control building density, building heights and street widths, but no comprehensive planning concepts were developed. This is well illustrated by the Building Law of 1882, the first piece of Turkish legislation to lay down principles for the planned growth of urban settlements.

Most towns were built at high density using timber and other inflammable materials; the occurrence of fires was therefore not uncommon and there was thus a need to regulate the redevelopment of affected areas. The 1882 Law stipulated that when reparcelling city blocks destroyed by fire or other hazards, the land involved had to be regarded as undeveloped for planning purposes[3]. This meant that each plot then had to be indicated on an official map and, if possible, given a square or rectangular shape before being redistributed to the original owners. The law allowed for a loss in plot area of up to 25 per cent without compensation in order to widen streets and reduce the risk of future firespread, though this presented considerable problems for residents occupying already inadequate size plots. The 1882 Law also provided that when local authorities decided to establish a *mahalle*, any landowners wishing to sell their land had to cede a proportion to the state without compensation to provide sites for such public facilities such as schools, police stations and clinics, as well as a cash contribution towards the cost of paving roads. The residents of a *mahalle* were also required to contribute financially to municipal expenditure on the construction and maintenance of public infrastructure. This was an extension of traditional rural practice in which public works for a village were financed from two main sources – *imece*, a form of compulsory labour contribution, and *salma*, a tax levied on each household according to its means. Although it therefore dealt with several important aspects of urban planning, the 1882 Law tended to regard these individually in isolation, rather than in an integrated manner.

During the nineteenth century, town planning in Turkey was largely carried out by architects, engineers and administrators, there being no official town planning profession as such. The first municipal corporation was established in 1854, but technical matters were generally the responsibility of the chief architects (*mimarbaşı*), who were agents of the central government. They executed their duties of supervision in co-operation with the representatives of the *şehremaneti*, an executive organ of local government until 1868. In the early 1870s, a national commission was formed with power to supervise the improvement of national highways and buildings with staff drawn from the Technical School established in İstanbul during the 1770s. The regulation of streets, preparation of base maps and issue of licences for house construction were all covered by the 1882 Act and were administered by central government until the end of the nineteenth century.

Regional differences in development reflected the vestiges of settlement structures in the Ottoman Empire. Historically, major areas of population concentration were in the interior of Asia Minor up until the eighteenth and nineteenth centuries, when the Industrial Revolution in Europe and the change from overland to maritime trade routes gave towns and cities in coastal regions a new importance. Port cities throughout Turkey were amongst the most heavily populated throughout the nineteenth and well into the twentieth centuries[4]. During this period, nothing was done to try and ensure a balanced development of the nation's disparate regions.

The balance of the socio-economic order had, in fact, started to change as early as the eighteenth century, as the Ottoman economy began to decline and external economic pressures and controls from Western European nations increased. For example, the monopoly of commerce in the Black Sea was ceded to Russia late in the eighteenth century, and the 1838 Trade Agreement with Great Britain reduced the Empire to a semi-colony. The capitulations accorded to European economic powers and an ever increasing foreign debt load made the Empire practically dependent on foreign manufactured goods and imported capital. By the beginning of the twentieth century, almost one-third of the total public revenue was used for the repayment of accumulated debts to foreign creditors, and a special organization was established under the name of the *Düyun-u Umumiye* (Public Debts Administration) to handle the problem.

Traditional industries were unable to compete with the rise of industrialism in the West, and many of the older cities of the Empire became simple trading centres supplying raw materials to the West. This change in the economic structure necessitated a new transportation system more suited to improving commercial relationships with Europe, with Istanbul, both as a harbour and as a base for Western institutions, playing an important role as a trade and industry centre. Its population was nearly 1.5 million at the turn of the century, and most of the country's service industries and merchants specializing in foreign trade were located there. The growth of Istanbul only served to increase the inter-regional differences which had developed as the Empire declined.

## THE EARLY REPUBLICAN ERA (1920–45)

Although the Turkish Republic was proclaimed in 1923, a National Assembly was established as early as 1920, and a government elected by the Assembly was entrusted with the task of governing the country. The Republican period, therefore, effectively started from 1920 when Mustafa Kemal, popularly known as Atatürk, became the country's first leader. Atatürk immediately committed himself to the complete national independence of Turkey, and then to its modernization.

By modernization he understood not only the secularization of society, but also the restructuring of its political and socio-cultural institutions. The six cardinal principles of Atatürk can be summarized as Nationalism, Republicanism, Populism, Secularism, Etatism and Reformism. They have greatly contributed to shaping the legal and socio-economic structure of contemporary Turkey, and Atatürk's emphasis on the development and modernization of Ankara was inspired to a large extent by these principles. He wanted to combine form and substance by constructing Ankara not only as a symbol of new ideals and a new national identity, but also as a new urban form benefiting from spacious streets, green spaces, public housing, sanitation facilities and civic buildings. In order to appreciate adequately the nature of urban growth and planning policies during this inter-war period, it is necessary to describe briefly some of the fundamental changes through which Turkey was passing, and the role played by the state in shaping events.

The founders of the Republic, and particularly Kemal Atatürk, considered it essential to transform Turkish society by removing the religious and cultural links with the past, and by emulating the political, economic and institutional structures evolved during the nineteenth century in Western Europe. It was recognized, for example, that economic expansion in Europe had gone hand-in-hand with industrialization and urbanization, though the fact that this initially occurred on the basis of an agricultural surplus perhaps received less attention. Accordingly, high priority was given to the growth of industry, and the importance attributed to agriculture in investment policies steadily declined. Socially, emphasis was placed upon encouraging secular Western attitudes and values, and urbanization was seen as a means of achieving both economic and social objectives. National development strategies, then, were often represented as a move towards 'Industrialization, Modernization and Urbanization'.

The state took a strong interest in the implementation as well as the formulation of policy goals. A law creating the Agency of State Industries was passed in 1932, giving the state powers to establish its own industrial concerns, and in 1933–34, a number of state banks (e.g. Sümerbank and Etibank) were established to finance public investment in textiles, mining and other industries. The lead which the public sector thereby established did not, however, threaten the commercial or financial interests of an existing private industrial sector, since during the early days of the Republic these were virtually non-existent. 'State capitalism' or 'etatism' as it became known, was intended instead to *establish* an industrial sector. As Lewis[5] has observed, 'local capitalist enterprise was lacking in both capital *and* enterprise', a situation which he attributed to traditional Turkish disdain for commerce and industry. It was also due to the fact that during the Ottoman period these functions were largely carried out by religious and ethnic minorities, whose contribution was effectively terminated during the transition to the Republic.

Analysts have been mixed in their assessment of 'etatism'. The World Bank[6] has commented favourably on the progress which it made possible; and Griffin[7] has noted that nearly all investment during the 1930s was financed from internal sources, though he accepts that the approach became inflexible and less efficient after Atatürk's death. With the benefit of hindsight, it is probably fair to claim that its greatest limitation was the low priority it gave to agriculture and rural development.

It was sometime, however, before economic policy directly affected the growth of urban areas and this period experienced only a slow increase in urban population. Urban areas (settlements of 10,000 or more inhabitants) numbered only sixty-six and accounted for a mere 16.4 per cent of the total population in 1927. There were only two cities (Istanbul and Izmir) with more than 100,000 people and a further three (Izmit, Adana and Bursa) with more than 50,000. Between 1927 and 1939 average annual population growth for the whole country was 2.3 per cent, slightly less than the comparable growth figure of 2.5 per cent for the urban population. Partly because of this slow pace of urbanization, Ottoman building regulations continued to be employed in the major urban areas until the late 1920s, whilst town planning activities were restricted to the drawing up of sketch plans for small towns affected by fires or other natural disasters such as earthquakes[8].

There were, however, four laws passed during this period which were subsequently to have a major impact upon urban development and town planning practice. The Illegal Buildings Act (Law No. 486) was passed in 1924 to permit the demolition of any building constructed on land for which the occupant did not have legal title. As will be seen in the case study of Ankara (see pp. 189–95), however, the usual interpretation of the law required that a court order be obtained before an *inhabited* building could be demolished, and this was commonly invoked by settlers to delay and eventually frustrate the authorities. Then, the 1930 Public Hygiene Act (Law No. 1593) empowered municipalities to introduce a form of land use zoning by distinguishing between residential and industrial zones, making possible the isolation of establishments diffusing noxious and unpleasant effects (smoke, dust, odours, etc.).

The third important Act passed during this period was the 1930 Municipal Act (Law No. 1580) which established a number of local authorities in accordance with the Constitution of 1924. Prior to this Act, local government had no statutory powers and even after 1930 municipalities were given a relatively minor role and were denied independent sources of revenue. Even local property taxes were paid direct to the state Treasury and councils were dependent upon grants from central government to carry out their mandatory functions, one of which included the preparation of master plans. This contradiction between financial and administrative dependence and political autonomy at the local level strongly influenced the nature of government action in several sectors, particularly housing and urban development. The demands upon central government created a bureaucratic chain of command which seriously delayed and undermined project planning and implementation. When Turkey became a multi-party state in 1946, political parties at local level frequently attempted to exploit such administrative bottlenecks in an attempt to frustrate what they considered to be unacceptable policies of the national government of the day, which in turn retaliated by threatening to cut off the supply of grants and other revenue to troublesome councils. Inevitably, this process inhibited the effectiveness of both central and local government still further.

The fourth significant piece of inter-war legislation was the 1933 Municipal Roads and Buildings Act (Law No. 2290), which required all municipalities, regardless of their size, to prepare a fifty-year development plan within a period of five years. The scope of such plans was limited to the regulation of street and block dimensions, building densities and day-lighting regulations; little attention was given, however, to planning for future city growth and development.

It should be remembered, of course, that the 1933 Act was passed at a time of slow urban growth when municipal councils had scant financial, technical and human resources. As urban growth rates began to increase during the 1940s and 1950s, the inadequacy of the Act's provisions and of local government in general became all too apparent. By 1957, when the law was superceded, only 58.5 per cent of municipalities had actually prepared their plans and not one had been effectively implemented.

During the years preceding World War II, government policies exhibited a concern for urban form rather than function. The main policy considerations were the appearance and arrangement of individual buildings rather than their use or location within the city. Rigid zoning regulations were put into effect to achieve these objectives and the approach tended to reflect, in a crude way, the theories of foreign planners who were active in Turkey at this time (see for example, Jansen's Master Plan for Gaziantep – figure 6.2).

Rural–urban migration was significant enough in the inter-war period to put

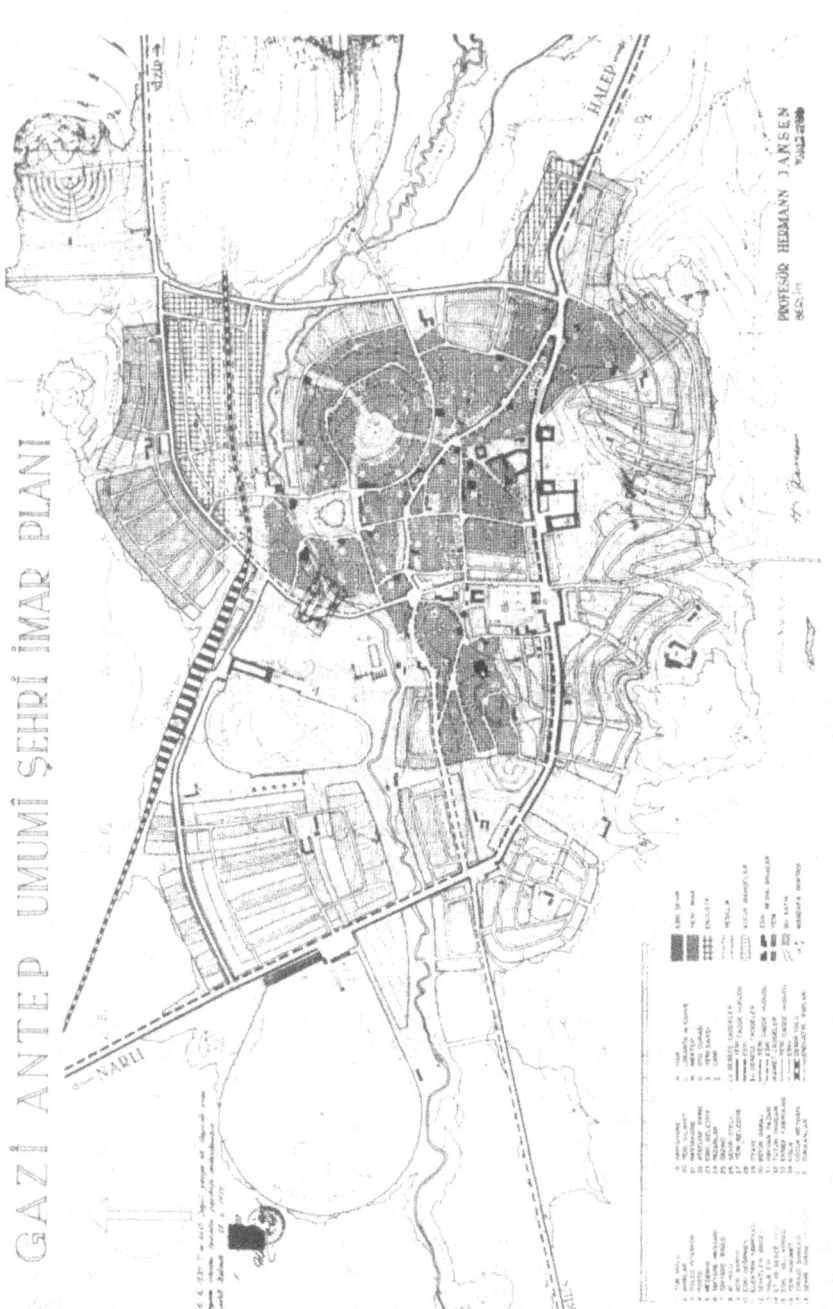

FIGURE 6.2. The master plan for Gaziantep prepared by Hermann Jansen. The main land-use zonings are: old city (eski şehir), proposed areas of new development (yeni imar), industry (endustri), green zones (yeşillik), small gardens (küçük bahçeler), and existing/planned offices (eski/yeni resmi binalar).

pressure upon governments to deal with the growth problems of the metropolises. Ankara received top priority simply because its new status as the national capital caused an unexpected influx of population into the city, together with the related problems of a housing deficit and land speculation. T. R. Aras, the then Foreign Minister, complained that the government was incapable of keeping the ambassadors of foreign states in the capital because accommodation and urban facilities were largely lacking; and even the government's decision to provide free urban land lots for the construction of official residences for such personnel had no immediate effect[9].

Measures taken to ensure the planned development of Ankara and other major cities were influenced by aesthetic rather than economic considerations. However, as was the case with the Municipal and Public Hygiene Acts, the health of people living in urban centres was accorded prime importance by Atatürk, and his etatist economic policies attached great impoortance to the balanced distribution of wealth and decentralization of population. It was, however, some time before these policies began to show results; and indeed, the centralized nature of the administration was reflected in the 1933 Municipal Roads and Buildings Act, which established detailed planning and construction standards for all cities regardless of their individual characteristics.

### Ankara in the Inter-War Period

In keeping with the fluctuations of history in Anatolia and the Near East generally, Ankara has had a chequered past. It was a local centre as early as the Hittite period (about 1700–1200 BC) and became a major provincial town under the Romans because of its strategic location on the Trans-Anatolian highway. Subsequent events were more varied and it was attacked by Persians, Arabs, Crusaders and Seljuks before settling into comparative obscurity as a market town in the Angora wool area, a name at one point given to Ankara itself. Throughout this period, the need for strong defences led to the majority of the town's population living at high density within the citadel, or one of the outer walls surrounding what is now Ulus; only a few summer houses belonging to merchants existed in the hills surrounding the city (figure 6.3). Following a major fire in 1915, which destroyed two-thirds of the town, the population in 1918 was about 20,000, and, compared to other provincial towns such as Konya and Kayseri, Ankara was unimposing.

The town's revival and rapid growth during the present century stems partly from its strategic location in the centre of Anatolia, Turkey's neglected heartland, and partly from the support which the town gave to Mustafa Kemal Atatürk during his campaign to save the country from dismemberment after World War I. It was nominated as the new capital in 1923.

The first plan for the city was prepared by a German named Heussler in 1924, and was partly implemented. The plan located the main administrative

174   PLANNING AND URBAN GROWTH IN SOUTHERN EUROPE

FIGURE 6.3. Housing in the old part of Ankara.
Many of the hills surrounding the city (background) have experienced illegal *gecekondu* development since the war.
*Photo:* G. K. Payne.

and commercial complexes, called Yenişehir (literally 'new city'), on flat land about 2 km south of the old town Ulus, which was left to perform its traditional functions as a regional market centre. To assist implementation of the plan, a special Expropriation Act (Law No. 583) was passed in 1925 to provide the city authorities with the necessary powers to expropriate about 4 km² of land at values which were fixed beforehand at fifteen times the level declared in 1915 for tax purposes[10]. Since this was based upon agricultural use, such a valuation was extremely low; indeed, the area now occupied by Atatürk Boulevard – the city's main commercial street – was acquired for as little as 1 TL a square metre, or less than half a U.K. penny at 1980 prices[11]. In 1928, the Ankara Planning Department was established as the agency responsible for implementing the city plan. It consisted entirely of appointed members responsible directly to the Ministry of the Interior and thereby ensured central government control over decision-making. The Department was also authorized to approve master plans for other cities as required.

At the initiative of Ankara Şehremaneti (municipality), an international competition was held in the late 1920s to select a more comprehensive plan for the city. The winning solution (figure 6.4) was also designed by a German planner – Hermann Jansen – and was formally approved in 1932. The Jansen Plan provided the main structural features for the subsequent growth of the city and projected a 'final' population of 300,000. It placed great emphasis upon

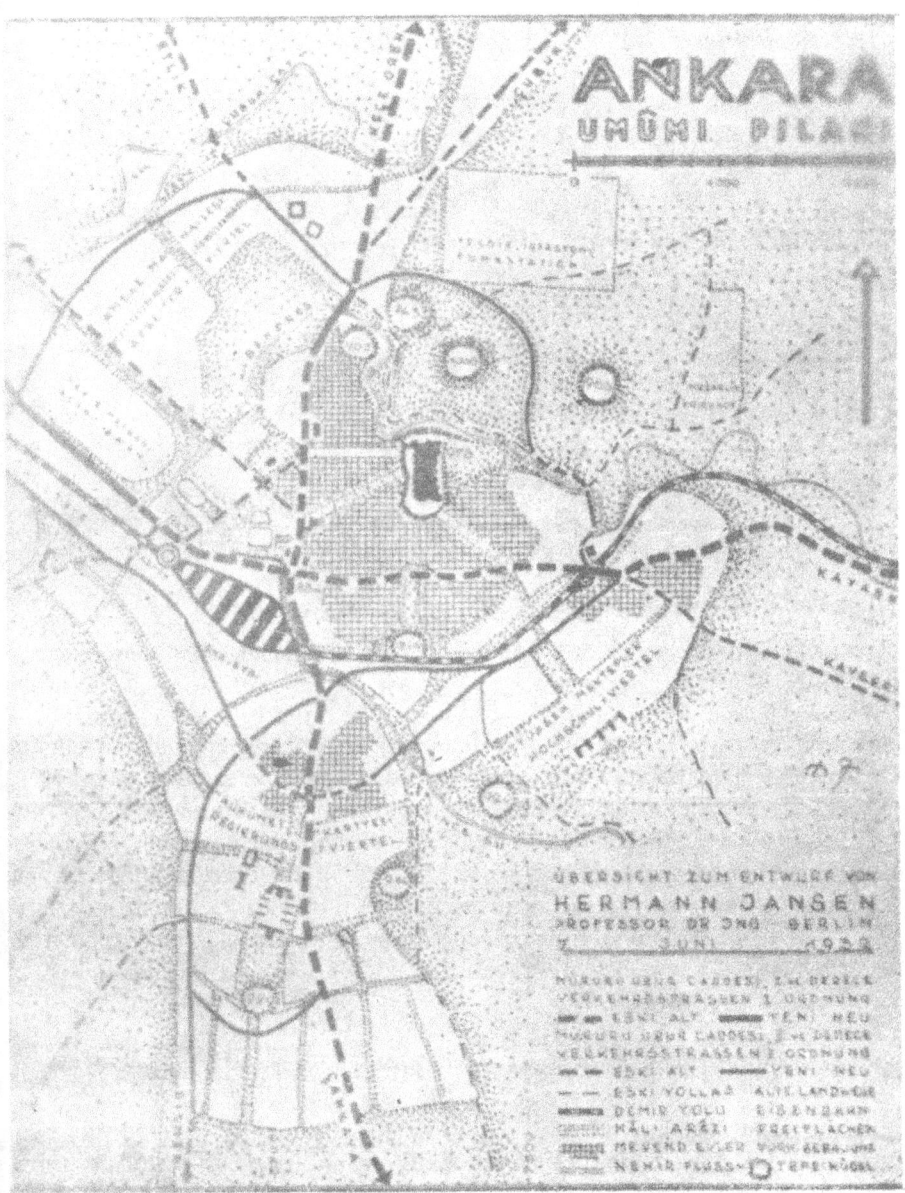

FIGURE 6.4. The Jansen master plan for Ankara, 1932.

the need for planned growth, the rapid provision of housing, control of land speculation, the provision of parks and other public spaces and the conservation of the medieval citadel area. Central government undertook to provide housing or rent subsidies for all civil servants transferred from Istanbul, whilst most private companies did the same for their own employees (figure 6.5). Incentives

FIGURE 6.5. Typical suburban town house, built for early middle-class households. *Photo:* G. K. Payne.

were also given to co-operatives, so that most people were able to obtain adequate housing within a reasonable period despite the rapidity of growth. The 20,000 population of the small market town in 1920 grew to 75,000 in 1927, and by 1945 Ankara was a city of almost a quarter of a million people. Rural–urban migration only started at the end of this period and was not numerically significant, so that at this stage of Ankara's development, its planners could justifiably congratulate themselves on having effectively regulated both the rate and the nature of growth.

### MIGRATION AND URBAN GROWTH IN THE POSTWAR PERIOD

Turkey's socio-economic history in the postwar era may be divided into two parts. The first is a liberal period extending up until the early 1960s, during which time there were no attempts to intervene in the market economy. Reliance upon foreign aid and capital to fuel the development process was the striking characteristic of economic policy; the development of the highway network for example was accomplished largely with foreign aid. The need for a centrally planned economy for a developing country was not accepted by the political elite of the time, and this pro-Western multi-party system continued up to 1960.

The second period, starting from the early 1960s, is marked by an official commitment to central economic planning. All economic sectors were viewed as a whole in an attempt to increase productivity. In national-economic development plans, attention was paid to the location of investments and to the role of cities in national development. For the first time, the importance of housing, urbanization, regional development and rural settlement was given official recognition in development plans. Although the targets of these plans were indicative for the private sector and imperative only for the public sector, they nevertheless influenced the geographical distribution of population and economic activities in the following years. Most of the legislation enacted during the last two decades has been rooted in the proposals laid down in these development plans. It is worth underlining, however, that even in this planned development period, a mixed economy and the characteristics of a pro-Western multi-party democracy still prevailed, although in the late 1970s and 1980s this has been punctuated by periods of military rule.

An important consequence of economic changes following World War II has been the rapid urbanization of the country, a process specifically encouraged by government policy throughout the period. Turkey's urban population increased from 18.1 per cent in 1945 to 42.0 per cent in 1975, bringing an additional 12 million people into urban centres; and it is estimated that at least 20 million more people will be living in urban areas by the end of the century. As table 6.1 shows, national urban and total populations grew rapidly in the 1950s and 1960s as growth of the rural population decreased. Although the crude birth rate has been declining since 1955, the death rate has declined even faster. Data published by the World Bank[12] indicate that the birth rate remained relatively high at 39.6 per 1000 in 1966–67 with a reduced but still high death rate of 14.6 per 1000 (compared with about 10 per 1000 in Western Europe). Since 41.6 per cent of the total population in 1970 were in the 0–14 age group, it can be expected that high population growth rates will be maintained for at least the near future. Indeed, the State Planning Organization

TABLE 6.1. Urban and rural population growth 1950–80.

| Year | Urban Population* No. | % of total | Rural Population No. | % of total | Total Population |
|---|---|---|---|---|---|
| 1950 | 3,923,852 | 18.74 | 17,010,818 | 81.26 | 20,934,670 |
| 1955 | 5,414,884 | 22.44 | 18,715,894 | 77.56 | 24,130,778 |
| 1960 | 7,189,122 | 25.85 | 20,620,709 | 74.15 | 27,809,831 |
| 1965 | 9,343,006 | 29.76 | 22,048,201 | 70.24 | 31,391,207 |
| 1970 | 12,734,761 | 36.02 | 22,870,415 | 63.98 | 35,605,176 |
| 1980 | 20,330,065 | 45.40 | 84,406,882 | 54.60 | 44,736,957 |

*Settlements with a population of 10,000 or more.
Source: National Population Census, State Institute of Statistics

TABLE 6.2. Urban population growth 1927–80.

| Population of Urban Area (thousands) | Percentage of Total Urban Population (and Number of Cities) | | | |
|---|---|---|---|---|
| | 1927 | 1945 | 1975 | 1980 |
| 10–20 | 24 (38) | 23.2 (58) | 12.5 (154) | 10.8 (166) |
| 20–50 | 28.9 (23) | 25.0 (30) | 16.5 (89) | 15.2 (112) |
| 50–100 | 9.3 (3) | 11.5 (6) | 9.5 (24) | 10.7 (23)* |
| Over 100 | 37.8 (2) | 40.3 (4) | 61.5 (25) | 63.3 (29) |
| Total | 100.0 (66) | 100.0 (98) | 100.0 (292) | 100.0 (330) |

*Source:* National Population Census, State Institute of Statistics.
*The decrease in the number of cities in this category is explained by an amalgamation of municipalities of this size in the late 1970s.

recently predicted a population growth rate of 2.75 per cent for the period 1980–85, declining gradually to 2.01 per cent by 1990–95[13].

The substantial transfer of population from rural to urban areas has not been spread evenly over different urban size categories. Instead, migratory movement has focused mainly on the largest and medium size cities with populations of 100,000 or more (see table 6.2). Thus, although the annual growth rate of the total population has been above 2.5 per cent since 1950, the greater part of urban population growth has been the result of rural–urban migration.

As in most countries, there are several reasons for this phenomenon. The emphasis placed on industrial expansion since the inter-war period inevitably reduced investment available for agriculture at a time when it had still not recovered from nineteenth-century administrative abuses. In addition, the concentration of land hoildings caused by the commercialization of agriculture in large parts of Western Anatolia and the continued power of feudal ağas or barons in the east, combined to make the already marginal productivity of labour even lower. Attempts at land reform in the inter-war years had made little impact and a further attempt in 1945 aroused intense political opposition from both the right and left, so that this too met with only limited success. Not only was agricultural productivity therefore low, but the prospects for many villagers obtaining adequate land on which to earn a reasonable living were remote and the situation was not getting better; a survey conducted in 1970 revealed that although agriculture accounted for 66.41 per cent of the country's economically active population, it only received 30.8 per cent of aggregate national incomes and within the sector, the lowest 20 per cent of the population received only 6 per cent of incomes, whilst the highest 20 per cent received 49.6 per cent[14].

Under such conditions, the attraction of urban areas was obviously considerable, and soon after 1945 the opportunities for gaining access to them improved. Among the massive programmes initiated under the Marshall Aid

Plan following World War II was a rapid expansion of the national road network. In 1947, Turkey had only 12,000 km of all-weather roads, but by 1967 this had increased to 42,000 km and the number of vehicles increased from 15,000 to 225,000 during the same period[15]. Although this programme was intended mainly to serve military objectives (enabling army units to get quickly to Turkey's borders), it also opened up or improved access to many of the country's rural areas and unintentionally linked them to the major cities. It was not long before people put the roads to use and began to move to the cities.

In the initial stages of migration, the attraction of the main centres of population lessened with distance, since increased distance raised the costs which had to be set against anticipated income. This was subject to considerable variation, however, and appears to be decreasing recently as further improvements have been made in transportation and the information available to potential migrants. The first migrants were generally adult males who arrived in cities on their own to establish a foothold in the urban economy before bringing their families to join them. Extensive informal networks quickly developed between towns and villages and migrant groups in the cities, to help new migrants with jobs and housing and also to help them to adjust to city life[16].

Despite limited access to the small and primarily capital-intensive industrial sector and subsequent confinement within the less productive but labour-intensive service sector, migrant groups consistently demonstrated an ability to increase their incomes to well above those attainable in the rural sector and frequently higher than the income levels of the indigenous urban poor. They also manifested lower levels of un- and under-employment and remitted considerable sums in small amounts to their home town or village.

A further feature of migration in Turkey which deserves mention is international migration. Although this was negligible until the 1960s, it grew rapidly to reach a level of 189,000 people in 1966 and 625,000 in 1972 *excluding* considerable numbers of illegal migrants[17]. Paine[18] has estimated that by 1973 there were over half a million Turks working in West Germany alone. The remitted earnings of such workers represented a major source of Turkey's foreign exchange, but tended to generate inflation in land values within rural areas and provincial centres which in turn generated secondary migration to cities[19] and, as such, further intensified urban growth rates.

Migration has inevitably strained the ability of cities to generate adequate productive employment or services such as housing. Rather than becoming the dynamic centres of economic development, absorbing surplus agricultural labour, as had been envisaged in national strategic planning, cities witnessed instead major expansion in their less productive but labour-intensive service sectors[20].

The impact of these changes upon individual cities naturally varied. Istanbul, the old Ottoman capital, had always had a large industrial and commercial sector with a number of diversified employment and housing areas.

Access for new migrants to a place of work was therefore relatively easy from any part of the city. Ankara, on the other hand, was never an industrial city and although it became the fastest growing city in the country, it was only fourteenth in terms of industrial production by the late 1970s. Spatially, the old centre of Ulus became the main reception area for incoming migrants, though later on the entire city was surrounded by low-income settlements.

Although the drive to industrialize was a major generator of urban growth, by the early 1960s it was clear that it had failed to keep pace with urban population growth. Furthermore, the emerging form of urban development exacerbated regional and rural-urban imbalances, together with those between different city size categories and the striking socio-economic imbalances and class contradictions within large urban centres. For example, a World Bank study showed that in 1975, 35,000 villages lacked electricity and 22,000 were without running water. Less than one-sixth of all rural households had electricity or running water in 1970, while two-thirds of the urban households had water, and more than three-quarters received electricity. On the other hand, the concentration of major urban centres in western Turkey has affected the distribution of a wide range of activities, resources and services among the different sections of the nation. In 1970, the most developed regions accounted for 45 per cent of all public credits, while eastern Anatolia received only 22 per cent[21].

Whether these differences serve to radicalize the political behaviour of the urban poor remains to be seen, though the violence which erupted during the 1970s reflected serious political instability. The nature of intra-urban imbalances can be illustrated by income differentials. A survey conducted in Istanbul in 1971, for example, indicated that the poorest 24 per cent of households received only 5.2 per cent of the total city income, whilst the wealthiest 13 per cent received as much as 46 per cent[22]. It also showed that 42 per cent of households in the areas occupied by unauthorized settlements received monthly incomes of less than 1000 TL (about U.K. £16 in 1975).

It is, in fact, the predominance of these low income levels, combined with the inability of the public sector to provide substantial quantities of inexpensive housing, which led to the most dramatic aspect of Turkey's urban growth, the *gecekondus*. This term (literally 'landed by night') was originally applied to settlers who occupied a plot of land and, with the help of friends and relatives, actually built and inhabited a house overnight, thus making a court order necessary before demolition by the authorities could take place (Illegal Buildings Act, 1924). It has since been applied to *all* housing built without an official construction permit, irrespective of land tenure status (figure 6.6). For example, a house built without a construction permit on land for which the occupant had freehold title was officially classified as a *gecekondu*, along with squatter dwellings on public land. Yet even those settlers without formal title could claim traditional precedent for their actions, since anyone was entitled under Ottoman law to occupy unclaimed state land to farm or build a house,

FIGURE 6.6. Unauthorized construction even included upper-income housing in many Turkish cities. In this example, from Ankara, traditional *gecekondus* are built on the hills with multi-storey *gecekondus* in the valley. Neither are officially approved.
*Photo:* G. K. Payne.

TABLE 6.3. The growth of *gecekondus* and *gecekondu* population, 1955–1980.

| Year | Total Urban Population (1) | Gecekondu Population (2) (000s) | % (2/1) | Total Urban Housing Units (3) (000s) | Number of Gecekondus (4) (000s) | % (4/3) |
|---|---|---|---|---|---|---|
| 1955 | 5,324,397 | 250 | 4.69 | 1050 | 50 | 4.76 |
| 1960 | 7,307,816 | 1200 | 16.42 | 1440 | 240 | 16.67 |
| 1965 | 9,395,159 | 2150 | 22.88 | 1880 | 430 | 22.87 |
| 1967 | 10,437,233 | 2250 | 21.56 | 2100 | 450 | 21.43 |
| 1970 | 12,734,761 | 3000 | 23.55 | 2800 | 600 | 21.43 |
| 1980 | 20,330,065 | 4750 | 23.36 | 4500 | 950 | 21.11 |

*Source:* Inkaya, Y., Türkiye-De Cumhuriyet Devrinin Başindan Günümüze kadar konut sorunu *Mimarlik*, 72/9, p. 55

providing he paid taxes for the right to use the land. Such practices conflicted, of course, with the development plans and zoning regulations being applied in the cities, and initially *gecekondus* were therefore demolished. The scale of in-migration gradually made such approaches ineffective however, and by 1946, when Turkey became a multi-party state, politicians in opposing parties realized the potential votes the *gecekondu* residents represented. Consequently, more pragmatic policies were developed to upgrade and regularize *gecekondu* areas and their numbers grew rapidly, as shown in table 6.3.

If the *gecekondus* illustrate the substantial socio-economic disparities within

Turkish cities, it should also be stated that as a *form* of housing provision they have considerably mitigated the impact of such imbalances. Households were able, at least until recently, to obtain a plot of land free or at modest cost levels near centres of employment, and to control the extent and phasing of their expenditure on housing. The tendency since the mid-1970s for *gecekondus* to be incorporated into speculative land transfer markets, and for building costs to be integrated into a system of petty commodity production, has changed the nature of *gecekondu* processes and considerably reduced their advantages to settlers, so that the impact of existing economic imbalances is now at least as extreme as the data indicate.

### PLANNING LEGISLATION AND MACHINERY IN THE POSTWAR PERIOD

The development of new planning machinery began early in the postwar period, after police provoked a riot in İstanbul by demolishing a number of *gecekondus* in 1947. The issues raised by this event, and the consequent awareness of public officials that such settlements were emerging in the centre of the national capital, led to two acts being passed in 1948. The Squatter Areas Act (Law No. 5218) recognized the contribution that low-income households made to the urban economy and empowered municipal authorities to upgrade squatter areas and allot parcels of land to potential builders. The Building Subsidies Act (Law No. 5228), on the other hand, permitted land to be sold on a cost basis to co-operatives, and assisted individuals who could prove that they did not already own a house. Tax concessions were offered and credit for up to 75 per cent of the cost was made available through the State Housing Bank.

These progressive pieces of legislation did not, however, achieve their objectives, since only those with some capital and the willingness to accept long distances to work from poorly-located new estates could benefit. The growth of *gecekondu* areas not only continued but in some cities actually escalated[23]. Despite police attempts at demolition, many settlers enlisted the support of Democratic Party leaders and Sewell has cited a case in which police resorted to cutting off a settlement's water supply, only to find that a local politician authorized a municipal water tanker to be sent to the area. With politicians vying for support after 1950, attitudes towards the *gecekondu* areas became even more ambiguous, a situation which was reflected in the Building and Unauthorized Construction Act (Law No. 6188), passed in 1953. This laid down that state owned land lacking a specific use could be acquired by municipalities for allocation as housing sites. As the area of land affected was often substantial, many *gecekondu* settlers subsequently claimed legal tenure and some titles were actually issued.

In 1957, the Ministry of Reconstruction and Resettlement was established with extensive responsibilities for the formulation of settlement policies and the planned development of towns and cities. To coincide with this and to clarify urban policy, a new Town Planning Act (Law No. 6785) was passed and, although amended in 1972, it is still in force today. This Act established responsibilities for the preparation of master plans and required all municipalities with populations in excess of 5000 to prepare such plans. Two types of plan were required: urban development plans, showing major urban land use zones and strategies, and implementation plans, including a phased programme of development.

Under the 1957 Act, central government was entrusted with the approval of development plans, and responsibility for this was vested in the Ministry of Reconstruction. The Ministry could act in one of three ways on the receipt of a plan from a municipality: it could reject it, refer it back for specified changes, or adopt it after making any changes considered necessary. However, the central government's representative in each city – the governor or sub-governor – exercised control over local councils in both the preparation and implementation of master plans. Plans were required to be based upon detailed surveys of economic and social conditions and local land-use characteristics, and were prepared for periods of twenty years. No public discussion was permitted during the plan preparation period nor were people invited to express opinions on the proposals. However, once a plan was approved by the Ministry, it was made public for 30 days before being put into effect to enable interested parties to appeal to the Council of State, Turkey's administrative court of appeal.

The law required that development plans be prepared by one of several institutions – the municipal councils, the Ministry of Reconstruction and Resettlement or the publicy owned Bank of Local Authorities (İller Bankası). The latter was empowered to give municipalities interest-bearing loans for capital construction and to provide them with various kinds of financial and technical assistance. The sources of its aid were national tax revenues and the contribution of local government units to its capital. Eighty per cent of the urban allocations of national taxation were divided between all cities according to their population size[25], and the remaining 20 per cent went into a special fund to provide smaller cities of 50,000 people or less with interest-free loans. The bank then acted as a co-ordinator between the central government and local authorities. Central government assisted the bank by making transfers direct from its budget to guarantee municipal debts. Its technical services included mapping, the preparation of master plans, and designing and constructing water supply and electrification projects. Another public bank attached to the Ministry, the State Housing Bank (Türkiye Emlak ve Kredi Bankası) was established to assist low- and middle-income families participate in large housing projects, and it soon became the country's largest source of mortgage finance, with most of its funds coming from the central Treasury.

Finally, the 1957 Act required all prospective builders to obtain a construction permit or licence from their local authorities to ensure that they conformed with the relevant master plan as well as relevant building regulations and bye-laws. In practice, however, most plans failed to anticipate subsequent urban growth rates, and many buildings were completed without permits – hence their inclusion under the label of *gecekondu*.

With many police forced by low salaries to live in *gecekondus* themselves, the occasional attempts at demolition during the late 1950s were at best half-hearted. Sewell[26] lists another reason as the reluctance of officials to be seen to force inhabitants, especially women, to leave their houses for fear of being charged with assault; and he suggests that a policy of 'selective' demolition followed, in which the worst house out of a given group was demolished and the others left. Not surprisingly, this acted as a good incentive to build a house well and maintain it in good condition!

The First Five Year Plan, introduced in 1963, insisted that further urban growth be limited to match the availability of employment opportunities and proposed the balanced growth of the country's regions (with priority given to eastern Anatolia). It also identified three policy objectives for urban centres: the renovation of existing squatter areas by providing them with service infrastructure, the clearance of the poorest quality squatter settlements, and the prevention of the development of new squatter areas. These objectives were subsequently incorporated into the first legislation specifically concerned with *gecekondus*, the Gecekondu Act (Law No. 775) of 1966. This spelt out in some detail the approach to be adopted and the intended means of implementation. The definition of *gecekondus* used in the Act was somewhat sweeping and thus included a large proportion of the total urban housing stock. The Act provided for the improvement of *gecekondu* areas through credit loans to householders for house renovation, and by improving physical infrastructure and services. *Gecekondus* were to be cleared where the cost of improvement was prohibitive or where the area was subject to landslides, floods or other dangers, and a four-point policy to relieve the pressures generating *gecekondus* was introduced. Apartments were to be built for low-income households on longer-term, low-interest mortgages, and 'core-houses' constructed with loans made available for their completion. Serviced plots and prepared building projects were also set aside for low-income groups and sites and credits provided for co-operatives.

The emphasis which this legislation put upon the upgrading of all *gecekondu* housing represented a radical departure from conventional approaches to unauthorized housing in an urbanizing country. Also significant was the acceptance by the government of responsibility for the rehousing of families cleared from the worst *gecekondus*. This not only gave them extra security, but ensured that no demolition could take place unless alternative accommodation was available. In view of the limited resources of local government, this in effect meant that its role was a modest, supportive one. An additional clause stated that the Act only applied to houses existing at the time it was passed, though it appears that the extension of such deadlines has almost become an annual event. A new law (No. 2805) was passed in 1983 and modified in 1984 'pardoning' all squatter houses built before June 1981 and all illegal buildings constructed before October 1983. It is estimated that about 1.5 million dwellings or other buildings will benefit from this law. Where possible, they will be given occupancy permits and land titles.

The same approach was followed in the Second Five Year Plan (1968–73), but under the terms of the Third and Fourth Five Year Plans (1973–77; 1978–83) greater emphasis was laid upon public sector provision of large-scale housing projects and the acquisition of urban land to reduce speculation and increase access for those unable to obtain a plot at market prices. Then, with the approval of a new Housing Act (Law No. 2487) in July 1981, a Public Housing Fund, based on a yearly 5 per cent of the state budget, was set up to increase the supply of social housing. This marked the abandonment of the idea that direct state investment in housing was unproductive. The Act introduced various incentives for the operation of housing cooperatives, their unions and social security agencies. These included long-term mortgage credit, lower interest rates and facilities for obtaining cheap land. Generally speaking, smaller housing schemes of 750 to 1000 units will tend to benefit from the incentives provided, though their longer term impact upon housing demand remains to be seen.

In 1972, an amendment (Law no. 1605) was passed to the 1957 Town Planning Act. This raised the size of settlements for which urban development plans were to be prepared from 5000 to 10,000 except in the case of towns which were provincial centres, or others which were expanding rapidly. The latter was at the discretion of the Ministry of Reconstruction and Resettlement and a further clause empowered them to prepare such plans for any other settlements in special cases. These included areas where natural disasters (fires, earthquakes, etc.) had occurred, towns where the prevention, rehabilitation or renovation of squatter settlements made a development plan necessary, and metropolitan centres comprising more than one unit of local government. The amendment Act also made it necessary for settlements between 5000 and 10,000 and for the sub-provincial centres to designate the main roads along which future development should take place. On balance, therefore, the law only exempted a number of very small settlements from previous responsibilities, but tended to increase the control of central government agencies over planning machinery in all other urban areas.

When urban growth began to accelerate immediately after World War II, much of the land outside city boundaries was both undeveloped and unclaimed. As such, it was officially state property and could be acquired for development by government departments. Some areas had become virtually freehold, however, and were acquired on the basis of a fixed cost as discussed previously (see p. 182).

As demand for land increased, public areas came under pressure from low-income migrants for *gecekondu* construction, whilst the price of freehold land rose steadily. By the 1970s, most available public land within and beyond city boundaries had been occupied (figure 6.7) and freehold land costs had

FIGURE 6.7. Illegal development crammed between the formally planned areas of Ankara, built as part of the early master plan.
*Photo:* G. K. Payne.

TABLE 6.4. Land prices in Ankara, 1924–69.

| Year | Total Land Value (1973 equivalent prices) TL 000s | Area (ha) | Wholesale Price Index |
|---|---|---|---|
| 1924 | 38,325 | 21,000 | 21 (the year 1938) |
| 1953 | 2,363,800 | 21,000 | 100 |
| 1969 | 45,856,535 | 21,000 | 299 (the year 1965) |

*Source:* Mimarlar Odası (1973) *Kent Topraklari Sorunu*, p. 52.

escalated dramatically (see table 6.4 for an example from Ankara); the lack of land for development had become one of the major impediments to orderly urban growth.

The first official attempt at control came in 1969 with the creation of the National Land Agency, which had the responsibility to curb speculation and provide sites for industrial and tourist establishments and low-cost housing projects. The agency lacked the finance to achieve these objectives, however, and has consequently been regarded as a failure[27]. From 1970 to 1982, property and land taxes were introduced to discourage speculation. These required anyone selling land to pay a sum equivalent to between 15 per cent and 50 per cent of the difference between its value at the time of acquisition and sale, the rate increasing with the value of the site. While in force, such taxes were paid directly to central government rather than to the municipalities or to the Land Agency which needed them for land purchase.

A number of other means for exerting land control were available to municipal or central governments. Among them, the Municipal Act of 1930 empowered councils to buy agricultural land in peripheral locations, but few were able to afford the market costs as required by the 1961 Constitution, since these values were based upon 'developmental' rather than 'existing use' value. City authorities also had certain powers of land expropriation where a site was required for roads, open spaces, etc., providing that at least 75 per cent of the area was redistributed back to its original owners. These powers and rules for compensation were revised by a new law in December 1983. Other controls provided under the 1957 Town Planning Act covered land-use zoning and the height, density and nature of development, but as detailed subdivision plans had to be approved by the Ministry, delays were considerable and speculators or other interested parties were able either to ignore the regulations or revise their declared tax valuations with a view to exacting increased compensation.

The net result of these processes has been the erosion of originally extensive areas of public land within and adjacent to many Turkish towns and cities. Measures taken to control the emerging private land market and land speculation have been too limited and too late. In consequence the opportunities for implementing development plans have steadily declined.

## METROPOLITAN AND REGIONAL PLANNING

In 1968, the problems created by rapidly growing cities and the inadequacies of municipal authorities forced the government to establish metropolitan planning bureaus, charged with research and planning in the country's major cities, including İstanbul, Ankara, İzmir and Bursa. These bureaus are branches of the Ministry of Reconstruction and planning directors of the cities concerned are ex-officio members. The bureaus work in close co-operation with the municipalities within their jurisdiction and have to date surveyed the socio-economic and land-use characteristics of their areas, completed projections about future development and formulated planning policies.

İstanbul Metropolitan Planning Bureau, with an important loan from the World Bank, was involved in producing development plans for the area covering such sectors as urban development, transportation, housing and sewerage systems. Similar development plans have been prepared at regular intervals for Ankara. Since the proposals of these bureaus cannot come into effect until they are approved by municipal councils as the formally constituted authorities, and since these councils have limited financial resources, considerable problems have emerged in translating development proposals into action. Recent emphasis has therefore been placed upon setting up metropolitan government with a certain degree of administrative and financial autonomy. Until recently, however, the 1961 Constitution did not allow central government to establish such intermediate levels of administration, though local authorities had the right to create local unions or consortia to improve the operation of specific functions. Several municipalities (e.g. Zonguldak-Çatalağzi-Kilimli) did make use of this right to set up appropriate metropolitan administrations; and a law enacted on 8 December 1981 (Law no. 2561) empowered the Council of Ministers to merge surrounding smaller municipalities and villages with central, larger municipalities of 300,000 or more inhabitants, in order to ensure the more efficient provision of urban public services. In January 1984, a new law (No. 2972) under article 127 of the new Constitution (1982) authorized the reorganization of the administrative structure of metropolitan areas. In accordance with this law, in March 1984 the government set up a two-tier administration for İstanbul, Ankara and Izmir, with a metropolitan council at the upper level and district councils at the lower level.

At the regional level, demographic evidence suggests that Turkey conforms to the pattern of imbalances found in many rapidly urbanizing countries. Recent trends have indicated a move away from the primacy of major urban centres such as İstanbul towards the increased growth of several medium sized cities, even in the underdeveloped south and eastern regions. This may well be due in part to high costs and unemployment levels in the larger cities, but the tendency must nontheless be seen as a welcome trend for those concerned with achieving a more diversified basis for regional development. Major imbalances still exist, however, and the pro-urban bias of government policy continues.

The statutes of the Ministry of Reconstruction and Resettlement and of the State Planning Organization empower them to prepare regional plans. The former is more concerned with land use and physical development planning and the latter with social and economic development and investment planning. This distribution of responsibilities creates problems of co-ordination and is not without friction, but between them they have prepared projects for Marmara, Çukurova, Keban, Antalya and Zonguldak.

The emphasis on regional planning between 1959 and 1966 gradually increased, with most projects prepared during this period being detailed studies of socio-economic structures, containing a mixture of development proposals. Many of these failed because they did not establish formal mechanisms for project approval and implementation, and because the State Planning Organization did not use its discretionary power in favour of the investment proposals made in the regional plans.

Whilst the need for regional planning has therefore been accepted by central government (which has taken responsibility for it), there is no provision for a dialogue between various levels of government. Plans are merely proposals depending for their implementation upon the State Planning Organization to allocate resources. Legislation requiring the preparation of local development plans in accordance with regional plans is non-existent. Similarly, principles for integrating regional plans with national development plans are not clearly defined.

It is to be hoped that the situation will improve now that a new generation of planners is establishing itself from the planning schools in Ankara, Istanbul, İzmir, Trabzon and Adana. According to the figures of the Chamber of Planners, the number of city and regional planners trained in these institutions plus those educated abroad has reached 350 during the last twenty years. Whilst the size of city or region for which a professional planner is authorized to assume responsibility varies according to his or her age and experience, there is now adequate expertise to meet the country's needs. It is to be hoped that it will be put to good use.

### The Growth of Ankara since the War

The rapid increase in urbanization throughout Turkey since 1945 has had a dramatic impact upon the development of Ankara. Being the national capital and located in the centre of an underdeveloped region, it naturally became the focus of intense migration as peasants were displaced from their land and the traditional products of craftsmen in small towns were replaced by those of new urban industries.

The combination of planned and 'unplanned' growth was such that by 1950 the city had already reached 289,000, near the limit proposed by the master plan only eighteen years earlier. Furthermore, the income levels of the migrants were generally much lower than had been envisaged previously, and most migrants were unable to obtain work or accommodation in the formal private or public sectors as had been assumed when preparing the master plan.

Initially, these pressures led to increased densities in existing built-up areas, especially in the medieval part of the city. This 'solution' soon became inadequate, however, and by the late 1940s, a number of open areas near the old citadel were covered with *gecekondu* settlers exploiting the traditional practice of claiming undeveloped public land (figure 6.8). Most land in Ankara, however, was either in freehold tenure or reserved by the planning authorities for specific uses, so that customary practices conflicted with the master plan, and the police were frequently ordered to demolish offending structures. The ability of the various planning agencies to prevent *gecekondu* construction was restricted, however, by a number of factors.

One of these was the 1924 Illegal Buildings Act which was discussed previously (see p. 170). This required that a court order be made before an inhabited building could be demolished, so any intending settler built as quickly as possible in order to be in occupation before police noticed his dwelling. Traditional rural practices of co-operation were applied to meet this need

FIGURE 6.8. Early *gecekondus* in the old part of Ankara.
*Photo:* G. K. Payne.

and it was common for houses to be built literally overnight. On receipt of a demolition order, the settler simply applied to the courts stating that the building was inhabited. The courts were inundated with such applications and land titles were often far from clear, so the authorities could never guarantee obtaining the necessary orders and gradually ceased to attempt comprehensive demolition.

The financial and technical weakness of the Ankara Council also restricted its ability to provide legal alternatives to *gecekondus*. Municipal budgets were totally inadequate to carry out major projects and in 1948 central government recognized the problem by passing the Squatter Areas and Building Subsidies Acts (see p. 182). Unfortunately however, though progressive in intention, these Acts largely benefited middle or lower-middle income households. In any case, Ankara's master plan was not amended to match the new urban situation, and the basis of decision-making in urban planning gradually moved away from agencies responsible for the master plan towards more pragmatic municipal departments. The authority of the master plan was further eroded in 1946 when Turkey became a multi-party state. No politician wanted to be seen as hostile to the large *gecekondu* population, and many actually joined settlers in opposing police action.

During the 1950s, Ankara continued to grow rapidly. From a population of 289,000 in 1950, it reached 650,000 by 1960 (more than twice the limit proposed by Jansen's master plan), and Robinson has estimated that over half of this increase could be accounted for by the growth of *gecekondus*[28]. By

FIGURE 6.9. Low-income public housing under construction in north Ankara. *Photo:* G. K. Payne.

1963, 64.4 per cent of the city's housing stock consisted of *gecekondus*, accommodating 385,000 people or 59.22 per cent of the city's population. Considering the high total growth, this represented a phenomenal level of locally controlled construction and was one of the highest to be found in an urbanizing country[29]. Central government attempted, in 1958, to impose more conventional policies by replacing part of a densely settled area in the east of the city with medium-rise apartment blocks. The adjoining areas became even more densely settled, however, as extra people moved in to claim elegibility for the legal tenure of a subsidized apartment and the scheme had to be abandoned. Following the military coup in 1960, a final attempt was made to contain *gecekondus* by restricting the provision of public utilities, but within two years this was reversed by a special Act on providing urban public services to *gecekondus* (Law No. 327) in time for the 1963 local elections.

The supportive approach to unauthorized settlement was consolidated in 1966 with the Gecekondu Act (Law No. 775). The main proposals of this Act (see p. 184) were immediately incorporated into Ankara municipality's programme and a number of housing projects were carried out in different parts of the city (figure 6.9). Numerically, however, these constituted a minute proportion of total housing demand and primarily benefited middle-income groups. 'Core' houses were also constructed at Yildizevler, but excessive control over what type of extensions were permitted inhibited their success. Finally, the serviced plots approach also met with failure. Termed *akkondus* by the municipality in order to emphasize the open, legal and acceptable opposite of that implied by the term *gecekondu*, they never attracted popular interest, probably because costs were higher and controls greater than in informal settlements. Delays in developing sites and allocation to potential applicants also

FIGURE 6.10. *Gecekondus* and middle-income apartments in Ankara.
*Photo:* G. K. Payne.

FIGURE 6.11. High-density, high-cost housing in the older residential areas near Ankara city centre.
*Photo:* G. K. Payne.

contributed to their failure, and so these projects were of significance for propaganda purposes only.

Despite such limitations, the support which the Act authorized central and local authorities to give to *gecekondus* enabled most low-income households to obtain housing and services at a cost they could afford. Whilst *gecekondus* did not actually reduce economic disparities between income groups, they did provide migrants with control over the main elements of housing, i.e. location, cost, design, construction, use and management. So successful were they, in fact, that by the late 1960s housing conditions for many *gecekondu* residents were agreeably better than for many middle-income households living in expensive apartments within polluted and overcrowded central locations[30] (figures 6.10 and 6.11).

Another major element in the consolidation of Ankara's *gecekondu* areas was the role performed by *mahalles*. These had been retained from the Ottoman period, and although they possessed no statutory powers or budget, they constituted the smallest unit of urban administration and were also the most common form of government in villages. The head man, or *mukhtar*, of a *mahalle* is legally a representative of the government and is required, amongst other tasks, to keep registers of births, marriages and deaths and of males eligible for military service; but he is also elected by local residents to safeguard their own local interests.

Despite the ambiguous role of *muhtars* and the lack of official status of the *mahalles*, they have proved to be an extremely flexible institution under conditions of rapid urban growth. If the population in any given *mahalle* increased to the point where people were unable to obtain a fair share of municipal budgets, they simply applied to be subdivided into separate *mahalles*, each with its own *muhtar* and claim on municipal revenues. In addition to being a system familiar to everyone in Turkey, *mahalles* provide a local scale to urban government and enable the varied needs of different parts of the city to be identified. They also extend the range of self-help practices into the field of local urban planning by encouraging local communities to participate actively in the affairs of their *mahalle*, leaving government agencies free to concentrate on those tasks for which they are best suited, namely the allocation of appropriate resources to each locality within a framework of strategic development.

The availability of large areas of publicly owned land in most parts of the capital was also a major factor in facilitating *gecekondu* construction and improvement. If they could afford it, most settlers purchased private land, but those who could not afford this were able to obtain a plot on public land within reasonable distance of major centres of employment. At the same time, local control over development enabled settlers to build more leisurely and to a higher standard. Teams of labourers were able to obtain secure employment in house construction, and local building materials suppliers even began to produce their own concrete blocks, doors and window frames to meet demand.

Up until the 1970s, this *ad hoc* basis of public intervention served the city well, though it rendered conventional town planning redundant. There is little reason to assume, however, that the planners would have been more effective. In 1955, when the city had exceeded Jansen's 300,000 population target, an international competition was launched to prepare a new plan. This was won by two Turkish architects, and although their plan allowed for a population of up to 900,000 (with a proposed maximum of 1 million), it was restricted to the existing administrative boundary and therefore excluded much of what at the time was peripheral settlement. As it happened, the projected total population was reached within eight years of the plan's acceptance, making it redundant before it could be effectively be put into practice. By 1970, the population was 1,209,000 and still growing fast.

During the 1970s the limits of *ad hoc* planning began to emerge. There were

FIGURE 6.12. Luxury apartments being built in Ankara on sites previously occupied by *gecekondus* (remaining in the foreground).
*Photo:* G. K. Payne.

FIGURE 6.13. Recent *gecekondu* development on the edge of Ankara. Steep, rocky hillsides make building expensive.
*Photo:* G. K. Payne.

several reasons for this change, but the lack of economic development in the city as a whole was probably the greatest constraint. Ankara's lack of industry and its rapid population growth held incomes down, and Akçura[31] estimated that the state had become the largest single employer, accounting directly or indirectly for one worker in three, whilst most of the remainder worked in the informal service sector.

The sheer size of the city was another major constraint on the success of *ad hoc* planning, in that new migrants had to accept long and expensive journeys to work and were less able to find a piece of public land on which to build a house. Not surprisingly, the increased pressure on remaining land fuelled speculation and even plots without full title began to attract high prices. Few *gecekondu* occupants could afford to resist the opportunity of realizing large profits and becoming the owners of one or more apartments (by selling the 'use-rights' they had to their plot to *emlakcis* (land agents) and *gecekondus* in favoured locations quickly became commercialized (figure 6.12). Instead of obtaining a cheap plot near friends or relatives, new settlers often had to move well out of the city, pay large sums for a plot on exposed hillsides which were difficult to develop, and then live surrounded by strangers (figure 6.13).

Several attempts have been made to assert a measure of control over these speculative pressures, though limited municipal funds and legislation for compensating landowners have impeded the creation of land banks to regulate prices and supply. At the same time, other policy options such as property taxes and land-use controls have not proved effective. Large-scale projects are being developed to the west of the city, though they are several kilometres beyond the present city boundary, and are unlikely to make a significant impact on their own.

The needs of Ankara, now that its population approaches 3 million, are very different to those of twenty years ago, when pragmatic locally-based decision-making served the city so well. It is difficult on present evidence to see how existing trends can be reversed or even contained, without considerably increasing both the powers and resources of local government and the Land Office. So far, the grounds for optimism are limited.

Concluding Remarks: Urban Planning in Historical Perspective

As the case study of Ankara has shown, urban planning in Turkey has been based upon static and conventional concepts; it has been viewed not as a process contributing towards socio-economic development, but as an end in itself. In formulating the goals and methods of plans, no provision has been made for public participation, and the secrecy with which planning decisions were reached left ample scope for vested interest groups to assert their influence. In fact such groups have become extremely successful in modifying plans, and it has become relatively common, for example, for landowners to effect a change in land-use zoning regulations where they find them restrictive.

Thus land officially designated for recreational open space would suddenly appear coloured as suitable for high-rise residential development on official plans. To prevent frequent changes from distorting the integrity of the plans, the Ministry decided in 1978 that no modification could be made to an approved development plan within four years of its approval. Regulations also required adequate and full justification for changes made after this period to prove that they were in the public interest. The reduction of public open space was stated to be an unacceptable basis for such a change. This regulation was, however, abrogated within two years on the basis that the planning process had to be dynamic and flexible under conditions of rapid change[32]. At the same time, it *is* true that the twenty-year period covered by development plans is too long. Their comprehensiveness is also more apparent than real, since there are no linkages between national, regional and local plans to integrate them. More specific strategies are required into which flexible elements and new projects can be fitted.

Another problem concerns the relationship between technical and political aspects of planning. Planning independent of politics, of course, has no validity, though officially this was the view until the 1960s. Later on, close contact between planners and politicians, especially at the local level, gained importance, but the experience of the 1970s suggests that this went too far and enabled vested interest groups to exert too great an influence. A more balanced basis for co-operation would no seem to be needed. So far, planning in Turkey has still to evolve an effective means of coping with the rapid urbanization of a changing society, and urban development has not followed the plans; instead the plans have tended to follow accomplished facts.

NOTES

1. See Berger, Morroe (1964) *The Arab World Today*. New York: Doubleday, pp. 86–90.
2. Ergin, Osman Nuri (1944) *Türk İmar Tarihinde Vakıflar, Belediyeler Ve Patrikhaneler*. Istanbul.
3. Ottoman 'Law on Buildings' (Ebniye Kanunu) (1882) amended by Turkish Law No. 642 (April 22, 1925).
4. See Kaleş, Ruşen (1977) *The National Settlement Patterns and Policies of Turkey*. New York: U.N. Centre for Housing, Building and Planning; Tekeli, İlhan (1973) Evolution of spatial organization in the Ottoman Empire and Turkish Republic; in Carl-Brown, L. (ed.) *From Madina to Metropolis*. Princeton: Darwin Press, pp. 252–9.
5. Lewis, B. (1969) *The Emergence of Modern Turkey*. Oxford: Oxford University Press, p. 283.
6. World Bank (1975) *Turkey: Prespects and Problems of an Expanding Economy*. Washington: IBRD, p. 9.
7. Griffin, K. (1976) *Land Concentration and Rural Poverty*. London: Macmillan, p. 229.
8. Plans drawn up by foreigners for Turkish towns in the 1920s included: a plan

of 1925 for Izmir by Rene Danger, a French planner; a plan for the old part of Ankara by Heussler, a German, in 1925; and other plans for Manisa, Aydın and Nazilli. For more detail see İmar ve İskan Bakanlığı (1973) *50 Yılda İmar Ve Yerlesme: 1923–73.* Ankara, p. 15.
9. Ulug, N. H. and Ankara Kulübü (1973) *Hemşehrimiz Atatürk,* Ankara: Türkiye iş Bankasi, p. 232.
10. Yavuz, F. (1952) The development of Ankara. *Town Planning Institute Journal,* September, p. 251; and Yavuz, F., Keleş, R. and Geray, C. (1978) *Şehircilik,* 2nd ed. Ankara.
11. Erson, L. (1974) Housing in Underdeveloped Countries and in Turkey as a Problem of Underdevelopment. Unpublished Mc.P Thesis, Middle East Technical University, Ankara, pp. 142–3
12. World Bank (1975) *op. cit.,* p. 145 (see note 6).
13. *Ibid.* p. 146.
14. Sunar, I. (1974) *State and Society in the Politics of Turkey's Development.* Ankara University, Faculty of Political Science Publication No. 377, p. 92.
15. Boratav, K. (1972) *Gelir Dağılımı.* Istanbul: Gerçek Yayinevi, p. 195.
16. For a general discussion of such practices, see Payne, G. (1977) *Urban Housing in the Third World.* London: Leonard Hill.
17. World Bank (1975) *op. cit.,* p. 155 (see note 6).
18. Paine, S. (1974) *Exporting Workers: The Turkish Case.* Cambridge: Cambridge University Press, p. 26.
19. Abadan-Unat, N., Keleş, R., *et al.* (1976) *Migration and Development; A study of the effects of international labour migration on Boğazliyan District.* Ankara: Ajans-Türk Press.
20. See Payne, G. K. (1978) *Ankara: Housing and Planning in an Expanding City* (3 vols.), SSRC Research Report, Vol. 1 Part 2.
21. Danielson, M. and Keleş, R. (1980) Urbanization and income distribution in Turkey, in Özbudun, M. E. and Ulusan, A. (eds.) *The Political Economy of Income Distribution in Turkey.* New York: Holmes and Meier, p. 288.
22. *Ibid,* p. 293.
23. Half the entire increase in housing stock between 1950 and 1960 has been estimated by Robinson to have consisted of *gecokondus.* See Robinson, R. (1958) Turkey's agrarian revolution and the problem of urbanization. *Public Opinion Quarterly,* 22, p. 400.
24. Sewell, G. (1964) Squatter Settlements in Turkey: Analysis of a Social, Political and Economic Problem. Unpublished Ph.D. Thesis, M.I.T., pp. 71–2.
25. This arrangement was modified by the Local Government Grant Law (No. 2380), passed in February 1981, in which municipalities received 5 per cent of all tax revenues.
26. Sewell (1964) *op. cit.,* p. 73 (see note 24).
27. Government of Turkey (1976) *Report to the United Nations Habitat Conference.* Ankara: State Planning Organization, p. 20; World Bank (1975) *op. cit.,* p. 173 (see note 6); Erson, L. (1974) *op. cit.,* pp. 204–5 (see note 11).
28. Cited in Sewell (1964) *op. cit.,* p. 71 (see not 24).
29. See World Bank Sector Paper (1972) *Urbanization.* Washington IBRD, Annex 1, Table 6., p. 182.
30. See Payne (1978) *op. cit.,* Vol. 1. Section 3 (see note 20).
31. Akçura, K. (1971) *Ankara.* Ankara: Middle East Technical University, p. 154.
32. *Official Gazette* No. 16959, April 13th, 1980.

# 7
# Concluding Remarks

## MARTIN WYNN

This book set out to examine the processes of urban growth in Southern Europe, and the role planning has played in each of the countries studied, in regulating that growth. In a study such as this, the full story – enormously complex and interwoven with other factors and events as it is – can never be recounted or explained in its entirety, and individual authors' political and ideological standpoints will inevitably influence their historical perspectives. Nevertheless, there are clearly some common features and particular landmarks worthy of final comment.

### TOWN PLANNING ORIGINS AND THE FIRST TOWN PLANS

There is no clear pattern in the emergence or form of early town planning which is common to all five Southern European countries examined in this book, although some similarities between two or more countries are evident. The pace and scale of both urbanization and industrialization, and the relationship between the two, varied considerably from country to country. In Italy, for example, a network of established urban centres within the region-state system preceded nineteenth-century industrialization, whilst comparable urbanization and industrialization came to countries such as Greece and Turkey only in the twentieth century. In all five countries, however, the advent of industrialization was a critical factor in speeding rural-urban migration, and worsening the overcrowded and insanitary conditions which were in part responsible for the early attempts at regulated development and planned growth, albeit on a rather *ad hoc* and piecemeal basis.

The eighteenth and early nineteenth century forerunners to the town plans of the industrial age were born out of different circumstances, but in none of these cases was there a conscious attempt to plan and control growth. Rather they were projects brought about by man-made or natural events on a macroscale. In Portugal, the earthquake of 1755 destroyed half of Lisbon which was subsequently rebuilt in accordance with a gridiron street plan, whilst the demolition of a large part of the Barcelona old city (to make way for the citadel) led to the planning and construction of Barceloneta, the first planned extramural development in Spain.

In a similar category were the 1801 plan for the Bonaparte forum in Milan, which reflected the new cultural and scientific ideas brought by the Napoleonic invasion, and the 1833 plan for Athens, the new capital of the recently founded Greek State. During the eighteenth century the pressure for outward expansion and opening-up of the old cities was only strongly experienced in the major Spanish cities, where the military necessity of retaining the old medieval walls and the early arrival of industrialization led to intensive infilling and upward growth in the old cities from 1750 onwards, and subsequent opening up of new roads and small-scale clearance operations.

It was not until the second half of the last century that the pressures of population and need for more orderly development gave rise to the first major pieces of planning legislation and the first major town plans, although again it is dangerous to generalize for all Southern Europe. In Greece, for example, planning activities sprang essentially from the need to manage competing property and speculation interests, above all in Athens which, in 1860, had a population of only 53,000 (cf. Madrid, 275,000 in 1853, for example). And in Turkey, where the modern state was not founded until the 1920s, the nineteenth century was dominated by the semi-feudal and largely agricultural Ottoman society, although the 1882 Building Act *did* establish significant principles for rebuilding and new development, particularly as regards the cession of land for service infrastructure. But as industrialization and rapid urbanization made their impact in Spain and Italy, and then Portugal, so the first major plans of expansion and renewal appeared, accompanied by legislation that attempted to provide solutions to related issues and problems – road and general service provision, expropriation and property redivision, public management of the implementation of development, and inner-city renewal and conservation.

Of the plans for this period, those for the areas of *ensanche* in the major Spanish cities, and above all that of Ildefonso Cerdà for Barcelona, stand out as conceptually and technically superior to Italian and Portuguese counterparts. Whilst the *ensanche* plans for Madrid (1860) and Barcelona (1859) were all-encompassing blueprints for future city growth, those for Turin (1852), Naples (1888) and the Haussmann-inspired *Avenidas* project for Lisbon in the 1890s were concerned with limited areas of renewal and expansion, reflecting the *ad hoc* conceptual basis for planning and development contained in the major pieces of related legislation. In Portugal, in fact, such legislation was virtually non-existent, and although the 1865 Expropriation Act in Italy drew the distinction between expansion and redevelopment plans, it was not until the twentieth century that the concept of comprehensive town plan appeared. Only in Spain was there even the semblance of a body of legislation setting out the ground rules for planning and growth on a citywide basis (the Acts of 1864, 1875, 1892 and 1895), but these lacked the necessary teeth to provide any effective control on speculative development. At the same time, the need for new plans to encompass the areas beyond the *ensanches* soon became apparent, a shortcoming which was paralleled in other Southern European countries and which led to the need for supra-municipal planning after the turn of the century.

### New Planning Concepts in the Early Twentieth Century

The turn of the century ushered in a new era in the development of Euro-American planning thought. Howard's book, *Tomorrow – Path to Peaceful Reform*, later *Garden Cities of Tomorrow*, was published in 1898 and Camillo Sitte's *City Planning According to Artistic Principles* appeared a year later in German, following on the heels of Stübben's *Der Städtebau*, first published in 1890. A series of international congresses was held in the first twenty-five years of the century, at which new planning ideas and concepts were aired. In general, however, they had rather less impact on planning in Southern Europe than in Britain, Germany or France, for example, whilst Southern Europe itself contributed relatively little to international trends, with the notable exception of the Linear City of Arturo Soria.

It was probably in Spain, in fact, that the cross fertilization and exchange of indigenous and overseas planning concepts and experience were most actively pursued. The failure of the plans of *ensanche* to provide adequate solutions to sprawling radiocentric growth led to the adoption of a new set of plans for the country's major cities in the early part of the twentieth century, with the frequent and significant involvement of architects and planners from abroad. The Garden City concept flourished in Barcelona in the immediate pre-war years under the stewardship of Cebriu de Montoliu and subsequently figured prominently in the 1929 plan for Madrid drawn up by the German planner Herman Jensen and Spanish architect Fernandino Zuazo. In this period, the activities of certain individuals, such as Fernando Mercadal and Hilarion Gonzalez de Castillo, were critical in fostering this exchange of ideas which involved not only the proponents of the Garden City, but also the French architect Jaussely, Stübben and, in the 1930s, Le Corbusier, all of whom drew up plans for major Spanish cities; and it also encompassed the birth of regional planning in Spain, with plans for both the Madrid and Catalan regions appearing in the 1930s. It is, however, the Linear City, closely allied to the Garden

City by some of its major supporters, which alone has made some impact on European and American planning thought, with the Brussels and London plans of Gonzalez de Castillo being two early examples of adaptations abroad.

Elsewhere in Southern Europe, involvement in the international planning scene was also having repercussions on domestic developments in planning. In Italy, the German concept of town planning came to dominate planning thought in the early decades of the century. Stübben's *Der Städtebau* was translated into Italian and became the standard work for the technical aspects of planning. The Garden City movement, on the other hand, had only limited impact in Italy in the early years of the century (mainly under the influence of Schiavi in Milan) but it did resurface in new town schemes both in the Fascist era and in the progressive liberal period immediately after the Second World War, when the plans for four satellite cities outside Milan were drawn up.

Meanwhile, in Portugal, the rapid growth of Lisbon (which passed the half million mark in the 1920s) continued apace within the spatial framework provided by the *Avenidas*, and only in the late 1920s and 1930s were new plans for the city drawn up. As in the *Avenidas* project, the authors of these plans were foreign planners and architects from Northern Europe, but this time no formal approval was given and their impact was minimal. In Turkey, French, German and English planners were also commissioned to draw up master plans for the country's major cities. The most influential was Herman Jansen (co-author of the 1929 Plan for Madrid) whose plan for Ankara in the 1930s embodied the concepts of land-use zoning and functional segregation of space, which he had gleaned as much from his involvement in the international planning scene as from his Germanic background.

In Greece, Athens continued to grow anarchically, with *a posteriori* piecemeal extensions to the city map (still based on the 1833 Kleanthis-Schaubert plan), without any overall planning policy or co-ordination of service and infrastructure provision. Athens passed the 250,000 mark in 1907 (c.f. Madrid, 570,000 in 1900) at a time when the urban primacy of the capital was becoming increasingly marked – a dominance which has become more exaggerated as the century has progressed. However, partly because of Greece's involvement in a succession of wars, the country remained relatively isolated from international planning until the 1920s, when foreign architects, including Frenchman Ernest Hebrard (who was professor at Thessaloniki University), became involved in the design of new rural settlements and city reconstruction. Architects dominated planning practice in Greece and, although many were deeply influenced by rationalism and Le Corbusier in the 1930s (the 1933 Athens Charter followed a CIAM conference in the capital), the unfettered speculative nature of the development process changed little in practice. The influence of CIAM and CIRPAC was also felt in Portugal, briefly, and above all in Spain (under the Second Republic) in the 1930s, and later in Italy after the end of Fascism.

## CONCLUDING REMARKS

### THE FOUNDATION OF MODERN TOWN PLANNING

The inter-war period was an era of emigration and massive rural-urban migration in Southern Europe, an age of World Depression that saw the growth of an urban poor on an unprecedented scale. The provision of housing became a major problem as the early shanty towns sprang up outside the major cities, and the first housing Acts and state-built estates date from this period. This was also the period that produced major new planning legislation in Southern European countries, some of which still provides the basic framework for urban planning today.

The 1923 Town Planning Act in Greece established regulations for the preparation and approval of urban plans at citywide or local level. Although municipal councils were identified as a major plan-making and approval authority, in practice their lack of financial and technical resources meant that central government agencies and the private sector played the leading role in drawing up plans. At the same time, the responsibility for providing public service infrastructure was laid at the door of the local councils which also proved to be unrealistic given their lack of capital. Corruption, political patronage and kinship ties have also played their part in destroying the credibility of the Act, but it remains on the Statute Book today and still provides the basis for planning procedure.

The 1934 and 1944 Planning Acts in Portugal failed to function effectively for similar reasons. The 1934 Act made it compulsory for *all* municipalities to draw up and approve urbanization plans when only a handful could realistically do so. By 1945, only 3 per cent of councils had started work on their plans and the 1944 Act in effect transferred all plan-making and approval responsibilities to the central government. Even then, however, the rate of plan-making remained low, and in 1980 only one in three municipalities had approved plans. Nevertheless, the two Acts, together with the compulsory purchase powers given to the state in 1933 Expropriation Act provided a procedural and legislative framework for plan-making and approval which survived until the 1970s.

In Italy, the 1942 Town Planning Act was technically more advanced than its Greek and Portuguese counterparts. A hierarchy of plans was identified at extra-municipal, municipal and local levels, with all major city councils being made responsible for plan-making; and procedures for the advertisement and approval of plans by local, regional and central governments were established. The municipal *Piani Regolatori Generali* (PRG) became the standard plan type and the Act was of significance in the legislative and procedural framework it provided for plan-making. As regards development on the ground, however, the machinery created by the Act failed to control the urban growth process, largely because it failed to come to terms with the economic and political forces which shaped the nature of development.

Having led the way in the nineteenth century, the evolution of planning legislation in Spain this century in some ways lagged behind that of its Southern European neighbours. Individual plans and local government initiatives in the planning field clearly underlined the need for new plan types to encompass the entire municipality and, in some cases, to go beyond the municipal limits. The 1924 Municipal Statute, however, only consolidated and synthesized previous legislation, and identified three main types of plan – *ensanche*, *extensión* and inner-city reform – all on a sub-municipal scale. It was, in fact, almost a retrograde step back into the previous century, and although the Gijon Congress (inspired by developments within CIAM and CIRPAC) set out the guidelines for more appropriate legislation in 1934, this was not forthcoming until 1956, when the Land and Urban Planning Act created a comprehensive planning machinery comparable with any other in Europe at that time. Again, however, as in the rest of Southern Europe, the functioning of this machinery was severely hampered in practice by lack of local authority resources, contraventions by state authorities themselves, and widespread collusion with private vested interests who exploited certain loopholes and vagaries in the Act itself.

In Turkey, Atatürk's modernization of Ottoman society brought the enactment of new legislation to govern planning and development in a country where the pace of urbanization in general remained slow and yet the primacy of the country's major city (Istanbul) was more marked than in the rest of Southern Europe. The 1933 Municipal Roads and Building Act required all municipalities to prepare fifty-year development plans within five years of the Act, which with hindsight appears absurdly unrealistic and overambitious. The content of such plans was conceptually very limited, containing street and block dimensions, building densities and daylighting norms, although, the influence of foreigners such as Jansen meant that some cities had more sophisticated plans. However, despite the fact that almost 60 per cent of municipalities had approved plans by 1957, their impact on guiding urban growth was limited.

The 1957 Town Planning Act, however, introduced some much needed improvements in planning, with central government ministries and the publicly owned Bank of Local Authorities, as well as municipal councils, being entrusted with plan-making powers. The Bank of Local Authorities was also authorized to make loans for implementing development, thus helping to alleviate the chronic lack of finances suffered by local governments. Twenty-year plans replaced their fifty-year forerunners, and implementation programmes became an integral part of plan documentation. Plan approval powers were vested in the Ministry of Reconstruction and the development control system was tightened up.

Thus, the legislative basis for modern town planning was established in Greece, Italy and Portugal prior to the postwar period, whilst in Spain and Turkey significant advances on the previous existing legislation took place in the 1950s. These planning Acts differed considerably in their scope and in technical and conceptual aspects, there being no reference to land-use zoning or functional differentiation of space in, for example, the Portuguese, Turkish or Greek Planning Acts. In all five countries, however, great emphasis was put on municipal level planning as the corner-stone of the planning system. Even in Italy and Spain, where the 1942 and 1956 Acts envisaged the municipal plan as but one in a hierarchy, it was, in practice, the municipal level plan that constituted the major planning instrument. What all these Acts failed to do, to a greater or lesser extent, was to provide adequate institutional, financial and technical support to enable the town plan and its municipal overseers to function in any workable fashion. Thus in Portugal planning activity remained extremely restricted, whilst in Greece and Turkey, although plans were produced in some quantity, they were technically poorly developed and openly flouted. And in Spain and Italy, although as a technical activity planning made considerable strides in the 1940s and 1950s, it failed to confront effectively the problems of rapid speculative growth in the countries' major urban systems. Let us now turn, then, to examine the resultant form of postwar urban growth in Southern Europe.

PLANNING AND URBAN GROWTH IN THE POSTWAR YEARS

The history of planning and urban growth in the postwar era exhibits certain parallels and common patterns in the countries of Southern Europe. War damage and intensified country-city migration produced enormous housing deficits – an estimated 2.5 million in Italy in 1951 and 1.5 million in Spain in 1955, for example. The typical government response was to encourage the private sector to take the dominant role in housing provision, and resultant city growth frequently paid scant regard to approved plans and regulations[1].

In a period of rapid urbanization, housing deficits remained high, and illegal shanty dwellings spread into the marginal land areas of Southern Europe's major cities, from Oporto and Lisbon to Istanbul and Ankara. At the same time, speculative private development and the increasingly large public housing estates have often been allowed to contravene approved plans, with the resultant high figures for illegal housing. Thus the *bairros clandestinos* in Portugal, the *vivienda marginal* in Spain, the *gecekondus* in Turkey, and the *borghetti* in Italy encompass not only the *de facto* shanty towns, built by the inhabitants themselves, but also a range of other dwelling types all of which have been built illegally. Indeed, in Greece, this phenomenon is so common that no special term is used: between 1945 and 1966, for example, almost half a million people – 45 per cent of the net increase in population in the city – were illegally housed in Greater Athens.

Increased congestion of the city centres and densification of the inner areas has been another characteristic of postwar urban growth, as tertiary activities have come to dominate city centres. This tendency has been recognized in a number of plans which have tried to create new decentralized service (and industrial) centres, and new transportation systems within metropolitan or regional frameworks. Such were the *Planos Directores* for Lisbon and Oporto, Madrid and Barcelona, the supra-municipal plans for Milan, Bologna and Turin, the 'Capital 2000' plan for Athens, and the Metropolitan Development Plans for Istanbul, Ankara and Izmir, all dating from the 1960s or 1970s. None of these plans succeeded in its proclaimed objective however, partly because of the lack of legislative or institutional machinery necessary for implementation; thus they have been overtaken by events, losing both credibility and viability on the way.

This scale of plan has generally represented a departure from terms of reference for planning established in national planning Acts, which is in part a result of the general inadequacy of existing planning machinery to deal with the problems of metropolitan planning and growth. Whilst these more sophisticated plans were left to gather dust, the succession of ministerial reorganizations, continued contraventions of existing planning law by state agencies, and the introduction of urgent measures and special laws have signified increasingly desperate attempts by national governments to ameliorate the results of rapid and largely unfettered urban growth.

In the last decade, reforms and amendments to the existing planning legislation have been introduced in an effort to provide more workable solutions to these problems. The need for such change had an added political dimension with the moves to democracy in Portugal, Spain and Greece in the 1970s, and the heightened awareness and militancy of resident groups throughout Southern Europe. Whilst these reforms have established formal guidelines for metropolitan and regional planning and provided increased flexibility at the city level, it has been at local level that some of the more innovative and significant advances have been made. The Urban Development Areas Act in Greece, the Special Plans of Interior Reform and Immediate Action Programmes in Spain, conservation schemes in Bologna (Italy) and Oporto (Portugal), and shanty area projects in all five countries, are initiatives which have attempted to incorporate local resident preferences in schemes focusing on improvement and renewal, rather than on the green-field site development which characterized much postwar peripheral growth.

Devolution of power and finances to regional and municipal governments has made considerable strides in recent years, again linked very much to democratization of national politics in Portugal, Spain and Greece. The chronic lack of resources which so hampered local governments in the boom periods of the postwar period is slowly being attended to, but the availability of local level finance and technical expertise still remains generally low.

Whilst there are signs that planning institutions and plan types are evolving to become better geared to the realities of the urban growth process, doubts must remain about their capacity and effectiveness in the long term. The enormity of housing, service and infrastructural deficits is such that, at best, attempts to redress these imbalances are likely to be little more than a 'holding operation' for some time to come. Although the pace of rural-urban migration has slowed in some areas, regional imbalances and the concentration of economic (and other) activities in a few major centres remains, and the move from country to city continues. At the same time, formal planning and the bureaucracy which surrounds it suffer from a lack of credibility which it will take time to re-establish. Planning in Southern Europe has been plagued by a range of quasi-legal or blatantly illegal activities undertaken by both public and private agencies, resulting in a lack of public confidence in the system as a whole.

Considerable political resolve, increased capital investment and legislative and institutional reform will be required if the array of political, economic, bureaucratic and psychological problems which planning now faces are to be overcome. The chaos of the inner areas, the degraded old cities, the mixed zones of industry in close proximity to other uses, and the varieties of ill-planned, low-quality housing are striking reminders of the failings of urban planning in the recent past. Whilst there *are* signs of recent change for the good, the overall picture remains bleak, and new initiatives will continue to be needed in what will inevitably be an uphill struggle in the future.

# Index

Ankara, 173–176, 186, 189–195, 202, 206
Antolini, 38–40
Antonelli, 47–49
Aprilia, 50–51
Atatürk, 169–170, 173
Athens, 2, 5–6, 8–11, 15, 20, 29–31, 200, 202, 206

Barcelona, 2, 111–155, 200, 206
Biasioli, 47
Bologna, 63
Bonaparte Forum, Milan, 38–40, 200
Braga (Portugal), 71

Cassa per il Mezzogiorno, 59
Castro, 117–119
Cerdà, 115–120, 157, 200
Chania (Greece), 15, 22–23, 27
CIAM, 15, 127, 202, 204
CIRPAC, 127, 129, 202, 204
City Expansion Act (Spain), 1864, 120, 201
Coimbra (Portugal), 71, 86
Commissione d'Ornato (Planning Commissions, Italy), 39, 41–42, 46
COPLACO, 147, 155
Costanzo Ciano (Italy), 54

DEPOS (Greek Public Corporation of Housing and Urban Planning), 13, 25
Doxiadis, 18, 24, 29, 32

Ermoupolis (Greece), 5, 8

Garden City, 41, 59, 121–122, 124–126, 201–202
GATEPAC, 127, 129
Genoa, 2, 37, 58
Giovannoni, 41

Haussmann, 81, 200
Hebrard, 12, 13, 14, 202
Heussler, 173
Housing Acts (Portugal), 85–87, 92; (Spain), 135, 142, see also Shanty/squatter housing

Illegal Buildings Act (Turkey), 1924, 170
INA-CASA (National Institute of Housing, Italy), 52, 67
Istanbul, 2, 165, 170, 180, 187–189, 206
Izmir, 170, 187–189, 206

Jansen, 125, 171–172, 174–175, 193, 201–202
Jaussely, 123, 201

Kleanthis, 8
Klentze, von, 9–10

Land and Urban Planning Act (Spain), 1956, 136–141, 204; 1976, 151–153, 204
Land Law (Turkey), 1858, 167
Le Corbusier, 15, 129, 201, 202
Linear City, 121–122, 201
Lisbon, 2, 71–107, 200, 202, 206
Littoria, 49–50
London, 2

Macia, 130–131
Madrid, 2, 111–156, 200, 202, 206
Milan, 2, 37, 48, 54–56, 58, 200
Municipal Act (Turkey), 1930, 171, 187
Municipal Roads and Buildings Act (Turkey), 1933, 171, 173, 204
Municipal Statute (Spain), 125–126, 157, 204

Naples, 2, 4, 37, 43, 58, 200
National Administration Act (Italy), 1865, 42, 45
New towns, 49–51, 54–56, 104–105, 150–151
Nunez Granes, 124

Oporto, 71–107, 206

Padova (Italy), 44–46, 60–61
Padua—see Padova
Palermo, 2
Paris, 2
Patras, 2, 5, 8, 22
Planning Acts (Portugal), 1934 and 1944, 87–88, 92–93, 203; 1971, 95
Poggi, 42
PRG (Piani Regolatori Generali), 53, 65–67, 203
Public Hygeine Act (Turkey), 1930, 170

Ressano Garcia, 81–82
Rome, 2, 37, 43, 58, 65–66
Rovira i Trias, 115

Salazar, 84–87
Salonica, 5, 25
Santos, 74
Schaubert, 8
Schiavi, 41, 202
Shanty housing, 66, 96–98, 105–107, 112, 129, 180–182, 184–185, 189–195, 205
Squatter—see Shanty
Stübben, 41, 201, 202

Town Planning Acts (Greece), 1923, 16–18, 203; (Italy), 1942, 53, 203; (Turkey), 1957, 183, 204; 1972, 185
Turin, 2, 37, 46–51, 58, 200

UDA (Urban Development Areas, Greece), 26–28, 30, 206

Venice, 24
Verona, 44–46, 60–61

Zuazo, 125, 201

For Product Safety Concerns and Information please contact our EU representative GPSR@taylorandfrancis.com
Taylor & Francis Verlag GmbH, Kaufingerstraße 24, 80331 München, Germany